Colonial

THE ENGLISH SPIRIT

THE ENGLISH SPIRIT

Essays in History
and Literature

BY

A. L. ROWSE

Fellow of All Souls College, Oxford

LONDON

MACMILLAN & CO. LTD

1944 SHIT

TO

G. M. TREVELYAN

ADMIRABLE EXEMPLAR OF
THE ENGLISH SPIRIT

PRINTED IN GREAT BRITAIN
BY R. & R. CLARK, LIMITED, EDINBURGH

PREFACE

In bringing these essays together — composed over a number of years — I am a little surprised to find how consistent and strong is the theme that runs through them : something more than pride in, a deep love for, English things, for our countryside and towns, with their memories of the people who inhabited them and of the things that took place there — all so much alive for me ; for places associated with names that are the very stuff of our tradition, Thomas More and Elizabeth, George Herbert and Hampden and Clarendon, Swift and Horace Walpole, William and Dorothy Wordsworth ; the Tower and Hampton Court, Rycote and Great Tew, Trinity Great Court and the High, Wilton, the Close at Salisbury ; for our tradition itself and the literature in which it is expressed and handed on. It comes as something of a surprise to see how that theme runs back beyond the years when these things have been so imperilled. And just as it has been something in the spirit of those things which has helped us to survive the danger, so the danger to them has heightened our sense of their value, of their being very precious to us. In the usual English way, perhaps we were shamefaced and shy at saying what they meant for us. Not being English, alas — except by conviction — but hopelessly Cornish, I am not ashamed but proud to say it for them. The stress we have been through in these last years has brought that deep unspoken current of love to the surface. I dare say we have all been somewhat surprised at how strong it really was all the time underneath.

I bring together these essays as evidence that with me it went back long before the years of war, and — in spite of unlikely and, indeed, discouraging political associations — I think I may claim that some of these essays, even though historical and literary, express a feeling of urgency, of apprehension, such as the political leaders of the time did not share — or if they did share it, did nothing about.

With this, then, goes another recurrent theme : not merely dislike of the second-rate and the mediocre, but a proper

v

appreciation of the danger that comes from giving them responsibility and following their lead — dangers which we have brought down upon ourselves before in our history and of which we may see the moral sometimes pointed in this book. This may be the century of the Common Man — it certainly is of the common *cliché* — but I prefer to look for the uncommon man, the man of genius or ability. Such men are in themselves more interesting, more rewarding, and in the end the country has greater need of them.

The positive side of this theme is a proper recognition of what we owe to our great men.

I cannot understand the meanness and obtuseness of mind which refuses to recognise not merely the quality or the genius, but quite simply the services that such men have rendered us in the past — Drake, Marlborough, Clive, Warren Hastings, Lloyd George — and for which we have such reason to be grateful. It is only right intellectually and good for our education, let alone our mere understanding of the past, to appreciate what they did and what they were, their greatness as well as their littlenesses — they were only human. And I hope that besides my admiration, my approach to them, whoever they may be, is a human one. Historians can quote the very words they spoke. It is a historian's business neither to be monotonously laudatory (as Victorian biographers were apt to be), nor to crab and denigrate (as is the way with the inferior today), but simply to understand and make clear what these men were trying to do and what their contribution was to the story of our people.

Why should we not be reasonably and instructedly proud of the extraordinary record and achievement of this country? Why should we be expected to apologise for it, as if it were something to be half ashamed about? I say *reasonably* proud, meaning " not without reason " ; and for the instruction, I hope that these essays may have something to offer.

Granted that there is nothing sillier or more offensive than an ignorant and uninformed chauvinism, which does not know why or what we have to admire in the past — on the other hand, the habit of depreciation, of being afraid to recognise what there is to be proud of, is no less deleterious, if anything more so. It opens the way to a defeatism of which we have had too much in the last two decades — when Heaven knows what the world owes to this country for standing alone quite simply for civilisation in the struggle against scientific barbarism, overwhelmingly strong in the technical equipment of a machine age, and all the more criminal because its nihilism, its will to destroy, was conscious and deliberate. Besides, this habit of depreciation is liable to be taken by foreigners *au pied de la lettre*. It is stupid of them, and also bad for them. Really obtuse foreigners, like the Germans, are apt to get some nasty shocks when they believe what their own propaganda told them for a second time in a generation — that we are a decadent people. Once, one would have thought, was enough for a mistake like that. But the Germans, as Coleridge observed, have a " nimiety ", a " too-muchness " about them.

It is important, then, both for us and for the world that the English should understand themselves and that the outside world should know what kind of a people they are to whom they owe (as a Cornishman I say it) so much.

On the side of literature and landscape, a theme that recurs, that rises from many of the essays, is the naturally poetic character of the English at heart. That should not surprise us in the people who have contributed the greatest poetic literature to the world — even greater than Greek, a distinguished Greek scholar assures me — more varied and of greater *envergure*. Yet what rises from my reading of these essays as a whole is the constant way in which English literature, even when prose, with such prose-figures as Horace Walpole or Clarendon or Froude — we expect it of Virginia Woolf or D. H. Lawrence — aspires to the condition of poetry. It is like the incurably romantic turn of English painting. It testifies to the latent strain in us which makes our literature and our life one and binds each together, giving strength to the one and an imaginative contour to the other.

So perhaps no apology is needed for bringing together in one volume essays and reviews which deal with both English life and literature.

The longest study, with which the book begins, " Mr. Churchill and English History ", was delivered as a Friday

Discourse at the Royal Institution. Such essays as "The Elizabethan Exhibition", "Elizabeth at Rycote", "Pictures in a Deanery", though written at various times in the past ten years, have not been published before. In the case of some of the other essays I have appended the dates at which they appeared : the dates add their own commentary on what was passing at the time, the background, often menacing or apprehensive or poignant, to all that one wrote. For these remaining essays and reviews I am indebted to the editors who provided the occasions for which they were written — of *The Times Literary Supplement, Observer, New Statesman, Spectator, World Review, Britain Today, Evening Standard,* and to the B.B.C., to whom I make my acknowledgments.

My chief obligation is to Mr. Jack Simmons, whose literary judgment has been invaluable and saved me from many errors.

A. L. ROWSE

OXFORD, *February* 1944

CONTENTS

I

MR. CHURCHILL AND ENGLISH HISTORY

I WONDER how many people, when they see that so familiar, endearing, bulky figure on the films or railway platforms returning from one of his innumerable journeys, think how much of English history is embodied in it ? There are ironies, and there are proprieties in history. And one of the most striking among the latter is that in these years when we have been fighting the closest struggle in our history for our existence, and have held the door open for the existence of others, the whole inspiration of the Grand Alliance against the aggressor should be a Churchill — descendant of the great Marlborough who did the same thing two hundred years ago.

I always think of it : it moves me to think of these patterns in our wonderful long record as a nation. It is evident that Mr. Churchill himself is conscious of it ; but then he is a historian, who educated himself by reading history, whose whole mind is impregnated with the historical outlook and has been dominated from his boyhood with the desire to play his part in the nation's story. In a most revealing little speech to the boys of Harrow the other day, he said :

" I can see myself as it seems but yesterday sitting a little boy here in these audiences, always feeling the thrill of your songs, and always feeling the glory of England and its history surrounding me and about me, and always praying that the day might come when I should have the honour of doing something to help forward the great association with which our lives have been connected."

There can be few people who have had their dearest wish so completely fulfilled. For I suppose it is true to say, as a mere matter of historical fact, that of all the figures to whom the nation has owed much for its safety and security in the past, for guidance in times of peril — Queen Elizabeth, Drake, Cromwell, Marlborough, the Pitts, Nelson — we owe most of all to Mr. Churchill, for never has it been a closer thing than it was in 1940. We have never, since we became a nation, been through greater danger than that through which he brought us then.

It is a great thing to have a historian as Prime Minister ; since he understands the exigencies imposed upon us by our position in Europe and the world, the tradition of our policy and its whys and wherefores, our historic role and all that depends upon it. Moreover, the statesman who is also a historian sees these things unfolding quite naturally as part of the evolution and life of the State and society ; he knows their origins and their causes and is not taken aback when they develop according to form. Mr. Churchill was not surprised during the dreary decade from 1931, when everybody in English politics was engaged in humbugging himself and other people, at the developments in Germany. He knew what to expect ; he had been there before. He was almost the only political leader to warn the country of what was before it. But then, he was the only political leader who was a historian.

It is no unfairness to say that Mr. Churchill's immediate predecessors, two Midlands industrialists, did not understand what was happening : they were not students of history. Mr. Churchill understands these things to his finger-tips. He has, we may say, a double advantage. They are in his blood ; but, more important, he has studied them long and carefully in the most exact (and exacting) way — that is, in writing about them.

He is in himself an embodiment of much in our recent past, the last three centuries, of which we have good reason to be proud. The Churchills are old West Country stock, of the lesser gentry when they first emerge upon the scene of history with the original Winston. But what an extraordinary fate was his ! This plain and impecunious Devonshire gentleman, who varied the slow excitements of frequent paternity and litigation with the itch of writing voluminously upon history and genealogy — and all in a quiet way in a remote West Country manor-house — became the father of the most famous general in English history, the victor of Blenheim, and through his daughter Arabella, the grandfather of the next most distinguished English general of the age (only he happened to be fighting on the other side) — the Duke of Berwick. Mr. Churchill says of Sir Winston :

" Had he lived the full span, he would have witnessed within the space of twelve months his son gaining the battle of Ramillies and his daughter's son that of Almanza ; and would have found himself acknowledged as the progenitor of the two greatest captains of the age at the head of the opposing armies of Britain and of France and Spain. Moreover, his third surviving son, Charles, became a soldier of well-tried distinction, and his naval son virtually managed the Admiralty during the years of war. The military strain flowed strong and clear from the captain of the Civil Wars, student of heraldry and history, and champion of the Divine Right. It was his blood, not his pen, that carried his message."

What a stock this was, to be sure !

We do not know whether this record was all of old Winston's doing. We can never be sure of these things ; but it would seem only fair to put down some part of it to his wife's credit — all the more so since she was one of the Devonshire Drakes of Ashe, a much older and more substantial family than the Churchills, a family of which Sir Francis Drake considered himself a cadet (and borrowed their arms). Lady Drake, whose daughter Sir Winston married — thereby doing rather well for himself — was on her mother's side a Villiers ; and so the Churchills came by a streak of that romantic, glamorous blood which runs in the veins of some of the more vivid specimens of the English aristocracy, among others in those of Chatham and Pitt, as well as Marlborough.[1] It gives one interesting cause to reflect.

The Drakes of Ashe were a Parliamentarian family, while the Churchills were Royalist. It is pleasant to think of Mr. Churchill's ancestry being suitably represented on both sides of that great divide. It was probably less pleasant for his namesake — since the Drakes came rather better out of the Civil Wars, being Parliamentarians — to have to bring his family up in his mother-in-law's house at Ashe, in pinched and straitened circumstances. While Sir Winston Churchill remained *perdu* in the depths of the country for ever writing

---

[1] Cf. " The Great Villiers Connection ", in Lord Keynes' *Essays in Biography.*

history, his son (and daughter) were making history at Court, before the eyes of the nation and ultimately of Europe.

On the Spencer side of his ancestry Mr. Churchill descends from a great merchant family of the Tudor period, and — very characteristic of the English aristocracy — one which made the most of the opportunities opened up by the Reformation and the dispersal of desirable church lands. The Spencers have always been an intelligent stock, bookish, highly political, and with a sound tradition of public spirit. From the Revolution of 1688 they have been Whigs, turning to Liberals in the later nineteenth century. Though less exciting than the Churchills, they have been solider and sounder, less up-and-down. It makes an agreeable symmetry for the historian to record that where the Spencers were Whigs and Liberals, the Churchills were Tories.

But enough of such matters. The last word on them was said two hundred years ago by old Sarah, Duchess of Marlborough, with her usual common sense and shattering candour :

" This History takes a great deal of Pains to make the Duke of Marlborough's Extraction very ancient. That may be true for aught I know ; But it is no matter whether it be true or not in my opinion. For I value nobody for another's merit."

In other words, what matters is for a man to prove himself. And how Marlborough and his descendant proved themselves we all know. The point is that each of them was the architect of his own fortunes.

This is not the place to review their careers but simply to regard them in the longer perspective of English history. Hardly any of our great historical figures have had such an effect upon the course of European history as these two : not even Elizabeth, nor Chatham — whose impact was to be seen more in the outer world. The historical significance of Marlborough's career is this. It is not merely that he was the greatest soldier we have ever had ; he was the ever-victorious leader of the armies of the Grand Alliance against Louis XIV, but he was also its diplomatic and political brain-centre. Everything in that long war came to Marlborough ; and often in the circumstances of war conducted by a coalition he was faced with impossible situations. He was not only never defeated in the field, the victor of four of the greatest battles in our annals and a master of strategic movement, he was responsible for the conduct of the war as a whole, in its political as well as its military, naval, and economic aspects. His was a European position. He led the Powers through all the complicated phases of that war to ultimate victory — even though he was thrown over by the Tories before the end.

The heroic Dutchman, William III, had died before all his plans for curbing Louis XIV's ascendancy in Europe could come into operation, on the threshold of war. Marlborough was his designated heir. He carried the plans through to success — greater than might have been William's, for he had far more military genius, and in more difficult circumstances, for he had not the full powers of the King. As Trevelyan says :

" Marlborough as a military strategist and a tactician, as a war statesman and war diplomatist, stands second to no Englishman in history. His powers resemble those of Chatham and Clive rolled into one."

We may observe, on a lower plane, that his ceaseless journeyings between this country and the Continent, of which he had such reason to complain, but which were so necessary to the conduct of a coalition war, parallel the global tours, no less necessary, of his descendant, in which the latter takes evident pleasure. (Doubtless the conditions are more comfortable. One way in which we have made a little progress.)

A more important parallel is their relation to parties, the internal politics of the country. For two-thirds of his life Marlborough was a Tory, the intimate of James II and of the Princess Anne, who became Queen on William III's death. At bottom Marlborough was motivated by the interest of the country — with which he, not unnaturally, identified his own. It is this which accounts for his desertion of James II, when he saw that that fool persisted in a course which was hopeless from everybody's point of view, including his own. With the country involved in a tremendous struggle with Louis XIV, in which Marlborough was the responsible leader, he inevitably took a point of view transcending party considerations and looked beyond to national support of the war. When the Tories began to withdraw their support, Marlborough was forced to look more to the Whigs and in the end to rely upon a Whig government to carry the war through successfully. The Tories were alienated and, when they gained power, threw him over, making peace without him. He was even driven into exile on the Continent ; but returned with George I, an indispensable support to the Hanoverian dynasty which was the choice of Parliament and of all moderate men who stood for a middle course. A constitutional monarchy was the logical conclusion of the Revolution Settlement.

It is interesting to observe the comments of Marlborough's descendant — who has twice made the difficult, not to say dangerous, journey across the House of Commons, who began as a Tory, became a Liberal, then a Tory again and finally emerged as the national leader of an all-party government in the crisis of the war — it is interesting to see what he thinks at similar turning-points in his ancestor's career. It throws a revealing light upon what he thinks for himself. In the crisis of 1707 when the Tories were ceasing to support the war, he gives the opinion that greater risks should have been taken to preserve the national character of the government. In 1709 when the best chance of peace was lost, he puts it down to the party conflict in Parliament : " Party government in time of war might show management and efficiency, but it lacked the deep-seated, massive strength of a national combination ". In the crisis of 1714, with the Queen's death, it was the men of middle views who turned the scale against extreme courses and brought in the Hanoverian dynasty in peace and quietness. It is they ultimately who govern England for her good.

Mr. Churchill's comment on the Tory majority of 1710, which deflected the course of the war, got rid of Marlborough and forced a less advantageous peace, is much to the point :

" The high circle of Ministers and ex-Ministers, most of whom were only slightly attached to party, except at election times, and several of whom were involved in the great trans-actions by which England had risen to mastery, were alarmed and perplexed by this development. They found themselves confronted by a mass of resolute, thick-headed, earnest gentlemen, who actually believed in the propaganda which had served its purpose at the election. Harley was deeply embarrassed. He, like all other Prime Ministers in such circumstances, having attained power, wanted to be quit of electioneering rant, and do his duty by the national issues."

One sees the close parallel to the enormous Tory majority of 1931, and the awkward problem it posed for Harley-Baldwin, which the latter dealt with in his fashion by neglecting the greatest issue of all, the country's safety. One reads Mr. Churchill's own mind, which has always been possessed by the idea of doing his duty by the country, rather than adhering to a narrow and one-sided party line.

In a most interesting essay on " Consistency in Politics ", Mr. Churchill says :

" A Statesman in contact with the moving current of events and anxious to keep the ship on an even keel and steer a steady course may lean all his weight now on one side and now on another. His arguments in each case when contrasted can be shown to be not only very different in character, but contradictory in spirit and opposite in direction : yet his object will throughout have remained the same. His resolves, his wishes, his outlook may have been unchanged ; his methods may be verbally irreconcilable. We cannot call this inconsistency. In fact it may be claimed to be the truest consistency."

He concludes :

" A Statesman should always try to do what he believes is best in the long view for his country, and he should not be dissuaded from so acting by having to divorce himself from a great body of doctrine to which he formerly sincerely adhered."

In the light of this we may more fully appreciate the meaning of Mr. Churchill's famous broadcast in March 1943 concerning the future shape our politics should take. It becomes very clear that he would prefer a truly national government to guide the country through the dangers and strains of the post-war period, one which would be able to follow what is the national interest rather than the line of one party or the other. In short, a government which was strong enough to be above party. Such a government is the proper environment for the activity of a great man dedicated to the welfare of the nation. " How vain," Mr. Churchill writes of Marlborough at his best, " how vain are those writers in so many lands who suppose that the great minds of the world in their supreme activities are twisted or swayed by sordid or even personal aims."

But history has its warnings, its lessons to offer. All through the slow unfolding of Mr. Churchill's magnificent portrait of his ancestor there looms the shadow of Harley : the sly, cunning party-manager, who spoke the language of Nonconformity (he was of Nonconformist descent), who was a pastmaster of party-manœuvring, preferring always to work underground, essentially a House of Commons man, an artist at being " hail-fellow-well-met " with everybody — moreover a kindly, generous soul, liking good cheer and good fellowship, appreciative of the company of literary men, fundamentally lazy, but with a gift for friendship. Such was Harley. Such also was the man who had the greatest power in English politics during the decades when Mr. Churchill's masterpiece was being planned and written.

In his portrait of Harley Mr. Churchill insists upon the element of shrewd party-cunning. One cannot but see something of Baldwin in that sense of timing, the finger upon the pulse of the ordinary man, the lying low, the canniness. They both of them in the end precipitated a disaster, and well-nigh ruined their country, by their indolence and fundamental irresponsibility towards the long-term interests of the State. But nobody can say that they had not a shrewd party-sense, and each of them kept out a far greater man with a far higher sense of his duty to the country. What each of them understood very well was that the Tory Party was their foundation in public life, without which they were nothing. Mr. Churchill observes : " Harley knew the Tory Party alike in its temporary weakness and in its latent strength. He saw that it was his foundation in public life." Mr. Churchill had observed another thing in the course of his own public experience : the alacrity with which the Tory Party threw over the great man who led us to victory in 1914–18, when he had ceased to be indispensable. Mr. Churchill pays Lloyd George this tribute: " He was the greatest master of the art of getting things done and of putting things through that I ever knew ". But he was not a Tory, and he was without an adequate party-foundation. So he was dispensed with, at the height of his prestige in the world, with his immense experience of men and affairs, in the prime of his powers. The Tories gave us a Baldwin for a Lloyd George. We are perhaps in a better position to understand Mr. Churchill's acceptance of the leadership of the party in 1940 — an offer which would never have been made to him if he had not already been Prime Minister.

It is obvious that the Prime Minister's book — he is as much a writing man as the first Winston Churchill — is a work of great contemporary, no less than of historical, interest : indeed the two are bound up together, the past throwing light upon the present, present experience illuminating the past. A student of politics who worked with Mr. Churchill in earlier years told me that it was his opinion that he came to maturity in writing that book. And it may well be so. The younger Winston had a certain *insouciance*, a gay irrepressibility that did not consort well with the gravity and judgment of a European outlook. But in writing that book he spent years pondering the greatest issues of peace and war at a crisis in our affairs, the long-term responsibilities of statesmanship involved in conducting the war of a Grand Alliance, its impact upon personalities and politics within the country. There is no doubt that the Churchill of today is a different man from the younger Winston : solider, graver, more monumental, a Roman figure, cast in the mould of one of the statesmen in the Abbey. Shall we be far wrong if we say, like his kinsman Chatham ? He has come late to maturity ; but there are unlikelier things than this, that it was the ten years he spent upon English history that matured him.

The book has all the qualities of his mind : magnanimity, a generous attitude towards opponents, a grand historic sense, great love of England, pride in the past, and a sense of duty towards the future. He pays a fine tribute to Marlborough's adversary, Louis XIV, for persevering against odds and holding out against adversity : " He wavered long ; but the outcome vindicated his final plunge, and in the after-light his grandeur amid appalling stresses shines forth. Here is another triumph

for perseverance against the enemy." That volume was
published in the year of Munich — but how different a spirit
it reveals ! If there is one thing we have reason to be proud of
at this moment it is that a man with such a spirit should be the
chosen leader of the English people. What a contrast it affords
with the congealed spite and meanness, the hatred and malice,
the combined megalomania and inferiority-complex of the
guttersnipe of genius who is the leader of the German people
and who faithfully expresses so much that is in the German
soul.

It is courage in adversity that most elicits Mr. Churchill's
admiration. He has a fine word for that rather dull woman,
Queen Anne : " her magnanimity and her sense of proportion
expressed the genius of the English race in adversity ". For
the English he has a word of warning : " The tale is rich in
suggestion and instruction for the present day ; for it illustrates
what seems to have become the tradition of Britain — indomitable in distress and danger . . . fatuous and an easy prey after
her superb effort had run its course ". That was written in
1936 — the year of the fortification of the Rhineland, of
Mr. Baldwin's surrender to Mussolini over Abyssinia.

There is all the sense of historic drama one would expect —
Queen Anne sitting in the big bay-window of the long gallery
overlooking the Terrace at Windsor when the news of the
victory of Blenheim was brought to her. You may still see in
the bay there the dominoes at which the Queen and her
husband were playing when Colonel Parke came into her
presence. He brought the famous note which Marlborough
had scribbled to Sarah on the back of a bill of tavern expenses,
on the same evening of the battle :

" I have not time to say more but to beg you will give my
duty to the Queen, and let her know her army has had a
glorious victory. Monsieur Tallard and two other Generals
are in my coach and I am following the rest."

More important than this, and a new contribution to history,
is the revelation of Marlborough's bias in favour of constitutional government for France, in place of Louis XIV's despotic
and aggressive monarchy. Marlborough wished to see France

governed by the Three Estates, " which I think is more likely
to give quiet to Christendom, than the tearing provinces from
them for the enriching of others ". How profoundly right his
intuition was ! It is the nature of a country's internal government which determines its external policy and dictates whether
it is possible for it to live in peace with other powers or no.
There are some régimes, Junker-militarist or Fascist, aggressive
and expansionist, which by their very nature make it impossible
for them to live at peace with their neighbours. If our political
leaders had known enough history to know *that* in the years
before the war, they would have saved a great deal of time in
trying to appease them ; they would have known that it was
impossible from the start and prepared for the worst. There
might then have been no war. It was indeed the only hope.

Mr. Churchill's comment on Marlborough's moderate
constitutionalism is most interesting :

" The idea of substituting for the despotic rule of France a
Parliamentary régime had long commended itself to him. It
is a strange speculation how the course of history would have
been changed if he had been able to enforce his policy upon
France. The French Revolution might have accomplished
itself gradually and beneficently in the course of the eighteenth
century, and the whole world have moved on to broader
foundations without paying the awful price in war and horror."

It would no doubt have been a good thing if a more drastic
peace had been imposed on France in 1709, rather than the
lenient Treaty of 1713. If Spain had been wrested from the
Bourbons then, it would have prevented the Family Compact
and perhaps the three subsequent wars we had to fight in that
century against Bourbon France and Spain combined.

But, alas, the one thing we learn from history is that people
never learn anything from history — though they might to
such profit ! One of the saddest of Mr. Churchill's utterances is on this theme, on the renewal of the German danger
(1935) :

" When the situation was manageable it was neglected, and
now that it is thoroughly out of hand we apply too late the
remedies which then might have effected a cure. There is

nothing new in the story.   It is as old as the Sibylline Books.
It falls into that long, dismal catalogue of the fruitlessness
of experience and the confirmed unteachability of mankind.
Want of foresight, unwillingness to act when action would
be simple and effective, lack of clear thinking, confusion of
counsel until the emergency comes, until self-preservation
strikes its jarring gong — these are the features which constitute
the endless repetition of history."

This unfortunately is all too true.   But need it always be
so ?   It states the gravest necessity for a historical education
permeating the whole nation.   We need so to have our noses
held to the grindstone that we cannot escape the lessons of
history, even if we would.   As Mr. Churchill said in Parliament
in March 1938, after Hitler's annexation of Austria :

" Look back upon the last five years — since, that is to
say, Germany began to rearm in earnest and openly to seek
revenge.   If we study the history of Rome and Carthage, we
can understand what happened and why.   It is not difficult to
form an intelligent view about the three Punic Wars.   But if
mortal catastrophe should overtake the British Nation and the
British Empire, historians a thousand years hence will still be
baffled by the mystery of our affairs.   They will never understand how it was that a victorious nation, with everything in
hand, suffered themselves to be brought low, and to cast away
all that they had gained by measureless sacrifice and absolute
victory — gone with the wind ! "

Mr. Churchill's mind was formed by the study of history —
and there could be no stronger recommendation for a historical
education.   In his fascinating autobiography, *My Early Life*,
he tells us how it came about.   Until he went to India as a young
officer in the 4th Hussars, he had received very little formal
education :   he was at Harrow.   But there he found the
restricted classical grind hopeless, and emerged (like Shakespeare) with small Latin and less Greek.   He wanted to go to
Oxford, like his father ;   but found compulsory Greek an
insuperable bar.   It was not until he found himself at Bangalore
in his early twenties, with plenty of time on his hands, that he
began to educate himself.   He started with Gibbon, since
some one had told him that his father was an admirer of

Gibbon and that it had greatly affected his style of speech and writing.

" So without more ado I set out upon the eight volumes of Dean Milman's edition of Gibbon's *Decline and Fall of the Roman Empire*. I was immediately dominated both by the story and the style. All through the long glistening middle hours of the Indian day, from when we quitted stables till the evening shadows proclaimed the hour of Polo, I devoured Gibbon. I rode triumphantly through it from end to end and enjoyed it all. I scribbled all my opinions on the margins of the pages. . . ."

That is the way to read. From Gibbon he went on to Macaulay, not only the Macaulay of the *Essays* but of the great History, a more serious proposition. From Macaulay to Lecky, and thence to Plato and Aristotle, Malthus and Darwin. " It was a curious education. First, because I approached it with an empty, hungry mind, and with fairly strong jaws ; and what I got I bit."

There can be no doubt about the impression that history — and these historians in particular — made upon that vigorous, tenacious mind ; all the stronger because he won it so hardly for himself. One can see the twin influences of Gibbon and Macaulay all through his writing and his speaking — with him, as with remote Sir Winston, writing came first. They are very strong influences, and only a mind of great toughness could absorb them and turn them to its own purposes. But this the Prime Minister has done. In his earlier books and speeches one notices the formal rhetoric, the balanced phrases, the pomposity of those classical models. But in course of time, with much labour and application, he has hammered out a style of his own, in which his masters are still visible peeping out between the lines, but in which he speaks simply and directly to the mind and heart of his people.

The people themselves, in these arduous years of their endurance, have given an indication of the soundness of their springs, an instinctive feeling for our language, in their extraordinary (and unexpected) responsiveness to the phrases and images of this master of its use. In these days when newspapers and wireless and films combine to flatten the language to a dead

level, without directness, crispness, vividness, without character
or savour, something in the heart of plain English people
leapt at the direct and vivid imagery in which they were
being talked to, and not without style, a certain classical
flavour — but the classics were English. His very quips and
jokes, whether against his appalling adversaries, or directed
good-temperedly against friends and colleagues, have had a
way of seeping down in these discomfortable years from the
circle around him to the ordinary citizen in bus or bar or train,
where the jokes are greatly appreciated and shed their warmth
upon the cheerless war-time scene. Everybody gets a laugh
out of the latest remark of Winston's. After so many years of
.humbug from high places — until the nation lost its way amid
the inspissated fog — one reflects that government by epigram
is better for all concerned than government by humbug.

Mr. Churchill's acute historical sense is not confined to the
manner or the presentation ; it is the very stuff of his mind.
One observes it in all his speeches. With what pleasure he
came to the House of Commons to announce the agreement
with Portugal, our ancient ally, over the Azores : " I have an
announcement to make arising out of the treaty signed between
this country and Portugal in the year 1373 [Loud laughter]
between his Majesty King Edward III and King Ferdinand
and Queen Eleanor of Portugal ". An ignorant House of
Commons, with no sense of history, which had in fact supported
all the fatuous appeasement ventures that made nonsense of
our history (until history ultimately made nonsense of them),
would of course find this merely funny. But to the Prime
Minister it would be more than a joke : it would be one more
link in the royal bonds that bind us to our own past. Or take
his speech on the rebuilding of the House of Commons, with his
infallible sense of how the very structure affects the character
of our Parliamentary system and answers to its purpose. Or
we may take his own conception of the role he plays in these
historic years : he sees it as part and parcel of our history ;
and hence an altogether higher sense of responsibility than that
of a Midlands ironmonger. We may be glad, indeed, that our
fate has rested in the hands of a man who has written one of
the historical masterpieces of our time. Indeed I cannot

remember when England was last governed by a Prime Minister who was a master of historical writing.

Like so many of the greatest men of action — like Nelson, darling of the English people, or Napoleon, or Lenin, or for that matter Caesar — with Mr. Churchill writing is bound up with action. They are not mutually exclusive activities, but complementary, each impulse seeking fulfilment in the other. The moment the great Coalition government which won the last war was brought down by the " avenging march of the mediocrities ", and Mr. Churchill was free to write, he turned to writing down his experience, as a Minister, of the years leading to the war and of the war itself. The result was a book, *The World Crisis*, which ultimately grew to six volumes, and is by far the best and most important of all English books on the war, with one exception. That exception is Lloyd George's *War Memoirs*. *The World Crisis* is only less important than that because Lloyd George as the head of the government saw the war from the very centre, and, from the level of the highest decisions, saw it as a whole.

But Mr. Churchill's book is not less interesting ; indeed it is fascinating, particularly the first volume which gives an account of his work at the Admiralty in making the Navy ready for the great challenge which grew all the time from Germany. (He, and the men who worked there with him in those years, deserved well of the State.) The book is not a history of the war ; nor is it — in spite of Arthur Balfour's gibe, " Winston's brilliant Autobiography disguised as a history of the universe " — mere autobiography. It belongs to the category in which French literature is richer than ours, *Mémoires pour servir à l'histoire*. Mr. Churchill makes this point, no doubt in answer to such criticisms as Balfour's, in the prefaces to successive volumes. He specifically disclaims the position of the historian in this work :

" It is not for me with my record and special point of view to pronounce a final conclusion. That must be left to others and to other times. But I intend to set forth what I believe to be fair and true ; and I present it as a contribution to history of which note should be taken together with other accounts."

The point is that only a writer with the instinct of the historian would trouble to make that clear ; one who was not would hardly see its point.

But all through these volumes Mr. Churchill adheres to the strictest principles of historical documentation.

" I have made no important statement of fact relating to naval operations or Admiralty business, on which I do not possess unimpeachable documentary proof. I have made or implied no criticism of any decision or action taken or neglected by others, unless I can prove that I had expressed the same opinion in writing *before the event*."

Few historians can or would wish to adhere to a principle so strict. But what strikes the reader of the book, even more than the absorbing, the thrilling interest of the story, is the transparent candour and honesty of the man who was involved in, and often buffeted by, the events he records. It affords a signal contrast with German literature of the war, whether the memoirs of the Kaiser, or Bülow, or Tirpitz, with their melancholy expression of the inherent German incapacity either to face or to state the truth.

" Documents written at the time and before the event are the only foundation upon which the judgment of history can be erected ", Mr. Churchill writes, if anything too austerely. " They alone reveal the perplexities of the situation at the moment." And in a later preface he adds, modestly, that his method " is no substitute for history, but it may be an aid both to the writing and to the study of history ".

His deep concern with both — to a degree beyond any other Prime Minister we have had and exemplified both in his own writing as well as in action — I think I have illustrated in full. My subject is Mr. Churchill's attitude to English history, for there is, to my mind, a deep moral in it. It is not my intention to deal with his own life and career as such ; it merely remains to point out the fact that much of it, by reason of its astonishing range and variety of experience, is part of the history of our time. It goes back to the days when a Spencer and a Marlborough were Viceroys enthroned in Dublin Castle. As a young man he saw his life-work in politics as a continuation and a fulfilment of his father's brilliant and tragically broken career. For a moment, in the critical year 1886, his father Lord Randolph, Chancellor of the Exchequer and Leader of the House of Commons, still under forty, was dictator of the fortunes of the Tory Party. He hoped to bring the party abreast with the developments of modern democracy and to capture its leadership. If he had lived, it is just possible that he might have brought it off : he had all the gifts for such a role, brilliance, popular convictions, a glamorous personality with an appeal to the broad masses of the people, an aristocrat equipped with all the arts of a demagogue. But he made one fatal mistake : he resigned at the summit of his power and influence : he never regained it ; the massive, static Conservatism of Lord Salisbury ruled in his place for some twenty years.

Lord Randolph might have revivified Conservatism and created, what he was out for, Tory Democracy. At least so his son thought when he wrote his biography in 1906 — the first of his important contributions to historical writing.

" Tory Democracy ", he wrote, " was necessarily a compromise (perilously near a paradox in the eye of a partisan) between widely different forces and ideas : ancient permanent institutions becoming the instruments of far-reaching social reforms ; order conjoined with liberty ; stability and yet progress ; the Tory party and yet daring legislation ! Yet narrow as was the path along which he moved, multitudes began to follow. At a time when Liberal formulas and Tory inertia seemed alike chill and comfortless, he warmed the heart of England and strangely stirred the imagination of her people."

The book concludes with an adjuration to that centre core of opinion, of neither party — or perhaps both — which has always been the pivot of his political thinking :

" There is an England which stretches far beyond the well-drilled masses who are assembled by party machinery to salute with appropriate acclamation [Gibbon !] the utterances of their recognised fuglemen [Macaulay !] ; an England of wise men who gaze without self-deception at the failings and follies of both political parties ; of brave and earnest men who find in neither faction fair scope for the effort that is in them. . . . It was to that England that Lord Randolph Churchill appealed."

There is nothing more affecting in the young Churchill than his touching devotion to his father. It is true to say that his father's memory, the thought of that eager, exciting, unfinished life, the determination to fulfil it in himself, was the inspiration of his early political years. He tells us in his autobiography how he longed as a boy to be able to help his father, stricken by defeat and fatal illness. It was because his father had admired Gibbon — so some one told him — that he began to read history. He had hardly made contact with his father's mind before he was dead.

Thirty years later, when he came to write his own *Early Life*, he was not so sure that his father would have remained a Tory :

" I can see my father now in a somewhat different light from the days when I wrote his biography. I have long passed the age at which he died. I understand only too plainly the fatal character of his act of resignation. He was ' the daring pilot in extremity '. That was his hour." But he thinks now that " from the moment Lord Randolph Churchill became Chancellor of the Exchequer responsible in large measure for the affairs of the nation, he ceased in vital matters to be a Tory. He adopted with increasing zest the Gladstonian outlook ; and in all social and labour questions he was far beyond what the Whig or middle-class Liberal of that epoch could have tolerated."

Independent and liberal-minded about Ireland, he would probably have opposed the South African War. In short, he would have become a Liberal : an opposite process to that figure of ill-omen, Joseph Chamberlain, with his nefarious influence upon the course of our politics. Lord Randolph would in all certainty have helped to push forward the great Liberal programme of social legislation, in which his son came to play an important administrative part.

We must not forget that on his mother's side Mr. Churchill is American. Lady Randolph was the descendant of French and English stock of old standing in the United States. The English regard the history of their kinsfolk overseas as part of their own history — and in a sense very rightly, though they may not know much about it. Just as with members of a family who go far away from home : they remain members of the family in the eyes of the old people.

Lady Randolph was not only a woman of great beauty, vivacity and charm, but a woman of courage and spirit. When her husband died leaving her with an obstreperous, ambitious, impulsive son on her hands, one with altogether more spirits than he knew what to do with, who might come to anything — or nothing — it is clear with what ardent devotion she backed him. It is equally clear from his autobiography how devoted he was to his mother : there was only twenty years between them, and " we worked together on even terms, more like brother and sister, than mother and son. At least so it seemed to me. And so it continued to the end."

Somewhere he records charmingly how " she left no stone unturned, no cutlet uncooked " on his behalf, with regard to some youthful campaign of his. It was she who lobbied and lunched and pushed for him. For, contrary to popular ideas, though it is something to be born a Churchill or a Cecil, the sons of younger sons have to make their own way in English life. It is not made for them. Winston Churchill's *My Early Life* is his *Mein Kampf*, and you can see from it how he had to make his career for himself, with the aid of his mother in the background. He was the architect of his own fortunes.

It is appropriate, too, that in these years when we have been fighting a second World War shoulder to shoulder with the United States, and when, as the Prime Minister has said, we have become somewhat " mixed up together ", an Englishman who springs both from the stock of the home country and the first of her offspring overseas should stand before the world as the leader of the English people in action. His has been an indispensable role as a link between Britain and America. Nor is it anything but profoundly right that there should be French blood in his heredity — his passionate love for, and faith in, France has been evident all through these cruel years of her submergence under the flood of barbarism ; since in Europe our relations always must be closest with France, the foundation of our European system.

It was an extraordinary and vitalising experience, ensconced as I was in my nook in the remote countryside of Cornwall, to

hear the Prime Minister making his first speech to a Joint
Session of Congress in Washington. After paying tribute to
his mother's memory — in his case, as we have seen, more than
a formal act of piety — he proceeded in his own inimitable
way : " It occurs to me, that if it had been the other way
round, and my father had been born in America, I might have
got here on my own. Only then the invitation to address you
would hardly have been unanimous." It was a tonic, in those
dismal days after Pearl Harbour, to hear the strong, truculent,
familiar voice coming over the air from three thousand miles
away, and to hear the cheers which greeted his " What sort of
a people do they think we are ? " It was for a moment as if
the years since 1776 had rolled away, and we were one again in
name as in spirit we have surely not ceased to be.

But it was a long and variegated, colourful career, with
some ups and downs, which led to that hour in Washington, the
summit of it all. It began in the army — in that unlike the
more regular routine of sedate political persons. One thinks
of William Pitt, " that terrible Cornet of Horse ". What
excitements and adventures that led him into : no Englishman
of our time has had more good fortune or fun : few can ever
have had such an all-round enjoyable life, and at almost every
point in contact with history ! Nobody in our time can have
had such an infallible nose for history on the wing : the
Spanish-American war in Cuba (this while on leave from the
army at home), expeditions on the North-West Frontier (sharp
fighting but good sportsmanship), Omdurman, the Boer War.
" Nothing like the battle of Omdurman will ever be seen
again ", he says. " It was the last link in the long chain of those
spectacular conflicts whose vivid and majestic splendour has
done so much to invest war with glamour. Everything was
visible to the naked eye." He describes the spectacle — from
the forward vantage point from which he saw it — of the
immense surge forward of sixty thousand Dervishes under the
sacred banners of the Mahdi against Kitchener's thin red lines.

Churchill's story as special correspondent in the South
African War is the most exciting of all. He was captured by
— of all people — Botha. It was the beginning of a lifelong
friendship. The story of how he escaped from the prisoners'

camp at Pretoria is as thrilling as anything that R. L. Stevenson ever wrote, with the additional advantage that it is true — part of history. He was in at the relief of Ladysmith. He came back from the war pro-Boer in sympathy, which was no doubt a factor in his leaving the Conservative Party and becoming a Liberal ; and this was an important influence when the time came for the government of South Africa to be handed over to the men, Botha and Smuts, whom we had fought but a few years before. Magnanimity pays its dividends. As a Liberal Minister Churchill played a full part in the great period of building up the social services before the last war, in administrative drive second only to Lloyd George. When the threat from Germany to our security at sea became serious, it fell to him as First Lord of the Admiralty to meet the danger. His job was something like that of old Sir John Hawkins in the years before the Armada ; and when the test came, he had a similar reason to be proud of the fleet he had built. Later in the war, he reverted to his old trade of soldiery and fought with the men in France : not ill equipped to meet Hitler on his own ground. From that he returned to take over Lloyd George's immense work at the Ministry of Munitions. No one since Sir Robert Peel has had such an all-round experience of the departmental work of government : Board of Trade, Home Office, Admiralty, Ministry of Munitions (the equivalent of the Ministry of Supply in this war), Colonial Office, Air Ministry, the Treasury. No one has held such supreme power in time of war since the great Chatham.

Perhaps there is some significance in the fact, as there is certainly a deep historic propriety, that at the moment of gravest danger to the State in May 1940, in the pass to which the rule of the business men had brought us, it was ultimately a coming-together of the old historic ruling class, under a member of one of its most famous families, with the solid representatives of the working class, that gave the country a new leadership and a new hope. Is it, perhaps, the past hailing the future ? That is the most important query over all our politics : will the future be worthy of such a past ?

In himself the Prime Minister exemplifies the grander and more robust standards of an age which was certain of itself, which had an infinite soaring confidence — when statesmen were not afraid to be poets, historians, philosophers, theologians, voyagers on uncharted seas of discovery. Ralegh was all these; Bacon was not only Lord Chancellor, the greatest lawyer of the age, its chief master of prose, but its greatest scientist. Mr. Churchill is made in an Elizabethan mould. But then he is a man to whom English history has been both inspiration and the call of duty.

II

THE RHYTHM OF ENGLISH HISTORY

PEOPLE are apt to think of the English State and polity, our institutions and their history, as a very conservative affair. This is a mistaken, or at least a very inadequate and one-sided, view. What makes the inner heart and rhythm of English society difficult to understand, and what is at the same time the clue to it, is the paradox of an outward conservatism with a continuing capacity for inner change and development. There is a saying that " you may change anything in England provided you don't change appearances ", and there is a good deal in it. Its truth is lost upon less subtle observers, who are misled by the retention of older forms — monarchy, House of Lords, the Church of England, and what not — and fail to notice how these and other institutions have adapted themselves to changed circumstances, sometimes with a complete change of function.

Yet, think : English history has been as dynamic as that of any country in modern times. If it has not had the somewhat staccato rhythms of French or Spanish history in the nineteenth century, it has not been the less inwardly flexible and changing for that.

What is the explanation of this paradox that makes the inwardness of our history and polity more subtle and difficult to lay hold of than that, perhaps, of any other country ?

There is no simple formula that one can give by way of answer. The explanation lies in our history itself, and in the nature of English society.

Modern England has emerged out of the experience of revolutionary changes just as much as the United States from those of 1776 onwards, or France from 1789, or Russia from 1917. All great countries, except perhaps Germany and Japan, have been through the experience of a real revolution. And England is no exception, only ours took place in the seventeenth century. The fact that it is further off in time does not make it any the less important in the development of modern society, for the experience, and the ideas that were thrown up in the course of it, exerted a prodigious influence upon the Continent all through the next century, and had a considerable part in inspiring the ideas of freedom behind the American Revolution, until indeed the great Revolution of 1789 set a new model for the nations.

But no one can think that English history during that formative period from the mid-seventeenth to mid-eighteenth century was unexciting, or that the English were necessarily a placid or phlegmatic, a dull and uninteresting folk. At any rate their contemporaries abroad, respectable French, Italians, Spaniards, did not think so : they regarded us then as the most restless, turbulent, and changeable of peoples. And not without reason ; for in the course of half a century we had had two revolutions, two civil wars and narrowly escaped another, executed one king and sent another packing, tried a Parliamentary Republic and a military Protectorate under Oliver Cromwell before arriving at a mixed constitution of our own making, after a pattern of our own, under which we settled down. After that record nobody need think of us as a wholly conservative people with no talent for change.

What was it that emerged from all those changes and experiments ? Well, in the first place, to take the most obvious, though not necessarily the most important : the English pattern of constitutional monarchy, which we have found to work satisfactorily ever since. It is a very convenient and useful form, and anything but rigid ; as it has developed, the monarchy has this great advantage, that it provides us with a symbol to which we can all look, whether overseas or at home, the visible embodiment of the unity of our peoples and form of society — a head which is at the same time separate from the centre of real political power.

That is a great advantage ; it is a very neat and practical division of function between the head of the State, with a very important social purpose to fulfil, and the political leadership whose job it is to carry on the work of government. It is an intolerable burden, in modern conditions, where one and the same man is expected to fulfil both functions. Only a superman can be expected even to attempt it — and the English do not much believe in supermen in politics. The monarchy serves the indispensable purpose of giving us continuity and at the same time flexibility : whatever the changes and chances of politics, there is a figure to which we can look, and that applies both at home and within the Commonwealth overseas. It is probable that no other constitutional form would fulfil that purpose anything like so well : it has shown a really remarkable flexibility and capacity for adaptation. In that sense the monarchy may be truly described as a democratic monarchy, an institution which is a help to the smooth and efficient working of democracy, and not a hindrance.

All this was implicit in the victory of the very moderate and English Revolution of 1688, though no one could be expected to have foretold it. What that cardinal event in our history meant, to put it in a sentence — and I do not think anyone has said it before — was a victory for constitutional flexibility and change : it kept the possibility of future development open. That was a great advantage compared with the rigid authoritarianism of Continental monarchies, of which the pattern was the oldest and greatest monarchy in Europe, the French *ancien régime*. When it became necessary in course of time to reform that, to bring it up to date, it needed a tempest with much uprooting of some things that were to be regretted, along with the dead wood. It would have been better for France if the old monarchy had had the capacity for change and self-development within itself. It would have saved France a great deal of trouble and suffering in the nineteenth century, and actually it would have given her greater stability, a less fractionalising polity.

The flexibility of the English constitution which emerged from the Revolution of 1688 has a similar advantage over the rigidity which the Fathers of the Constitution imposed upon the young United States a hundred years later. No one knows better than the Presidents of the United States themselves the almost insuperable difficulties such a constitution puts in the way of governing the country and the shifts they have been put to in order to get round them.

The peculiarity of English constitutional development goes

back then to the seventeenth century ; it is there that you must look if you wish to understand the *difference* between our course and that which other nations took — the almost universal tendency on the Continent at that time was towards authoritarianism, monarchy on the model of Louis XIV, bureaucracy, centralisation, and the subjection of the individual to the State. We took a different turning and held on a course of our own with a system of Parliamentary government, of voluntary local administration, an emphasis upon freedom of speech and person, a deep note of individualism in our public life which was given full play.

Sometimes it had too much play ; and there is no doubt that this course we took had some disadvantages and was more difficult to manage. We had to pay the price of political freedom in the hectic party conflicts of the reigns of Queen Anne and of George III. Foreign opinion — like that of Frederick the Great — often got the impression that you could not rely on Great Britain because of the conflicts between parties and the changes they involved. But that was a mistake : underneath these changes there was continuity of purpose and a deeper reliability. In the long struggles with Louis XIV and Napoleon no power was more constant or held more tenaciously to its purpose than Great Britain. And often the very flukes and alterations of party fortunes, in contributing flexibility, helped towards the success of the nation.

The Revolution of 1688 was not at all an idealistic affair ; it issued no lofty-sounding (and disputable) Declaration of the Rights of Man. It was essentially a practical solution of difficulties in government, full of moderation and compromise. Common sense was its keynote, and Locke, the philosopher of common sense, its prophet. It was the beginning of our modern period of government by a mixed polity, in which the aristocracy, the gentry, the business classes ruled, with the emphasis passing as time went on from one to the other. But even in the heyday of the aristocratic age, the eighteenth century, they never ruled *against* the people ; their whole art of governing was to retain the people's confidence and support. It was their success which exerted such a profound influence on political thinkers abroad, like Montesquieu and Voltaire, and later

Guizot, Royer-Collard, de Tocqueville.

The English political system proved its strength and flexibility in the course of the prolonged and double strain imposed upon it by the twenty years' struggle with Napoleon and by the Industrial Revolution. As the Industrial Revolution unfolded its tremendous developments, it created a new middle class which came in time to out-rival the older political classes in power ; it called into being a new industrial working class ; it altered the whole balance of forces in the English polity. It provided the greatest test the political system could possibly have. The whole question was — would it be sufficiently flexible to adapt itself to the new and changing balance of forces in the country, so as to guide and control them without a breach in continuity ; or would there be an upheaval ?

For a time in the 1830s, and again in the 1840s, the issue lay in doubt. On the Continent lesser strains produced many revolutions in those decades from 1830 to 1851. But in England, with the Reform Bill of 1832, the governing class decided upon the policy of concession ; they deliberately chose to share power with the growing middle class, and as the century went on they constantly increased the area of their support with extensions of the franchise, by the Reform Bills of 1867 and 1884, ending up with universal suffrage in our time.

Government in England in the last century has had, then, a constantly extending basis of support — unlike the constitutional July monarchy in France, which, in many ways France's most promising constitutional experiment, was yet ruined by having far too narrow and exclusive a basis of support — virtually the *haute bourgeoisie* alone. The keynotes of English government in this period have been — keeping close contact with the people, concessions and a spirit of comprehension on the part of the governing classes instead of exclusiveness, flexibility, and a capacity for adaptation in institutions. Both parties, Conservative as well as Liberal, contributed to the work of adapting the institutions of the old aristocratic State to the new circumstances ; the grand figure in this achievement was Gladstone, who started as a Conservative and ended up as an advanced Radical looking to the twentieth century. It is this that makes him such a symbolic figure in the English nineteenth century — as against Germany's Bismarck ; and this is the significance of the work he did for the State.

With the course of time — it is a long time since the seventeenth century — compromise, comprehensiveness, concession have come to be more than a policy ; they have become a habit, deep instinctive impulses in English political life — and perhaps they answer to something in the character of our people, as it has developed in modern times. So much is this so, that in the twentieth century the development of an independent working-class movement in politics has not on the whole been met with obstruction, as in many countries abroad, notably Bismarck's Germany, but with a recognisable desire to comprehend it and bring it within the political system, brought up to date and renewed. The result is that the English Labour Movement, so far from being revolutionary, is deeply the reverse. It takes an integral part in the work of the English State ; its part in guiding the country through the crisis of this war is far greater than its part in the last war ; more responsibility is passing to it, and will continue to do so.

The response of the British people to this crisis in their fortunes has proved their essential soundness — which some in the outer world had begun to question in the decade since 1931. The Germans talked once more of the decadence and effeteness of the British people, in spite of their experience of us in 1914–18. And that precisely because, like any civilised people, we preferred peace to war. Our marked preference for peace, in that decade of concessions, was yet another sign of the profound happiness of our people and their contentment in their own way, of the soundness of their impulses under the forms of government which they have evolved by the process of trial and error and by the method of compromise to suit their own circumstances and character.

Most thinking people realise that the end of the war and the social transition before us will provide another test of the combined strength and flexibility of our polity ; but we all believe that it will prove equal to whatever test comes, after what we have been through.

III

THE HISTORICAL TRADITION OF BRITISH POLICY

THE significance of the long tradition of British policy is not much understood or discussed in this country. English people, in their sensible, easy-going way, are content to take it for granted without thinking much about it. Continental writers, who have devoted more time to writing about it, have not been notably more successful in understanding it : they have been too apt to think of it in terms of undue simplification. German writers especially, like Treitschke, and even Eduard Meyer,[1] who should have known better, have regarded English policy through the centuries as a mere Machiavellian, self-seeking pursuit of power.

Naturally the first business of British policy, like that of any other state, has been to defend and look after the interests of the country. There is nothing that requires any explaining here. What else would you expect ? Anything other than that would have led to the country's downfall. No country knowingly pursues a policy that is contrary to its interests.

There is no ground for argument here. If British policy has been more successful than most, over the centuries, we must ask why. *There* is ground for open discussion.

Is it due to an excessive dose of Machiavellianism in the directors of British policy ? To British gold ? The consistent following of the principle of *Divide et impera* ? Goebbels is only the latest of a series of hostile commentators who have rung the changes on these themes.

They are really very crude over-simplifications, to say the least : they bear their inadequacy on their face to any reflective mind. There must be some more satisfying answer. We may find the clue to the answer in several lines of approach.

There is first the geographical. The fact of our being an island has been a great advantage all through our later history.

[1] Cf. his book on English history written in the last war.

It has given us the benefit of a time-lag, imposed a bulwark between us and the too violent impact of forces from outside. We were given time to work out our own solutions, to absorb the shock of new ideas and movements, to bide our own time and interpose with effect in Europe when the moment was ripe. Since the last war people have got into the habit of under-estimating the importance of our insularity ; they have been apt to say that the development of air power has annihilated it. Air power has, of course, made an immense difference ; but it has not annihilated it. It was our insularity that saved us in 1940.

But the explanation is still more to be found in historical circumstances — the relations of powers and forces upon the Continent of Europe, and the role Britain was almost inevitably called upon to play, herself being one of them, though slightly withdrawn. The constantly recurring pattern in modern European history is that of the Grand Alliance against an aggressive, aspiring state : a coalition of the smaller Powers whose independence, and sometimes whose very existence, were threatened by the domination of one Power too strong for the rest. It is very natural : one sees the same thing happen in the most elementary forms of human society, such as boys in a school. The sensible thing to do with a bully is to coalesce against him — not to give way to him, for that way leads to disaster (as with British policy under Charles II). Naturally England, as one of the Powers threatened by successive attempts at domination, formed part of such coalitions, and her geo-graphical position, and increasing power, enabled her to play a decisive part.

That was the *raison d'être* of the European struggles against the domination of Philip II, Louis XIV, Napoleon, the Ger-many of William II, as now of Hitler. If other Powers were willing to come into alliance with us — nay, often besought us to come to their rescue — the explanation is not to be found in anything so superficial as Machiavellianism or money — for after all Machiavellianism is very superficial and crude, and finds its devotees out ; but in our sharing a deep, common interest, the desire of each of us to live our own lives our own way.

The exception in this general run of our policy proves the rule. We were never strong enough ourselves to threaten other people's existence, except during the period 1763-76. The end of the Seven Years' War left us in control of the whole of North America, and with France and Spain defeated. Our ascendancy was such that when the colonies revolted we were faced with a European coalition against us. We were defeated ; and it was not to be wondered at. Nobody in this country has much regretted that defeat. Indeed, most of our best historians have taken the American side in the struggle, and said it was a good thing we were defeated — leaving it to modern American historians to rectify the balance and do a little more justice to our case than we did ourselves.

What, then, has been gained by this historic role of Britain in the evolution of Europe over three and a half centuries ? I mean, what has Europe, what has the world gained by it ? For Europe and the world — as a historian I state it bluntly — have gained, no less than we have ourselves. Few Englishmen have thought of the answer, and they would be shy to claim it if they had thought of it. Perhaps a Cornishman — one of the numerous minorities happily included within the creative amalgam that is Britain — may be allowed to answer for them : *something very precious to civilisation.*

The ultimate justification of policy lies not in the realm of policy, but in the values of life and civilisation. We must apply that standard. If British policy has not on balance advanced those, it must be condemned from the point of view of the world in general, however much it may have served the interests and advanced the power of this country.

Very well, let us apply the test. One of the most fruitful results of the first of our great modern struggles, that with Philip II, was the independence of Holland. And what a debt European civilisation owes to that ! — the tradition of Dutch freedom and independence which enabled such a prolific culture, such contributions to art, science, thought, to be made ; the example of religious toleration ; of free political institutions ; the lessons which Europe had to learn from Holland in commerce, banking, colonising activities, in agriculture ; the magnificent maritime tradition, one of the gallantest in Europe, which later became powerful enough to give our seamen the hardest knocks they ever got from anyone.

Again, it was our stand against Louis XIV, headed by the heroic Dutchman William III (King of England, 1688–1702) and continued by Marlborough, ancestor of Mr. Churchill, which mainly saved Western Europe from taking the too monotonous imprint of the Grand Monarque. Holland was saved again, from a nearer and more dangerous neighbour — and eventually an independent Belgium came into being, with a character of its own, something neither French nor Dutch, and a contribution to make to the magnificent, the infinitely creative variety that is Europe.

In the long struggle with Napoleon we helped again to save the independence of the smaller states of Europe — and even France, ultimately, from herself. Compare the artistic and cultural sterility of the Napoleonic régime with the astonishing outburst that came after. Everyone knows Napoleon's reply to an observation on the paucity of literature under his rule : " I shall tell my Minister of the Interior to look into it ". The result was that Madame de Staël, one of the two most distinguished writers in France, had to go into exile. When the Napoleonic Empire was overthrown, with its terrible concentration of French resources and manhood upon the mere pursuit of power, there followed in nineteenth-century France one of the greatest epochs in European culture, in literature and painting, in science, music, thought. One cannot express, one can only be deeply grateful for what France contributed in that age : the main source of civilisation in the last hundred years. It would never have happened if French energies had gone into holding down Europe.

Even apart from these ultimate considerations there are those of the real and relative strength of political forces.

A week or two before war broke out I was talking to a French officer in the *Place* at Nantes who was being called up to join his regiment. He blamed all the trouble Europe had had from Germany on the English for having destroyed Napoleon. It is a tenacious French view. But even apart from us the Napoleonic ascendancy in Europe could not have been maintained ; there were too many forces of national resistance arrayed against it. They could not have been held down indefinitely ; they were bound to burst through. Our national resistance was only one factor ; Austria was another ; Prussia, Spain, Russia yet others. Napoleon only won his success, like Hitler, by exploiting European divisions and striking rapidly before the overwhelming force of all the rest could be brought to bear. The underlying factors of real power were bound to come through in the long run, the balance of national forces to right itself. As is happening again in Europe before our eyes, with the revolt of Italians, Poles, Southern Slavs, Czechs, Scandinavians, French — a real *soulèvement* of the peoples.

This leads us to certain conclusions :

1. The lesson of European history would seem to be that no one Power is strong enough — let alone good enough — to run the rest of Europe.

2. Britain's role in this war is in keeping with the secular tradition of its policy. Its ultimate justification is that we shall have helped to keep the door open for what the Czechs, the Poles, the Jugo-Slavs, and all the subject peoples have to contribute to civilisation. Some of them are only at the beginning of what they have to offer.

3. The sane and sound policy for a people to follow is not a megalomaniac dream of sole power, but one which, while maintaining its own interests and idiosyncrasy, is also as far as possible in keeping with the interests of the great bulk of the others.

That has been the sheet-anchor of our security during four centuries ; it is the real explanation of the long success of our policy. We have only been defeated when we have departed from it.

A recent essay of Thomas Mann, " This War ",[1] shows us that there is one German who understands the British attitude on this subject, and the contrast it affords with the German. He says :

" The Germans cannot, in the last resort, blink their eyes to the fact that England's attitude to power is quite other, and incomparably more natural and straightforward, than their own. . . . To Englishmen power is in no way the darkly

[1] Printed in *Order of the Day : Political Essays and Speeches*.

emotional concept as viewed by Germans ; power, in English eyes, implies no emotion — the ' will-to-power ' is a German invention — but a function ; they exercise it in the gentlest and most unobtrusive manner, with the least possible display, and safeguarding as much freedom as is feasible, for they do not believe that power is a proclamation of slavery, and are therefore not slaves to power themselves."

It is a tribute, coming from a German, of which the English may well be proud.

IV

THE ENGLISH SPIRIT

IT may seem presumptuous on the part of a Cornishman to write about the English spirit, to attempt to define the indefinable, to sprinkle salt on the tail of a subject so elusive, so hard to catch — a spirit of which the essence is perhaps a quality of feeling, at heart a dream. Yet there may be some advantage too : there are things that a Cornishman can say, and even see, which an Englishman perhaps could not. For one characteristic of the English is their very unselfconsciousness : they do not know what they are really like — a charming trait. And one that is even more so is that they do not greatly care. We others are convinced that there is no people (except possibly the Germans) who entertain more illusions about themselves. The English think of themselves as a dull, plodding, humdrum, hard-working sort of people. They are, in fact, nothing of the kind. So far from being hard-working, they are lazy, constitutionally indolent. They are always being caught lagging behind, unprepared — again and again in their history it has been the same ; and then, when up against it — and not until they are up against it — they more than make up for lost time by their resourcefulness, their inventiveness, their ability to extemporise, their self-reliance. For they are by no means a dull, humdrum people : they are a most imaginative and creative people. With the single possible exception of the French, the most brilliant of modern nations.

A Cornishman, who is sufficiently of them to appreciate them and yet is different enough to see them with a certain objectivity, may say that. It would never occur to an Englishman : he would hardly take it seriously if put to him, would perhaps feel rather embarrassed if asked to. Yet this is surely a moment when we may remind him, and ourselves, of the astounding achievement of the English, a people who have contributed such names to the roll of the world's great men, to take a few at random : Shakespeare, Newton, Milton, Darwin, Dickens, Drake, Nelson, Marlborough, Swift, the Pitts — to say nothing of our kith and kin across the seas, Washington, Franklin, Abraham Lincoln.

Yet the achievement of the English, or even the English character, is not my subject, but something more difficult, more subtle and intangible. It is perhaps not without significance that the most careful and sympathetic, and therefore the most penetrating observers of the English spirit have been Americans — they were sufficiently close to know, and enough outside of us to see : Washington Irving, Nathaniel Hawthorne, Henry Adams, Henry James — and in our own time, most philosophical and reflective of all, George Santayana. The burden of the evidence, all these observers are agreed, is that at the core of the English spirit is happiness, a deep source of inner contentment with life, which explains the Englishman's profoundest wish, to be left alone, and his willingness to leave others to their own devices so long as they do not trouble his repose. (Some evidence of the truth of this diagnosis is the fact that he is so slow to wake up to the evident preparations made by others to trouble his repose ; it is not that he is unintelligent, but that being contented with life himself, he cannot understand others who are not.)

When one thinks of the specifically English note in our literature — after all the best mirror of a nation's soul — it is a merry, cheerful, happy note that comes to mind. It is there from the beginning with Chaucer — most English of poets — with his gay and chattering company, mine host of the Tabard, the full-bosomed wife of Bath, the agreeable and elegant prioress, all going down the road from Southwark to Canterbury. When we think of the poet himself, of whom we know so little (and yet so much !), we think of that gesture of his which brings him alive and makes him dear to us across all the centuries, of his throwing away his book when spring comes and going out into the meadows to hear the birds sing and see the flowers :

" Farwel my book and my devocioun ! "

It is the same spirit that one recognises in such poems as " Jolly Good Ale and Old " :

" Though I go bare, take ye no care,
  I nothing am a-cold ;
  I stuff my skin so full within
  Of jolly good ale and old."

Written in the sixteenth century, the song would not be out of place upon the lips of the men serving in the Forces now four hundred years later. The same note one hears in this and in Chaucer, one hears all through, in Skelton, Herrick, Bishop Corbet ("Farewell ! rewards and fairies "), in Dickens, in Chesterton. Of course one finds it in Shakespeare : think of Sir Toby Belch and Falstaff. Paradoxically enough, I hear it in

" When icicles hang by the wall,
  And Dick the shepherd blows his nail,
  And Tom bears logs into the hall,
  And milk comes frozen home in pail,
  When blood is nipped and ways be foul,
  Then nightly sings the staring owl,
        To-whit !
  To-who ! — a merry note,
  While greasy Joan doth keel the pot."

Somehow it brings the image of England to my mind more than any other poem : winter-contentment, cold outside, warmth within, the parson's saw in church, church bells and star-lit Christmas-tide. And straight the mind flies, across the years, to that other serene poet of England and his

" The time draws near the birth of Christ ;
  The moon is hid, the night is still ;
  A single church below the hill
  Is pealing, folded in the mist."

For all the extravagances, the historical fantasies of a Belloc and a Chesterton, there is some truth in the notion of merry England : the England of maypoles and church-ales and dancing on the village green, of harvest-homes and Twelfth Night. If you want one great name in English literature that sums up all that England does not stand for, a bitter spirit, sour, an extravagant, a worshipper of force and of the *führerprinzip*, it can be said in one name : Carlyle. As for Swift — well, the English spirit has changed what was the most damning indictment of human foolery into a children's fairy-tale.

I think we know where this spirit of happy contentment
in life comes from : it comes from the particular relation, the
secret compact that the Englishman has entered into with
nature. Santayana says somewhere that of all modern peoples
it is the English who provide the best example of a people in
harmony with their environment. That is why they are at
ease at heart : none of that overstrain which makes the Germans such bad neighbours to everybody, so uncomfortable to
themselves (though it is at the same time the source of their
achievement : Luther, Kant, Beethoven, Frederick, Bismarck,
Hitler). Santayana says :

" The Englishman's heart is perhaps capricious or silent ;
it is seldom designing or mean. . . . What governs the Englishman is his inner atmosphere, the weather in his soul. . . . He
carries his English weather in his heart wherever he goes,
and it becomes a cool spot in the desert, and a steady and sane
oracle amongst all the deliriums of mankind. Never since the
heroic days of Greece has the world had such a sweet, just,
boyish master. It will be a black day for the human race
when scientific blackguards, conspirators, churls, and fanatics
manage to supplant him."

That, written twenty-five years ago, has not lost its point
since : the issue has become all the more momentous, the
choice for the world between two totally different attitudes to
life, between one spirit and the other, more clear. It is fairly
evident what this detached philosophical observer from the
New World thinks of the consequences for civilisation if the
other should win.

That expected, so ardently desired victory did not take
place twenty-five years ago. Nor should it today ; for there are
other elements in the English spirit, of which those who are not
English, but have met them often on the battle-field, are again
more conscious than the English themselves : pride, courage,
tenacity. I once asked a German friend of mine what was the
specific quality among the English soldiers of the last war which
they noticed. His answer was surprising. He said, " Their
pride." When taken prisoner, battered, dirty, weary, wounded,
their spirit was unbroken, they never dreamed of submission ;

they retained their self-respect, they assumed no other. The Germans were taken aback by this; they were impressed. They will have reason to be yet again. Everybody who met the men who came away from Dunkirk knows how completely unbroken their spirit was. Bombed to blazes, with no tanks and few planes, with their defences crumbling right and left, they were undismayed.

These things are unchanging in our history. Here is a Gloucestershire recruit out of Shakespeare going to the war : " By my troth, I care not ; a man can die but once : we owe God a death : I'll ne'er bear a base mind : an't be my destiny, so ; an't be not, so : no man's too good to serve his prince ; and let it go which way it will, he that dies this year is quit for the next."

It is exactly the same sentiment as I heard from the lips of a young sailor in the train : " If you worry, you die ; and if you don't worry, you may die : so what's the use anyway ? "

It is perhaps at its highest moment of tension, as in 1588, in 1805, in 1917, or again today, that the English spirit is most revealing of its nature. The fighting men of those earlier great days expressed it no less well than the writing men, perhaps better. Where Shakespeare wrote,

" Nought shall make us rue,
If England to itself do rest but true ",

Drake and Howard of Effingham were writing with the superb eloquence the men of that moment had. I find myself often and often in these days, when the R.A.F. is gradually wearing down the numerical superiority of Goering's air force, saying over to myself Howard's words to the Queen as he fought Philip's Armada all that week up the Channel :

" By little, and by little, we pluck them of their feathers."

It would serve as a motto for the Royal Air Force today.

For what is clear in the end is that the spirit of the English at that moment, or in 1805 (Nelson wrote just like Drake), is not different from that in the present : there is a continuity of response to danger undismayed. The words and actions are interchangeable : one of Nelson's messages, with its natural eloquence, would serve to express the spirit of the Royal Navy

D

today. The men have their own way of expressing their spirit, as in the action against the *Graf Spee*, or in that splendid moving letter of a fallen airman to his mother.

That is the stuff of which the English spirit is made, no less than that dream of happiness and content which lies at the heart of every Englishman. Is it possible to think that such a spirit can ever be conquered ?

(*Written July* 1940.)

DRAKE'S WAY

MANY people — the Government itself, to judge from some of its pronouncements — have been struck by the similarity of our situation today [1] to that in 1587–8, that earlier and no less grave crisis in our history when we awaited the fruition of all the preparations throughout the Spanish Empire in Europe and America for a descent upon this island. At this comparable moment, in the same week as the Armada was brought to battle in the Channel, it is more than interesting, it is exciting to listen to the views of Drake himself on the absorbing question of offensive versus defensive, whether it is better to await the enemy's blow in your own waters, on your own soil, or whether the best defence is not to carry the war into his.

Here are Drake's views, as I took them down some years ago from the actual letters he wrote from Plymouth to the Queen (now, alas, no longer to be seen, since present circumstances have closed the Public Record Office). I seem still to see in my mind's eye the large folded pages covered with that firm, fluent, confident handwriting, the ink rather purplish in places as if some water had fallen upon it, the glisten of sand here and there as if it were not three hundred and fifty years ago that that hand scattered the sand upon the page. What memories it brings back ! Memories of ceaseless watching in the Channel and along the coasts, then, as now, of anxiety and courage in time of trial, of energy and spirit crowned with ultimate and deserved victory.

Drake's views are expressed at length and copiously ; none of your strong-silent-man nonsense with him ; he had the superb natural eloquence of the great man of action, like Nelson, like Cromwell, and he was not afraid to let himself go. The situation, it will be remembered, was that while Philip was completing his preparations in Lisbon, the cautious Burghley and Elizabeth were playing upon their second string, peace

[1] Written July 1940.

talks with Parma in the Netherlands. At the same time they wrote to Drake for his opinion as to the best way to break up the concentration of ships at Lisbon.

He declared himself in general in favour of a descent upon the enemy's coast, a surprise attack upon his shipping and transports, breaking up and destroying them so that there would be no invasion. And he had shown with brilliant success how it could be done the year before at Cadiz, " the singeing of the King of Spain's beard ". Now, in the spring of 1588, he urged again and again a descent upon Lisbon to break up the still greater concentrations there, before they became too vast an armada to attack with impunity. For various reasons the government hesitated, giving Philip the opportunity to draw his forces together, made up of the contingents from different parts of Europe under his control. They hesitated until in fact the Armada was assembled ; the invasion of England was possible, the issue doubtful.

To the Queen's inquiry what was now to be done, Drake replied :

" Truly this point is hardly to be answered as yet, for two special causes ; the first for that our intelligences are as yet uncertain. The second is the resolution of our own people, which I shall better understand when I have them at sea. . . . But if your Majesty will give present order for our proceeding to the sea, and send to the strengthening of this fleet here four more of your Majesty's good ships and those sixteen sail of ships which are preparing in London, then shall your Majesty stand so well, with God's assistance, that if the fleet come out of Lisbon, as long as we have victual to live withal upon that coast they shall be fought with, and I hope through the goodness of our merciful God in such sort as shall hinder his quiet passage into England."

As for morale — that much-abused, but still useful, word — Drake wrote :

" I assure your Majesty I have not in my lifetime known better men and possessed with gallanter minds than your Majesty's people are for the most part, which are here gathered together voluntarily to put their hands and hearts to the finishing of this good piece of work, wherein we are all per-

suaded that God the giver of all victories will in mercy look
upon your most excellent Majesty and us your subjects who
for the defence of your Majesty, our religion and natural
country have resolutely vowed the hazard of our lives."

(How Elizabeth took the godly element in all this we do not
know ; in general she could not bear Protestant sermonising :
she preferred to do her own. She once said of Hawkins, when
he tried a little on her, " God's truth ! This fellow went away
a soldier and hath come home a prating divine.")

Then follows a famous sentence which could not be bettered
as summing up Drake's general conception of strategy :

" The advantage of time and place in all martial actions is
half a victory, which being lost is irrecoverable. Wherefore,
if your Majesty will command me away with those ships that
are here already and the rest to follow with all possible expedition, I hold it in my poor opinion the surest and best course."

Still the Queen did not show her hand. A fortnight later
Drake returned to the attack :

" Most renowned prince, I beseech you to pardon my bold-
ness in the discharge of my conscience, being burdened to
signify unto your Highness the imminent dangers that in my
simple opinion do hang over us. That if a good peace for your
Majesty be not forthwith concluded (which I as much as any
man desireth), then these great preparations of the Spaniard
may be speedily prevented, as much as in your Majesty lieth,
by sending your forces to encounter theirs, somewhat far off
and more near their own coast, which will be better cheap for
your Majesty and people, and much the dearer for the enemy.
. . . I will continually pray to God to bless your Majesty with
all happy victories. From Plymouth this 23rd of April, Your
Majesty's most loyal, Fra. Drake."

In the end, Drake's view was accepted, but permission for
him to set sail was not given until too late ; the Armada did
indeed reach our coasts. Perhaps its ultimate destiny would
have been the same.

Such were Drake's views. Not that one puts them forward
as dogma to be followed in what may turn out to be very
different circumstances. But at a time like the present it is

inspiring to recall them, still more the man who held them and the memory of that great moment in our history when, an altogether smaller people with vastly inferior resources to what we have today, we faced undismayed the greatest Power in Europe and America.

VI

THE IDEA OF PATRIOTISM [1]

WHAT is it that we mean by " patriotism " ? We know the
word so well, we have heard it so often, that we are apt to take
for granted what it means without inquiring further. If we go
into it together we shall find that it is by no means so simple as
you might think, but a great deal more complex and subtle.
We shall want to know what other people have meant by
patriotism — what it has meant to other forms of society at
other times than our own.

And first, a word about the word itself, before we come
to the thing it describes. The word " patriot " came to us
through the French from late Latin, and ultimately derives
from the Greek word *patrios*, meaning " of one's fathers ". Its
stem is that very elemental word that runs through all the
Aryan languages, cognate with " father ". That already tells
you a good deal. It suggests two things : (1) that the idea of
patriotism hinges on to something very fundamental in social
life ; but (2) that in itself it is a comparatively late development
in society, an emotion or feeling which has been built up out of
more primitive ones. It is, in fact, a complex construction of
emotions and sentiments and associations, more sophisticated
and abstract than the simpler emotions like fear, anger, love
(though the last is perhaps complex enough !).

But that is not to deny its strength and power. Professors
Julian Huxley and Haddon tell us in their book *We Europeans*
that " patriotism has proved itself one of the strongest forces
known to history, second perhaps to religion alone ".

Now we can come to the definition of patriotism : the
Oxford Dictionary defines it as " love of or zealous devotion to
one's own country ". That fixes for us a further point in the
exact pinning-down of the idea. Patriotism, to be exact,
implies a *patria* : it is that particular kind of loyalty which is
directed to the nation, and without which the nation could

[1] A broadcast to schools, October 1940.

45

not exist. It did not come into existence, therefore, in the full sense until the development of the modern nation-state. We owe it, like so many other things, to the Renaissance. It is significant that we do not come across the word " patriot " in French until the fifteenth century : that period of prolonged war between the French and the English out of which the modern states, France and England, with their feeling of nationality, of distinctiveness, of a character of their own, developed. And the word does not appear in English until the end of the sixteenth century. I do not think that it appears in Shakespeare at all.

Patriotism is a form of group-feeling. Every kind of group — a cricket club, a church, a trade union, a university, a school — counts on the loyalty of its members and could not exist without it. Patriotism is that particular group-feeling called forth by the nation.

The most highly developed states of antiquity, the city-states of Greece, and Rome, had a very recognisable spirit of patriotism akin to our own. They had something to be proud about, and they were proud of their cities' achievements. It was Athens that was the beacon-light of the ancient world ; and the highest expression of their patriotism is to be found in that wonderful oration which Pericles made over the bodies of the Athenians who fell in the first year of the Peloponnesian War. It was a conscious celebration of the particular qualities that made Athens what it was, as against Sparta — the Nazi-state of the ancient world :

" They toil from early boyhood in a laborious pursuit after courage, while we, free to live and wander as we please, march out none the less to face the selfsame dangers. Indeed, if we choose to face danger with an easy mind rather than after a rigorous training, and to trust rather in native manliness than in state-made courage, the advantage lies with us ; for we are spared all the weariness of practising for future hardships, and when we find ourselves amongst them we are as brave as our plodding rivals. . . . In a word I claim that our city as a whole is an education to Greece, and that her members yield to none, man by man, for independence of spirit, many-sidedness of attainment, and complete self-reliance in limbs and brain. . . .

Our pioneers have forced a way into every sea and every land, establishing among all mankind, in punishment or beneficence, eternal memorials of their settlement."

That is magnificent ; but what is even more important, Pericles was justified in his claims for Athens. It will not have escaped your notice what a parallel there is between Athens and Sparta, and what England stands for as against Nazi Germany. When you think of the great achievements and the great men whom this country has produced — Shakespeare, Newton, Milton, Darwin, Cromwell, Nelson, the Pitts — our tradition of political freedom, the triumphs of modern industry, the British Commonwealth of Nations — I think we are not unjustified in saying that when Pericles spoke for Athens two thousand years ago he spoke also for us today.

Sparta too had her patriotism ; but it was a gloomy, repressive, and ultimately a sterile creed, like the Moloch-worship of the state which we see incarnate in Nazi Germany. Everything was sacrificed to the pursuit of power ; and when they had achieved power they found they had never faced the question — Power to what end ? to what purpose ? The whole thing crumbled, leaving nothing but a name to signify the cult of rigour and hardship for its own sake — Spartanism. While Athens was the creator, the seed-bed of western civilisation.

The Roman Republic exhibited the spirit of Sparta, and with it something of the same sombre, gloomy, exclusive patriotism. To me — and I think really to all of us — Rome begins to be much more interesting when she developed an empire, became more receptive of outside influences and developed the idea of universal citizenship based upon common allegiance to Rome, a sharing of her civilisation that was open to all peoples and languages and creeds. That was Rome's greatest contribution to the world, a common pride open to all in being able to say, as St. Paul was able to claim, " *Civis Romanus sum* ". That was a kind of patriotism, though a very different one from any that we have yet mentioned, or from what we are accustomed to in the modern world. Perhaps the nearest thing to it yet achieved is the free citizenship, the unforced allegiance that runs through the British Empire ; and who knows, before we are through our present trials, whether the greatest of English-speaking countries, the United States, may not come to be included in a wider unity ? Of the older civilisations, probably the Chinese came closest to Rome in its spirit of a quasi-universal loyalty. At any rate I am clear that it is this aspect of Rome — its ability to hold diverse peoples and tongues in a spirit of common allegiance — a sort of universal patriotism, that has most to say to us in the modern world.

Then came the break-down of the Roman Empire : the inrush of the barbarians, the Goths, the Vandals, the Huns : the oncoming of the Dark Ages. All these primitive peoples in that miserable, confused era — where " ignorant armies clash by night " — had their folk-loyalties. Read Tacitus on the Germans, Caesar on the Gauls : pretty dreary reading I find it, with all their squabbles and quarrels, and incessant inter-necine strife. Like the Anglo-Saxon Heptarchy. No wonder a civilised eighteenth-century gentleman like Gibbon thought its history the " battles of kites and crows ". But their tribal loyalties were not what we mean by patriotism.

That brings me to a further point. For patriotism to be true patriotism, it must attach itself to a really significant entity, a nation or a state that has achieved some greatness, that possesses a tradition and a record that means something to civilisation. We can all recognise French or German or Dutch patriotism — but then we get to a border-line with the smaller indeterminate nationalities which are really agglomerations of tribes with very little conscious corporate existence. I appreci-ate the point well as a Cornishman : devoted as I am to Cornwall and its history, is there such a thing as Cornish patriotism ? It comes, I think, under the heading of what we call " local patriotism " : not a bad thing — a good thing rather, provided it is kept in proper perspective.

Nor did the Middle Ages develop patriotism as we know it. The way they found out of the confusion of the Dark Ages was in a shadow-version of the Roman Empire, in which loyalty to the universal Church took the place of the Roman citizenship. On one side you had the universal claims of the Church — a great deal more real and effective than those of the Holy Roman

Emperor — and on the other the localism which went with feudalism. No place, no need, for patriotism there. You had a society which was ruled by a cosmopolitan upper class, speaking for the most part French in Western Europe, like the Anglo-Norman baronage or the English kings right up to Henry VI. It was with the break-up of that feudal, cosmopolitan society that the modern nations as we know them came into existence, and with them, patriotism.

First and most important were France and England, whose national consciousness was heightened by their long struggle with each other. For France that struggle produced a national hero, imbued with the purest spirit of patriotism, whose personality stands for all time as the symbol of national re-generation : Joan of Arc. She was a patriot, if ever there was one. (Read what Bernard Shaw has to say on the subject.) I doubt if our Henry V was : he was much more a con-queror, an imperialist, a medieval Napoleon. Shakespeare was reading back from his own time when he made Henry V say before Agincourt :

> " This day is called the feast of Crispian :
> He that outlives this day, and comes safe home,
> Will stand a-tiptoe when this day is named,
> And rouse him at the name of Crispian.
> He that shall live this day, and see old age,
> Will yearly on the vigil feast his neighbours,
> And say, ' Tomorrow is Saint Crispian ' :
> Then will he strip his sleeve and show his scars,
> And say, ' These wounds I had on Crispin's day.' "

Yet that is medieval enough in feeling, for it is just human, a natural human reaction of almost any time or place.

One English reaction in the long struggle with France, it is said, was the development of the University of Oxford, so that English students should not have to go to the University of Paris as in the earlier Middle Ages. But it was the French who in their poetry first expressed this new-found feeling of love for their native land as such, the foundation of all patriotism. Do you know that charming pathetic ballad of Charles D'Orléans, who was prisoner in England, and how one day upon the cliffs of Dover the desire to see France again overcame him ?

" En regardant vers le païs de France,
Un jour m'avint, à Dovre sur la mer,
Qu'il me souvint de la douce plaisance
Que je souloye oùdit païs trouver."

I suppose the most famous expression of all of this sentiment are the sonnets of Joachim du Bellay, the French Renaissance poet, written about France when he was an exile in Rome :

" Quand revoirai-je, hélas, de mon petit village
Fumer la cheminée : en quelle saison
Revoirai-je le clos de ma pauvre maison,
Qui m'est une province, et beaucoup d'avantage ? "

You see the poet thinking of France in terms of his own Anjou, his own little village, his small house there with the smoke coming from its chimney. I dare say at bottom we all think of our native country, see it in the mind's eye, in little imaginative glimpses like that. I know when I have been very ill before now, away from home, in London, I found myself taking refuge in images of home, little Cornish coves where one bathed in summer, a stream running down a moorland valley, the cool interior of a church, the sun printed on the wall. At the same time it was Joachim du Bellay who wrote the proudest of all patriotic lines :

" France, mère des arts, des armes, et des loix."

National sentiment, as we know it, was then the product of the break-up of medieval society. It comes with the Renaissance, the modern nation-state. Even that most sceptical, unbelieving intelligence, Machiavelli, was a great patriot in his way, both for Florence and for Italy : you know that his book *The Prince*, that text-book of political realism, not to say cynicism, concludes with a chapter " That Italy may be rid of the Barbarians ". It is fairly true to say, as a historical generalisation, that patriotism is at its highest and noblest when a people have been through and surmounted a great danger. That seems to bring forth all the latent capacities of a people, heighten them to the greatest tension of which they are capable. And it is such moments in their history that are apt to be the most creative. Such was the great age of fifth-century Athens after she had triumphantly withstood the Persian Invasion ; such the Augustan age at Rome after the long civil wars ; such the Elizabethan age in England after the stern test of the struggle with Spain ; the golden age of the Dutch seventeenth century, the age of Rembrandt and all the painters and seamen, when Holland had won her independence ; the great age in German history, the early nineteenth century, with the repulse of the French Revolution and Napoleon. May it not be that after we have come successfully through our present time of trial, we may be rewarded with an age of creative achievement which will place the twentieth century alongside the Elizabethan age in our history ?

For, in the end, patriotism to be good must be constructive and not exclusive. It must take justified pride in the great achievements of one's country, not in everything good or bad just because it is one's own. " My country, right or wrong " is a very questionable principle. It happens that the English people have a wonderful record of creative achievement : in their long record of political success, their poetry — the finest of modern poetries — their achievements in science and industry, upon the sea and now in the air. But other great peoples have similar achievements to be proud of : the French, the Italians, the Germans, the Russians, the Chinese. The ordinary man is perhaps not capable of looking further than his own nation, his own language : his own country is the mental world he inhabits. But he is the really civilised man who is capable of appreciating not only English poetry and English seamanship, but French and Italian and Dutch painting, German music, the Russian novel, Chinese art. For all the great nations have contributed greatly to civilisation, and are ultimately to be judged by that. Is it too much to hope that since men have grown from small tribal loyalties to that greater loyalty to the nation which we call patriotism, one day after these present troubles are over we may achieve some feeling of common pride in the best of each other's achievements and attain something like a European patriotism ?

VII

THE SPIRIT OF ADVENTURE : THE BRITISH INTERPRETATION [1]

I WONDER what your favourite books are ? What kind of reading you like best ? I should like to know, for I wonder if you like the same kind of books that were my favourite reading when I was at school. My favourite books, I remember, were two stories of adventure : Stevenson's *Treasure Island* and Q's *The Splendid Spur.* Then there were other books, too, that gave me the same thrill of excitement — *Westward Ho !* and Kipling's *Kim.* And for some odd reason I remember a whole summer day spent out on one of the lovely headlands of Cornwall — it was Trenarren, near my home — with my nose in a book. I forget its title now, but it was all about the Spanish Main and an Englishman caught in a conspiracy, fighting his way out of the narrow streets of the town in the dark. Whenever I looked up from my book I looked straight out to sea — westwards to the Spanish Main.

You could not help getting the feeling of adventure if you were brought up as a child in Cornwall. In my father's early days, thousands of Cornish miners had emigrated overseas to open up the gold mines of South Africa, Australia, the silver and tin mines of Montana. Pretty rough days those were in the mining camps of Johannesburg and Butte City, and many were the tales that came home to us of the happenings there — more like the tales of Bret Harte or films of the Wild West than our own sedate and necessarily sober life — since we were schoolboys at home in Cornwall.

Then there were all the little Cornish ports with foreign ships and sailors perpetually coming and going from the seven seas. And all round our coasts there were the places that spoke to us of the excitements of the Elizabethan age, the adventures of the Civil War. There was Pendennis Castle from which Henrietta Maria set sail for France ; there was Fowey harbour

[1] Broadcast to schools, October 1940.

into which the chests of Spanish treasure intended to pay Alva's troops were unloaded into the cellars of Mr. Treffry's house, Place ; there was Trematon Castle, near Saltash, into which the immense treasure of silver that Drake brought back from his voyage round the world was put for safety, until it was loaded into waggons and trundled away to the Tower.

How could you fail to be excited by the story of British adventure with such a background ? For the fact is that the tales you hear, the stories you read, the memories of the places, all fuse together into a tradition that calls forth a response in those who are born into it. So it is natural for West-countrymen to take to the sea as their field of adventure. It was natural for Trevithick, the great inventor, when he got discouraged at home to go off to Peru and stay there without a word for thirteen years, and suddenly, after the most extraordinary adventures, turn up again one day in Cornwall with nothing but his gold watch in his pocket ! The two Victorian writers who more than any brought back the spirit of the Elizabethan age into their writing — Kingsley and Froude — were both of them Devonshire men, cradled and brought up in the places which Drake and Hawkins, John Oxenham, Gilbert and Ralegh and Grenville haunted when they were alive.

There is a case, if you like, of transposing adventure into the realm of the mind : " Much have I travelled in the realms of gold. . . ."

I suppose it is true to say that of all modern countries it is this country, by and large, which has had the greatest and most continuous record of adventure, the longest and most varied list of great adventurers. The country that comes nearest to us in one way is that other small, seaboard, seafaring country on the western edge of the Continent, led on similarly by its geographical situation to adventure and discovery : Portugal. Portugal had a brilliant period in navigation and discovery at the end of the Middle Ages and beginning of the modern epoch. It was Portuguese navigators who first felt their way around the coast of Africa, rounded the Cape of Good Hope, and opened the seaway to the East. It was a great Portuguese, Magellan, who first found the way into the Pacific and crossed that ocean, so circumnavigating the globe. The Spaniards

followed in the wake of the Portuguese with their discovery
and conquest of America.

The English voyagers of the sixteenth century were inspired
by their exploits to follow suit, and so there came about our
own greatest age of adventure, the Elizabethan age.

What is the British tradition of adventure ? What has it
been ? What do we mean by it ?

Well, first and quite naturally because of our geographical
situation, an island out on the north-western outskirts of
Europe, our main field of adventure has always been *the sea*.
So it is that at the beginning of our existence as a nation, when
King Alfred undertook the education of his people, he translated
from the Latin a book of Voyages. Even before that, outstanding among what remains to us of Anglo-Saxon poetry are the
two poems which deal with the sea, and the life of the seaman :
the *Wanderer* and the *Seafarer*. But the Norman Conquest had
the effect of binding us more closely to the Continent, and
during the Middle Ages it may be said that France was the chief
field of English adventure. What names, and what memories
that has left in our tradition : Cressy, Poictiers, Agincourt.
Of course medieval Englishmen went further (and fared worse) :
some of them went on crusades to the Holy Land ; the seamen
made voyages to Iceland and into the Mediterranean.

But it is not until the sixteenth century, with the discovery
of America, that we began to come fully-fledged into our own.
Think how exciting the globe was to the men of that time : it
was a constantly expanding world that they inhabited. When
they first reached America they thought they had reached the
outskirts of the Cathay — the China — they were looking for.
They did not know that they had bumped into a new and
unknown continent, and it was only slowly that they came to
realise that it was a whole New World. Then they had no idea
at first how big it was : they were always looking for a quick
way round it into the Pacific and so to China : the North-West
Passage. The Pacific itself was a great surprise to them : they
did not realise how vast it was : the more they sailed into it the
larger it grew. The Spaniards kept the navigation of the middle
passage across from Mexico to the Philippines a dead secret.
Both Spaniards and English believed that there was a southern

continent somewhere in its spaces : they called it Terra
Australis. Sir Richard Grenville planned a voyage to discover
it when he was a young man, but he was not permitted to carry
it out ; Drake, who came after him and was allowed to go on
that voyage, in which he circumnavigated the globe, made a
feint in that direction on emerging through the Straits of
Magellan into the Pacific, before he went up the coast of South
America, and across by the usual Spanish route. And then in
addition to all that, there was the great dark continent of
Africa, which they learnt to sail round, but of which very little
of the interior was known until much later — until the nineteenth century.

So we were launched by the Elizabethan seamen upon our
long career of adventure across the seas : adventure leading to
discovery, discovery to exploration, exploration to colonisation
and settlement, and so to Empire. So that you might say the
British Empire was a product — almost a by-product — of
adventure. It certainly was not planned ; it came into being
naturally, gradually, as the result of the adventurous spirit,
the stout heart and courage of our forefathers looking for a
livelihood and an outlet for their energy and spirits across the
ocean.

That leads me to another point. We say the " British "
Empire — you know it was a Welshman who coined the
phrase in the sixteenth century, the distinguished geographer,
Dr. Dee. And I suppose I ought to say " the spirit of British
adventure ", not merely English. For I think the greatness
and variety of its record is partly due to the different elements,
the different contributions of temperament and character, of
English, Scots, Welsh, and Irish : it has made it all the richer.
Let us think, for instance : whom do you regard as representative figures of British adventure ? I should suggest, say : Drake,
Clive, Captain Cook, Nelson, David Livingstone, and, in our
own time, Lawrence of Arabia.

Let us look at where they came from, and what they were
like as types of Great Adventurers.

Drake was the son of a poor clergyman, and as everybody
knows, a West-countryman. Clive came from an old family
on the Welsh border. Captain Cook was the son of a Yorkshire

E

agricultural labourer ; Nelson an East Anglian, a Norfolk man, another parson's son. David Livingstone was a Scot who started life as a factory hand ; and T. E. Lawrence the son of an Irish baronet. So you see what different streams, from what different environments and social classes, have run together to form the British achievement in adventure.

Let us look a little more closely into them as men : I think you will find it revealing. There are certain common qualities they all have : they all have courage, spirit, daring. They all have extraordinary powers of physical and mental endurance. You will remember that terrible last journey of Livingstone when he was slowly dying, racked with fever and dysentery : they thought at home in England that he was lost, and Stanley went out on an expedition to find him ; when he found him, Livingstone refused to come away with him, but went on to the end. It is like Captain Scott in the Antarctic — or like Sir Richard Grenville in the *Revenge* : Grenville could have got away, but he just wouldn't ; he took on a whole Spanish Fleet on his own. You all know from *Revolt in the Desert* the incredible strain that the young Lawrence endured, being bumped out of an aeroplane, crashing in cars, making those long night marches in desert conditions, sleepless for nights and days. The truth is that all these men exemplify a triumph of *will-power* : that is what enabled them to succeed. The strain made some of them harsh — as Grenville was harsh, and Bligh of the *Bounty*. Perhaps Drake too — as certainly he was in his execution of Captain Doughty in South America, before breaking into the Pacific. Still you can't make an omelette without breaking some eggs. It is a mistake to be too soft ; one can't expect to achieve anything without grit. *That* they all had.

They have something else too : they are all of them resourceful, quick in finding a way out of difficulty, in inventing something. When Drake came back from Nombre de Dios to the coast, with all the silver that he and his men had rifled from the mule-train they had surprised, he found that his boat was missing : so he had to knock together a raft on which, in a sinking condition, he got to his ship. Grenville once boarded a Spanish prize in mid-ocean from a raft of sugar chests that he had roped together. There are any number of examples of

Livingstone's resourcefulness in tight corners in Africa, and of Lawrence's in the Arab Revolt.

Another common characteristic : none of them minded taking on odds, indeed they seem to have liked it better that way. Drake sailed round the world in a ship of 180 tons. Clive fought the battle of Plassey with less than 3000 men against 40,000 infantry, 15,000 cavalry, and 50 guns. Nelson always took on forces that were larger than his own, and at Trafalgar annihilated a fleet, two fleets, French and Spanish, that together were superior in strength. Lawrence ran the Arab Revolt with a handful of men ; Livingstone explored Central Africa practically off his own bat. It isn't mere numbers that count — as Goering found to his surprise with the R.A.F.

All these men have a dynamic quality about them — the specific quality of the heroic. But also they are very English heroes. And that means that in spite of the different standards of the periods in which they lived, they were humane men for the most part, sparing of human life, considerate of others. Of the great heroes of the Continent, I do not know that we can say so much : Frederick the Great and Napoleon, Cortes and Pizarro, were all ruthless and unsparing of human life. Even Drake, who was a tremendous fighting man, was well loved and popular with his men : he cared for them and looked after them ; they knew that there wasn't a thing about a ship that he did not know. Nelson too, a terrific fighter — who fought until he had lost an arm, an eye, his face marked with scars — was considerate of his men, and not only of his own men, but of the enemy as far as possible in war conditions. He refused to adopt the French habit of employing riflemen on board ship as inhumane, since it had no effect upon the issue of the action. At Trafalgar he twice gave orders to cease firing upon the *Redoutable*, because her great guns were silent and he thought she had struck. It was a rifleman in the mizzen-top of the *Redoutable* who fired the shot that killed him.

Captain Cook too was a humane, considerate, and kindly man. You know that wonderful three-year voyage of his ship the *Resolution*, in which he explored the coasts of New Zealand, Australia, and New Guinea — but the most important discovery of all in that voyage was the possibility of keeping a ship's company at sea without serious loss from sickness and death. On all earlier voyages a considerable proportion of the crew died from disease ; sometimes the mortality was terrible ; it is the melancholy side to so many of those magnificent stories of adventure we read in Hakluyt. But on this voyage Cook put into effect such measures that only one man out of a complement of 118 died. And we all know the trust and devotion that Livingstone's native boys had in him. I am not sure that Livingstone isn't the greatest of these heroic spirits : if the story of adventure may be said to have its saints, he is one of the first of them. Adventurous men are not necessarily very patient or tactful — indeed they are often impatient and hard to get on with. But when you think of Livingstone's wonderful patience, and infinite tact and wisdom in dealing with difficult situations and people, you cannot but admire him immensely. That simple Scots missionary was one of the truly great men of the nineteenth century. Probably his greatest gift of all was the absolute and transparent confidence that his personality inspired, so that he was able to move practically unarmed through the most savage and unexplored parts of Central Africa. Not that he was in the least soft either for all his gentleness : once when his party was attacked in the rear by a band of quarrelsome savages looking for trouble, the man of God got off his riding-ox and, sick as he was, whipped out a six-chambered revolver and presented it at the chief's stomach. It converted the latter from an enemy into a friend.

Livingstone had something else too : he had from his earliest years an extraordinary passionate spirit of scientific curiosity that made him learn everything that he wanted for his purpose. When a young lad working in a cotton factory, he contrived to fix up his book on the spinning-jenny so that he could catch sentences as he passed to and fro at his task. He studied botany and zoology and geology. On his way out to the Cape he got the captain of the ship to teach him how to use a quadrant and take lunar observations. Later on, when on holiday at the Cape, he put himself under the Astronomer Royal, and developed a skill at astronomical observations such as very few other travellers have ever had. He was just as observant and thorough at gardening and carpentry and mechanical work of all kinds as he was at native languages. I am not sure that such passionate acquisition of knowledge isn't Scottish rather than English. But there, Captain Cook was a superb and scientific navigator, and so was his 2nd Lieutenant, Bligh of the *Bounty*, both Englishmen.

We have seen that these men whom I have taken as types of British adventure, of the heroic spirit in our people, have certain qualities in common. In other ways they differ very interestingly. They are products of their period, and they respond to the atmosphere of their time. Drake belonged to the age of Elizabeth, the high Renaissance, and there went with that a certain magnificence of behaviour, a certain swagger in bearing such as you can see in his portrait, with Elizabeth's great jewel at his girdle, hand upon the pommel of his sword, in the background the globe he circumnavigated, and his arms with the Southern stars and a wave of the sea between. You can hear it in his speech. " We trust so to handle the matter ", he wrote to the Queen, when the Armada was in the Channel, " that the Duke of Medina Sidonia will wish himself ere long at St. Mary Port among his orange trees ". He did. Cook was a man of the eighteenth century, like Anson, that other circumnavigator of the globe : both of them rather cool, commonsense, rational natures. (You should read the narrative of Anson's *Voyage Round the World*, compiled by his chaplain, who recommends the story as that of " a very singular performance ". It is very good reading.) Then Livingstone is very much a man of the nineteenth century, a Victorian, with a Victorian's trust in Providence and his belief in his mission " to alleviate human misery " to guide him.

T. E. Lawrence, the last of my types, is very much a man of the twentieth century, impelled to action yet wondering whether action was worth while, to what end, having no belief to support him, nothing to fall back upon but his own courage and fortitude and determination not to fail the tests which he set himself. He had our modern passion for speed, for the conquest of the air, the absorbing interest in technical achievement for its own sake, which is serving us to such good stead with the young heroes of the R.A.F. today. How proud he would have been of them, for he was their forerunner, their type. He wrote of his first period with the R.A.F., " At Farn-borough I grew suddenly on fire with the glory which the air should be, and set to work full steam to make the others vibrate to it like myself ". That is the spirit of which these heroes are made. Throughout most of our history we have seen it at work on the sea, and it is that that has made us what we are and given us our Empire.

We sometimes depreciate our own twentieth century ; but a period which has produced such men as Captain Scott and Shackleton, the Antarctic explorers, the men of the Mount Everest expeditions, those two Englishmen who were first to fly the Atlantic, Lawrence of Arabia (not to mention that other Lawrence, D. H., a great adventurer too of a very different sort, in the realm of the mind) — such a period is a very rich one indeed, and one to be proud of in the annals of our people. It is for us to keep that spirit alive and contribute something of our own to that tradition ; the least we can do is first to remember those who made and created it.

VIII

SEAMEN AND EMPIRE

(i)

Now that the Empire, in the form at least in which we have known it historically, is changing its character, there is an extreme interest, partly nostalgic, partly inspiriting, in reading that wonderful story as told by a sympathetic historian. And what better guide could there be than J. A. Williamson, that retired schoolmaster whom the elect know to be one of the best historians writing in this country ? He has a very fine body of historical work to his credit, on various aspects of British expansion beyond the seas, on maritime enterprise, the great Tudor navigators, our sea history in general. He has his own special angle, his own particular qualifications : himself a sailor of craft, he knows the winds and currents, understands the conditions within which our forebears navigated the oceans, the limitations imposed upon them and their triumphs. He has, quite rightly for a historian — or for anybody else for that matter — a keen sense of pride in our past, four centuries full of achievement.

The story begins with the discovery of America, in which, Dr. Williamson makes it clear, the English part is much more important than is generally realised.[1] Some years before the voyage of Columbus, the men of Bristol were sending out ships beyond Ireland to search for Atlantic islands. It was very right that the lead should come from Bristol : the link-up that made for Atlantic discovery from that port is most exciting. In the fifteenth century Bristol was the chief port for the trade with Iceland, and in Iceland the knowledge of the tenth-century Norse discoveries in North America, Greenland, and Markland had never died out. Then, too, Bristol's contacts with Portugal and Spain, her ships trading to Madeira and later to the Azores, linked up with Spanish and Portuguese voyages into the Atlantic, and stimulated the imagination of

[1] J. A. Williamson, *The Ocean in English History*, 1941.

the Bristol merchants. John Cabot brought these early efforts
to a point, when he came to the town with the new Renaissance
ideas on world geography and the possibilities of the Atlantic.
He was no less remarkable a man than Columbus, " his
equal in originality and determination, his superior in knowledge and judgment ". Dr. Williamson says, " It is fairly
clear that Cabot had developed his plans before the success of
Columbus was known, and that he was an originator and not
an imitator of Columbus ". Unfortunately the records of him
are extremely scanty, and he died on his second voyage across
the Atlantic, whereas historical luck treated Columbus well.

But it seems probable that the English were the first to
recognise that it was a new continent that had been discovered,
and not, as Columbus insisted, the outlying coast of Asia.
Later, it was the Bristol merchants at Seville who got to know
the secrets of the Spanish Empire, its trade and navigation, and
were the chief agents in making them known in England. With
the reign of Elizabeth, English seamen forced their way into
the Spanish sphere : as Dr. Williamson says grandly in his
summing-up of the disaster to Hawkins and Drake at San
Juan de Ulua — " but the English were in the Caribbean, and
in one capacity or another they have been there ever since ".
In the next century, when after decades of triangular conflict
with Dutch and English, the Portuguese Empire was *en pleine
déchéance*, we were the successors to practically the whole
inheritance.

So the story proceeds : a tale of marvellous energy, ability,
and endurance, of foresight and ambition, that is not without
its romantic and even its pathetic sides, so different from the
disgraceful decadence, the complacency, and incompetence of
the last two decades, which have gone far to lose us the inheritance of four centuries. Dr. Williamson permits himself no
comment on this, except by implication when he says : " The
British Empire, indeed, was not founded in a fit of absent-
mindedness, by third-rate persons who could prosper at no
other undertaking. Its planning occupied the best brains of
thinkers and masters of action." (We know too well what kind
of minds are responsible for its losses.) Dr. Williamson gives us
exciting history in league-boots, as when he sums up the effects

of the English intervention in India : the early import of cotton fabrics contributing to the comfort and health of the nation, the accumulated wealth of the nabobs, their influence in politics, their country houses, the part their capital played in financing the Industrial Revolution, which then reversed the process with a large export of cotton to India in the nineteenth century, the mechanisation of the Indian industry in the twentieth : " The whole sequence was set going when Thomas Aldworth settled in 1612 at the head of the English factory at Surat ". It is somehow moving to think of the numbers of private Englishmen from the mid-seventeenth century onwards " making their living in all the ports of southern Asia. The great majority of them were obscure and unrecorded, but casual mention of them occurs continually in travellers' narratives."

There are chapters in this book on English enterprise in the Atlantic, on the Tudor Propagandists, the Hakluyts, Gilbert, Dr. Dee, Ralegh, on the opening of the Eastern seas, the development of trade in the Indian Ocean and the China sea, the discovery of the Pacific, in which our country had so large a part from Grenville and Drake to those wonderful years in the eighteenth century in which Cook solved all the major remaining mysteries of the Pacific. In his last chapter Dr. Williamson estimates the importance of the oceanic factor in the shaping of modern England. It has, of course, been decisive. It was trade and shipping which created the Empire, and it has rested throughout upon sea power. Dr. Williamson ends his story with the security of the last century, won as the result of a twenty years' struggle with Revolutionary France, in which, as he says, " the stakes were higher than in any previous conflict ". They are higher still today.

Dr. Williamson's special quality is a gift for communicating a sense of excitement with a plain statement of fact, of appealing in a way few historians do to the historical imagination. I know one or two members of the great public, with no particular knowledge of history, who have already found this book thrilling. So they all ought, for Dr. Williamson writes with the vigour and freshness and clarity that somehow go with those who love the sea. As for the historian, I can only say that this book gave me a day's pleasure coming up in the train from Cornwall to Oxford.

(ii)

What a wonderful fellow Nelson was ! G. M. Trevelyan says in his *History of England* : " Nelson is the best loved name in English ears. There is more in our relation to him than can be accounted for by his genius and our obligation." I am not ashamed to confess that I can never look upon his tomb in the heart of St. Paul's, or think of that last entry in his diary the night before Trafalgar, without tears.

Miss Clemence Dane's anthology of his letters makes it abundantly clear why English people feel as they do about Nelson.[1] It was a very good idea to make this selection ; and it would be ungracious to say that it might be better done by a historian, who could give us a stronger sense of the background, a fuller narrative to link up the sections, since it had not occurred to any historian to make the selection at all. Anyhow in this, Nelson speaks for himself to us, paints his own portrait, naïvely, unselfconsciously, irresistibly. Perhaps not many of us realised that the phrase " the Nelson touch " comes from Nelson himself. He wrote, on joining the *Victory* for the Trafalgar campaign :

" When I came to explain to them the ' Nelson touch ', it was like an electric shock. Some shed tears, all approved — ' It was new — it was singular — it was simple ! ' ; and from Admirals downwards, it was repeated — ' It must succeed, if ever they allow us to get at them ! ' "

What does the " Nelson touch " mean ? Evidently he meant by it the plan of attack which shattered the French and Spanish fleets at Trafalgar. There is something aesthetic in Nelson's pursuit of victory, a desire for completeness, perfection, annihilation — matched, of course, with dauntless courage, swiftness of vision, imagination, a spirit of flame.

But when one knows Nelson, in thinking of him the phrase comes to mean something more. " I am all soul and sensi-

[1] *The Nelson Touch. An Anthology of Lord Nelson's Letters* ; compiled by Clemence Dane.

bility ", he wrote to Lady Hamilton. And the other side to this intense fighting spirit was an extraordinary loving nature, all humanity and considerateness, generous to a degree and sensitive as a woman for others. It is this combination which makes him irresistible. The captains with whom he fought the battle of the Nile — many of them famous names now : Hardy, Troubridge, Saumarez, Hood — were his " band of brothers ". In his last years, when he was prematurely ageing, worn out by that indomitable spirit, half blind, one-armed, many times wounded, a famous figure throughout the world, they were his " darling children ".

What is so interesting about Nelson — and his letters portray him in his own words — is how different he was from the conventional idea of the hero. So far from being the strong, silent man of fiction and fools, he was sensitive, self-conscious, talkative, vain, and very much a writing man ; it is an endearing trait that he could not get over his sea-sickness, and a bull-fight in Spain quite upset him. His passionate love for Lady Hamilton threw him completely off his balance ; the thought that the Prince Regent was going to dine with her made him hysterical. Then there is his extreme considerateness for everybody — his family and friends, fellow officers, and the ordinary seamen who fought under him. One always finds him interceding for mercy, asking for sentences on offenders to be reduced No wonder the men adored him. About money he was generous to a fault, even careless ; he was for ever forking out for his relations or handing over sums to those in want. He seems to have been much more distressed over the wounds of his subordinates than over his own ; when one of them is killed, he grieves unaffectedly, spontaneously, simply, like a child.

Added to all this there were his technical abilities : he was a good pilot at an early age, a superb tactician, an inspired commander ; and all the while, from his early years to the end, there was the game-cock fighting spirit which impelled him to the forefront of every action. " I know it is my disposition ", he wrote, " that difficulties and dangers do but increase my desire of attempting them." He was undoubtedly a favourite, even with the Admiralty. It led him to take responsibilities and liberties, and even to depart from orders, which an ordinary man would never have dared. It was fortunate for him that he was always successful; if not, as he often said, he would have been " broke ". He could afford to take risks : he was a genius.

So, too, was Drake. But in spite of a West-country (and Elizabethan) prejudice, I cannot but think that Drake comes second among English seamen to Nelson. His personality is not so irresistible. Where Nelson cared nothing for money, Drake collected a fortune. He was not really a good collaborator, or perhaps even commander of a fleet. He was an individualist of genius, and the best navigator of his time. Like Nelson, he had the intense, the ardent fighting spirit, an aura which terrorised the enemy ; like him, he had the devotion of his men, an infallible way with him, a magnetic power. He too was a humane man, unlike the disagreeable Grenville ; he always had the affection of the native Indians of the West Indies and the Isthmus against the Spaniards.

Mr. Oakeshott's book is largely concerned with his doings.[1] He tells again in a pleasant, agreeable manner the stories of some of the chief maritime enterprises of the Elizabethan age which opened the way for the growth of the Empire. He makes an excellent point when he says that with us " the achievements of the seamen became part of the national tradition, part of the texture of English life, in a way that happened nowhere else, save perhaps among the Dutch ".

[1] Walter Oakeshott, *Founded upon the Seas.*

IX

PAGEANT OF LONDON

In these times, when we realise what a hostage to fortune we have given in London, how precious a possession of the English-speaking peoples it is, with its buildings and memorials of the past, its memories and continuing associations, it is very fitting that *The Great Chronicle of London* should be for the first time given to the public.[1]   The gift comes with a little poignancy just now : the book is itself such a tribute to all that past.   It is like a pageant of London's history.   As we read, the figures of those good citizens, mayors, sheriffs, aldermen in their scarlet cloaks, pass before our eyes year by year : now they are waiting by St. Magnus' church to receive Henry VII coming over London Bridge from Blackheath-field — very gracious he was after the victory, knighting the mayor, recorder, and sheriff on the spot before going on to offer at St. Paul's ; now they are standing in the streets to welcome Margaret of Anjou to her wedding, the craftsmen " all clothed in brown blue " and every citizen wearing a scarlet hood, " the which gave a mighty shew ".   Or it is sixty years later, and Katherine of Aragon is passing by to her wedding; an ominous shower falls (just outside the " Cardinal's Hat ", too) wetting her mantle and powdered ermines, so that " she was fain to be conveyed under the hovel of the drapers' stalls, till the shower were over-passed, which was not long ".   Or it is poor Henry VI being paraded through the streets, ever in the same long blue gown of velvet, " as though he had no mo to change with ".   Usually the citizens themselves are taking an active part : electing their officers for the year, sometimes not without discord and disturbance, banqueting, brawling, quarrelling, defending their walls against the Bastard of Falconbridge, or angry men of Essex who demand better prices for their " butter, cheese, eggs, pigs, and all other victual ".   So much of the pageant of our

---

[1] *The Great Chronicle of London*, edited by A. H. Thomas and I. D. Thornley. (Printed at the Sign of the Dolphin, for the Library Committee at the Guildhall, London.)   This review was written in April 1939.   Miss I. D. Thornley was killed in an air-raid on London in 1941.

history has been played upon that small, that adorable scene
with its familiar features, old St. Paul's, London Bridge, the
Tower : the coronations of kings, the wedding processions, the
feasts at Westminster or in the City, the executions, the burnings of heretics, the hospitality of the great, and their various
ends — satisfying like Henry VII's or tragic like the great
Kingmaker's, his body lying naked in St. Paul's before the
image of our Lady of Grace.

Though this is not a book for the general reader — it is a
sumptuous great volume like a family Bible, superbly produced
and printed, and edited with admirable care and scholarship
— it may easily be imagined what a readable book could be
made out of it. There are five hundred copies printed ; which
we owe to the double generosity of Lord Wakefield of Hythe,
in the first instance for purchasing the manuscript of the
chronicle and presenting it to the Guildhall Library, and
secondly for defraying the entire charges of the publication.
It is an example of public-spiritedness in the grand style of the
eighteenth century; and it is very right that the volume should
be such a superb specimen of craftsmanship, in printing and
binding no less worthy of that age. Perhaps it is not too much
to hope that other benefactors may be inspired by this example ;
that some members of the peerage, one or two dukes in especial,
may be incited to publish their papers in a series of volumes
like the Hatfield or Dropmore MSS.

The historical importance of the chronicle is considerable.
The late learned Mr. Kingsford regarded it as " perhaps the
most important for the student of sources of all the original
authorities for English history in the fifteenth century " ; and
it is following his usage that it has come to be known as *The
Great Chronicle of London.* Very appropriately, for it is in some
ways the fullest and most valuable of the London chronicles.
It falls into two parts, the earlier being very simple and factual,
though even here there are valuable public documents inserted.
As time goes on it gets fuller — it has the best account, for
instance, of the dispute between Beaufort and Gloucester which
held up public business in 1425. The insecurity was such that
all the shops of London were shut in one hour, we are told ;
while the Archbishop of Canterbury was employed riding eight

times that day between the Cardinal and the Duke trying to compose their quarrel. The second part of the chronicle, from 1439 to 1512, is apparently the work of one hand, of someone writing in the reign of Henry VIII. As the story comes down to the writer's own day, to events of which he was evidently an eye-witness, the record becomes more personal, develops a character of its own.

It becomes fascinating to read ; and to the historian a first-rate source with something new to tell us. For example, the account it gives us of the events in and around London during the Cornish Rebellion in 1497, when a motley army of Cornish-men marched all the way up through Southern England upon the City, is the fullest and best account we have anywhere. Similarly, we have all sorts of touches that are new, at any rate to me. At the dinner which the Mayor gave to the Scottish Ambassadors who had come to London to negotiate the marriage of Margaret Tudor to James IV, the chronicler tells us — he was evidently present : " In time of which dinner a Scottish priest sitting at one of the side tables made this ballad " — and then there follows Dunbar's famous poem in praise of London. It is pleasant to know the occasion upon which this so well-known poem was first produced.

" London, thou art of townes *A per se.*
    Soveraign of cities, seemliest in sight,
Of high renoun, riches and royaltie ;
    Of lordis, barons, and many a goodly knyght ;
    Of most delectable lusty ladies bright ;
Of famous prelatis, in habitis clericall ;
    Of merchauntis full of substance and of myght :
London, thou art the flour of Cities all.

Upon thy lusty Brygge of pillars white
    Been merchauntis full royall to behold ;
Upon thy stretis goeth many a semely knyght
    In velvet gownes and in cheynes of gold.
    By Julyus Caesar thy Tour founded of old
May be the house of Mars victoryall,
    Whose artillary with tonge may not be told :
London, thou art the flour of Cities all.

Strong be thy wallis that about thee standis. . . ."

The chronicler had a taste for poetry, and incorporates several poems, including the effective ballad against Empson, which he tells us was written by William Cornish, of the King's Chapel :

> " O myschievous M, fyrst syllable of thy name,
> Son to the devil, for the second part
> As Alexander in honour, so thow in shame
> May be remembered, that most wretched art :
> A cankered knave, a churl of the cart,
> Of venymous blood, of high presumpcion,
> A bond churl born in Towcetyr toun."

And there is a ballad against Empson's agent, John Baptist de Grimaldis, which only survives here. Students of early Tudor literature will be grateful for these bits.

As we read, the picture of the man writing forms in our mind behind the anonymity of the chronicle. We see him at his desk copying rapidly, adding things of his own to the record. He had his own slant on things ; he was shrewd and sensible, not over-credulous, though orthodox ; he shared the conventional horror of heresy, in those ways like everybody else ; he enjoyed a good execution, and did not fail to append the sentiment, " upon whose soul and all Christen, Jesus have mercy, Amen ". He had a sly sense of humour ; tells many a good story, like that of the handsome Edward IV kissing the good widow of Suffolk, who promptly doubled her contribution to his loan for the honour. He had a good news-sense ; the chronicle filled some of the functions of the Press today, and we know what popular reading it was. He was a draper : that is almost the only thing we know of him for certain, though we might have guessed it from his interest in clothes, the critical eye with which he appraises the dressing of every scene. The Tudor writers through whose hands the book passed, John Stow the antiquary, Foxe the martyrologist, perhaps Hall, took it for granted that it was written by Fabian, the chronicler, alderman of the City and Master of the Drapers' Company. And, indeed, if it was not Fabian, who can it have been ?

X

ST. THOMAS OF CHELSEA

THE psychology of the martyr is surely a very curious and morbid thing. Two main elements seem to be essential to it in conjunction ; and in these days of psychological analysis they are not difficult to identify. There is first a deep-rooted spiritual (or intellectual) pride amounting to an invincible obstinacy, and second a positive desire for pain ; the latter is in the end satisfied by the consequences brought on by the former. Both elements were present in a very marked degree in Sir Thomas More. It is not to be wondered at that so prominent and controversial a figure as he, taking so leading a stand on all the hazardous issues of the Reformation at its most critical phase, should have ended in martyrdom ; the wonder is that his canonisation should have been so long postponed. For surely no Englishman, with the possible exception of St. Thomas Becket, has more eminently possessed the qualities necessary for a saint.

From very early the ascetic impulse was developed in him : when a young man in London studying law, he lived for many months according to the Carthusian rule, and, by dint of a hair-shirt and sleeping on planks with a log for a pillow, he managed to keep awake for nineteen or twenty hours out of the twenty-four. We hear more of the hair-shirt and his flagellation from Roper : " He used also sometimes to punish his body with whips, the cords knotted, which was known only to my wife, whom for her secrecy above all other he specially trusted, causing her, as need required, to wash the same shirt of hair ". An unpleasant duty, one would have thought ; however, there were no bounds to the faithful Margaret's devotion. Later, when shut up in the Tower in the worst of his troubles, he assured her that " if it had not been for my wife and you that be my children, I would not have failed long ere this to have closed myself in so straight a room, and straighter too ". When discomforts were heaped upon him, his books and papers taken away and even lighting denied him, he said : " Me thinketh God maketh me a wanton, and setteth me on His lap and dandleth me ". Bishop Butler would have regarded it as all very horrid and perverted — which perhaps it was. However, we understand these things rather better ; we are not so surprised by them ; we know that there are these tendencies which recur in human nature.

As for intellectual pride, it was an unmistakable element in him — a sort of spiritual vanity, all the more interesting because on the surface his was a nature so agreeable, humorous, amenable. Henry can never have expected such an unyielding obstinacy from the charming companion, the whimsical, diplomatic *savant*. Professor Chambers owns that up to the inclusion of More's name in the Act of Attainder in February 1534, Henry had treated him well and with unexpected patience.[1] More told Chapuys, the Imperial Ambassador, that the matter of the divorce concerned him no less than his life, not only for the sake of the Emperor and his aunt, Katherine, but for the sake of Henry and the kingdom of England. But who was he to judge the well-being of Henry and his kingdom better than the King and his own government, who were in a far better position to see all the issues involved, from the very centre ? Why could he not have submitted his judgment as everybody else had — all the nobility, the Commons, and the clergy too — in fact everybody except Bishop Fisher and a pack of friars ? That was the rock on which More foundered — a deep-seated spiritual vanity. Clearly nobody wanted to take his life ; Henry genuinely regretted the political necessity ; Cranmer tried to save him by a dialectical subterfuge in taking the Oath of Supremacy as creditable to his intelligence as it was to his humanity. Only More refused to be saved. This was the issue that More had to face with his daughter Margaret when she tried to get him to yield. It is as if he were afraid of yielding his own self-will : " Too late, Margaret ? I beseech our Lord, that if ever I make such a change, it may be too late indeed. For well I wot the change cannot be good for my soul." He was a good deal too certain what was good for his soul ; it sounds more like self-will when he says, " There is no

[1] R. W. Chambers, *Thomas More.*

man living of whom, while he liveth, I may make myself sure ".
He fell back, of course, as they all do, upon his certainty with
regard to the next world — a weak position where the facts do
not warrant such certainty. At his trial, he reminded the
Commissioners that St. Paul had been present and consenting
unto the death of St. Stephen, " and yet be they now both
twain holy saints in Heaven, and shall continue there friends
for ever, so I verily trust that though your Lordships have now
here in earth been judges to my condemnation, we may yet
hereafter in Heaven merrily all meet together, to our everlasting salvation ". It is beautiful, it is touching ; but it is not
common sense to stake so much upon a hypothesis.

And so Dame Alice thought too. In all that brilliant circle
of so much wit and charm that centred upon the house at
Chelsea, Dame Alice has always come off rather badly at the
hands of historians ; it is time that someone saw her point of
view, with some sympathy for her good sense. After all, was
she not right about her brilliant, witty, incomprehensible
husband ?

" What the good year, Master More," quoth she, " I marvel
that you, that have been always hitherto taken for so wise a
man, will now so play the fool to lie here in this close filthy
prison, and be content thus to be shut up amongst mice and
rats, when you might be abroad at your liberty, and with the
favour and goodwill both of the King and his Council, if you
would but do as all the bishops and best learned of this realm
have done. And seeing you have at Chelsea a right fair house,
your library, your books, your gallery, your garden, your
orchard, and all other necessaries so handsome about you,
where you might in the company of me your wife, your children
and household, be merry, I muse what a God's name you mean
here still thus fondly to tarry."

It was after all much the same judgment that Edward Hall,
the chronicler, made, and he was representative of ordinary
sensible opinion : " I cannot tell whether I should call him a
foolish wise man, or a wise foolish man ". But it was all of no
avail : More went on to his magnificent and moving end. Nor
can we repine at it ; for by it a splendid story was added to the
tradition of the English people, and an addition made to the

slender stock of English saints in Heaven.

Professor Chambers has written what, it may be supposed, will long remain the standard work of ordinary compass on More. It is a pleasant, sensible, and very human book, scholarly and satisfying. Although it is clear that Professor Chambers has a definite point of view, and loathes Henry VIII and all his works, his sympathies are wide and his prejudices usually under control. There are only two large lapses from this, both dealing with the general historical effects of the Reformation : one is in Chapter II, the section on " Henry's England " ; the other is the whole of the final chapter on " More's Place in History ", which had been better omitted. For Professor Chambers' attitude to the Reformation is a purely sentimental, religious one, and devoid of real historical judgment. Henry's reign, for example, is divided into two halves ; the first tolerable because Catholic, the second one of complete frustration, ruin, and national degradation. This is nonsense. And when told that the reign was crowned with dynastic failure, we remember that Henry and Anne gave us Elizabeth, and through her the Elizabethan age. What more splendid, more convincing success could there be ?

XI

ERASMUS AND ENGLAND

(i)

It is only fitting and proper that we should commemorate the quatercentenary of Erasmus (he died on 11 July 1536), since so much of his life and work was bound up with this country : he owed to it some of his closest and most fruitful friendships, he derived from it an essential impulse to his life's work and in the end contributed something of his own spirit to the solution which we found for our religious difficulties in the sixteenth century and to the tradition which has been continuous with us since that time. A recent German scholar has said that Erasmus has always been best understood and treated with most sympathy in Anglo-Saxon countries : that they appreciate best his humanitarianism, his love of peace and liberty, his lifelong service to international ideals, his spirit of moderation and tolerance in religion. Of this greatest of Europeans, it might almost be claimed that he was half an Englishman. He first came to England, along with the young peer, Mountjoy, who was his pupil in Paris, in the early summer of 1499. Already his reputation as the most brilliant of the younger scholars there had preceded him. Colet and the young More had, for example, heard of him. Colet, but recently returned from Italy, was at Oxford delivering that famous course of lectures on St. Paul's Epistles which, in breaking through the crusted accretions of commentary which the Middle Ages had collected and going straight to the meaning of the text, had an influence in inaugurating the movement for reform in the Church, not less than Keble's Assize Sermon had for the later Oxford Movement. Indeed Colet's ardent spirit had a profound influence upon Erasmus at this decisive turning in his life. Less clever than Erasmus intellectually, Colet had that strong ethical passion which could give the more brilliant, more sensitive man a sense of direction. As the distinguished Dutch historian, Huizinga, says :

" It was Colet's word and example which first changed Erasmus' desultory occupation with theological studies into a firm and lasting resolve to make their pursuit the object of his life."

Hardly less important than this sense of purpose communicated to his life, were the friendships that Erasmus made here, which lasted to the end. For all the extreme sensitiveness and the thin skin of the man of genius, it is clear that Erasmus had a real gift for friendship. So too had Thomas More, the most delightful companion that ever lived, whom Erasmus was wont to call, in the language of the time, his " darling ". Then too there was Colet, eager and inspiring : how well we know the famous disputation that arose at dinner in the Oxford college, Colet presiding. Prior Charnock on his right and Erasmus on his left ; how inimitably Erasmus describes it all in the *Letters*, so that we see them all clear as in a portrait after the lapse of centuries. They were a charming circle, those Oxford humanists, drawn together by their common love of scholarship and by the ties of friendship. Their life has fortunately been described for us, with great sympathy and insight, by older English writers, by Seebohm in his *Oxford Reformers* and by Froude in his *Life and Letters of Erasmus*. But Erasmus himself has described the happiness he found in England among those friends in those early years :

" How do you like our England ? you will ask " (he wrote to Robert Fisher). " Believe me, dear Robert, when I answer that I never liked anything so much before. I have met with so much kindness and so much learning, both Latin and Greek, that but for the curiosity of seeing it, I do not now so much care for Italy. When I hear my Colet, I seem to be listening to Plato himself. In Grocyn, who does not marvel at such perfection of learning ? What can be more acute, profound and delicate than the judgment of Linacre ? What has nature ever created more sweet, more endearing, more happy than the genius of Thomas More ? "

Alas, he could have no idea of the wreckage that was to be made of the group of friends by the storms of the Reformation !

He was here again in the autumn of 1505, extending his acquaintance in the Church, the kindly, generous Warham,

Archbishop of Canterbury, Fisher, Bishop of Rochester, Foxe, Bishop of Winchester, the gentle, scholarly Tunstall. And for the greater part of the years 1509–14 he lived in England, partly in London with Mountjoy and More, partly at Cambridge. Of these fruitful, laborious years, certain abiding achievements remain. He wrote his greatest work, *The Praise of Folly*, in More's house in Bucklersbury. Much of his work on Jerome and for his great edition of the New Testament was done in London and at Cambridge. In the comparative freedom of England he wrote, though he never dared to acknowledge, the brilliant, scathing tract *Julius Exclusus*, his scoriation of the warlike Pope — a work of the same class in which Byron's *Vision of Judgment* comes. Then there are the innumerable pictures of English life contained in his *Letters* and *Colloquies* : the insanitariness of our houses, Dame Alice, More's shrew of a wife, the gaunt and saintly Fisher in his draughty palace at Rochester.

Perhaps, in the end, England was something of a disappointment to him, as all countries were to the fastidious soul of the idealist with the gift of irony, bent upon his own inner dream of perfection and reason. He had had a shock upon his first visit, when the money that he had so carefully collected for his journey to Italy was confiscated by the Customs at Dover under a Statute of Edward III prohibiting the export of coin : it meant five years' more drudgery in Paris before he was free at last to go. Then too the great hopes that were offered by his English friends on the accession of Henry VIII, which induced him to leave Italy, were disappointed. But Warham was generous, and presented him to the benefice of Aldington in Kent, from which he drew a pension of twenty pounds for the rest of his life. With the outbreak of Henry's French War he was no longer at ease, and complained that it had " altered the spirit of this island ". As soon as peace was signed he left the country, though with a graceful tribute upon his lips ; for when an Italian envoy tried to induce him to go to Rome, where he might enjoy the first place instead of living alone among a barbarous nation, he replied that England contained such a number of excellent scholars among whom he would be content to occupy the humblest place.

One recalls too that when he describes the things upon which various nations pride themselves, the Scots their nobility and logical sense, the French their breeding, he says of the English that they " particularly challenge to themselves Beauty, Music and Feasting ". What a change of values from the England of the Renaissance to the nation of shopkeepers !

In the great struggle over the Reformation which divided Europe into two camps, Erasmus was all for moderation and the appeal to reason — in vain. His last writing on Concord in the Church, his constant deploring of over-much definition of belief as likely to lead to only worse conflicts of dogma, is like nothing so much as the Anglican compromise that later developed. It was sad that his last years should have been filled with the sufferings of his English friends, More and Fisher ; nor could he know to what extent his own influence was to bear fruit in the *via media* of the Elizabethan Church. If the Church of England had a process of canonisation, Erasmus should certainly be its first saint.

There is indeed much that is English in his spirit ; his memory, then, should form one of the many, and not the least strong, of the historic bonds between the Netherlands and ourselves.

(ii) The Erasmus Exhibition at the Bodleian

The uncertainties of this extraordinarily inclement spring threaten, lift off, then descend upon the Library. A thunder-cloud lours over the Radcliffe Square outside, bringing out and making vivid and distinct the inherent colours of objects, the black and gold of the Camera, the white rim to the sky, the green of weather vanes. Rain patters against the panes of the long Exhibition Room ; wind and rain stir together among the trees of Exeter garden, bringing to mind the phrases of Arnold, of another, earlier spring, " the vext garden-trees . . . the volleying rain ". The shower over, a burst of sun comes in from the garden, the silver birch shivering and gleaming with wetness, the chestnut flowers now gone, alas, from the great tree in the corner, that sends the noise of innumerable leaves into the still and faded room. An unexpected finger of light lies along the cases pointing to the great Froben edition of

Chrysostom, sumptuously bound for Henry VIII with the royal arms engraved upon it, lighting up the gilt roses and the leopards.

The Bodleian authorities have followed up their charming More and Fisher Exhibition of last year with this to commemorate the quatercentenary of Erasmus, no less informative if a trifle less intimate than that. Anything to do with Thomas More has, for an Englishman, a charm and intimacy all its own. The personality of Erasmus, perhaps, has a less obvious appeal ; there are no jokes that survive by which we remember him ; his talk and all his writing were alike in the Latin of the Renaissance which comes between us and the realisation of a singularly vivid, vibrant, sensitive being, a character that should have an especial appeal for the moderns. Yet he was much in England, a well-known figure in that day, four hundred years ago, the friend of More and Fisher and Colet, taken notice of at Court by the young Henry, generously treated by Warham, Archbishop of Canterbury, his patron, and by the Lord Mountjoy, his former pupil. In fact, Erasmus' life was, more than any other, the thread which drew together the Renaissance in Northern Europe — Germany, the Low Countries, France, England. He resided here, at Oxford, 1499–1500 ; at Cambridge and in London for the greater part of the years 1509–14. He was a formative influence in the revival of learning in England ; a debt in part recognised, in part repaid by the fact that the greatest Erasmus scholar of our time was an Oxford man, the late President of Corpus. It is right and proper that Erasmus should be commemorated here ; it is graceful that he should be so well commemorated.

Most of the cases, all those lengthwise along the wall, are taken up by a very representative collection of early editions of his works, many of them of great interest and rarity. Altogether they give a very fair picture of his life, since so much of his life was in his books, from that early commendatory letter with which he was asked to fill up the blank page at the end of Gaguin's *De Origine et Gestis Francorum* — the Latinity of which was so much more elegant than that of the book itself that it called attention to Erasmus, a new-comer then to the literary world of Paris, rather than to Gaguin. This was Erasmus' first

appearance in print, in Paris in 1495 ; here is the third edition
of the work in which the merits of Erasmus' preface were recognised by placing it at the beginning of the book, as it always has
been subsequently. It was by this that his name was first noised
abroad among the world of scholars and by which Colet, when
studying in Paris, first heard of him. Next to it is a tiny
volume of poems, *De casa natalitia Jesu et paupere puerperio dive
virginis Mariè Carmen noviter emendatum*, which appeared in the
same year, his first separate work ; here is a copy, one of only
three that are extant, of the second edition. These are very
early works, products of the lean years in Paris, the plain living
and arduous study of the Collège de Montaigu from which so
much of the later work sprang, but of which he could never
afterwards think without a shudder. It was not until his visit
to England, and even after, that the full stream of his works
began to appear from the presses of the time. His sensational
literary career was in a sense the creation of the printing press ;
he saw the splendid opportunity opened up by it, leaped to it
with both hands, living with the press and by it.

It was by the *Adages* and the *Enchiridion Militis Christiani*
that he gained a wider and independent audience for himself ;
and here is an early edition (Antwerp, 1509) of the *Lucubrationes
aliquot*, among which the *Enchiridion* first came out, though it
was subsequently published separately, the first among his
more famous works. The first English version of it appeared
in 1518 ; here there is a copy of the second translation, said to
be by Tyndale, the translator of the Bible and (for his pains)
subsequently martyr. Others of his English connections are
brought to mind by the rare first edition (Paris, 1506) of the
translation into Latin of several of the dialogues of Lucian, so
popular an author with the Renaissance, a work in which
Erasmus collaborated with More ; it is dedicated to Fox,
Bishop of Winchester. Similarly, the beautiful Aldine edition
of the *Adages* (Venice, 1508), a product of the visit to Italy in
1506–9, is dedicated to Mountjoy. The number of items —
proverbs and phrases with their explanations and expansions,
sometimes into whole essays on important subjects like the
famous one on war, *Dulce bellum inexpertis* — amounted in this
edition to some three thousand, having increased from eight

hundred in the first collection. Next to it is the 1536 Froben edition of the *Adages*, no less beautiful than the Aldine ; it was the last to be issued in Erasmus' lifetime, and by then the number of entries had increased to over five thousand.

And so to a whole case devoted to various editions of *The Praise of Folly*, in Latin, English, Dutch, French, German, Italian, from the year it was published — it was written in More's house in Bucklersbury in 1509 — to the present day. Among them are editions of 1511 and 1521 (Basel), and the first English translation by Sir Thomas Challoner, with a beautiful Renaissance title-page decorated with caryatids and flowers and fruit, published in 1549. I suppose that this is the most popularly known and appreciated of all Erasmus' works : a contribution of genius to the remarkable literature of Folly of the Renaissance, a form of literary expression one would have thought even more suitable to our own time and circumstance. The *pièces de résistance* here are the fine Froben editions of the New Testament, the first and the last in his lifetime, Basel, 1516 and 1535 : both beautiful pieces of craftsmanship, though the latter has a more crowded text because of the increasing Annotations that the years brought : Erasmus' chief contribution to scholarship. There follow fine examples of the Froben texts of the Fathers, Cyprian, Chrysostom (Henry VIII's copy), and Ambrose in whom Erasmus had been interested from his earliest years ; the original edition of his work on Free Will, against Luther, *De libero arbitrio* (Froben, 1524), with Luther's reply, and the rejoinder which Erasmus put together in ten days in time for the Frankfurt Fair in September 1526. And there is a copy of Athenaeus which has his marginal notes ; one of them torn out for the sake of the autograph is now preserved in the Amsterdam University Library. So are the fragments of the great, the relics of genius, treasured up.

But what is of most interest to us are the two cases containing a number of his last letters, written in his own hand, and now belonging to the Bodleian, together with some relics of his English friends. Among the latter is a large Greek book which once belonged to Grocyn and has his name inscribed upon it ; and a charming little account-book which once belonged to Linacre, open at the page which gives, " Md. for my costs

when I went to maydstone for ye greke boke ". There are the
charges for barge hire from Gravesend, and so to Halling and
Maidstone and back again ; " for carynge of ye hamper from
ye colege to ye water syde id. ; for karyage of ye sayd hamper
to London vid. ; for caryage from ye water to yor howse iid."
Trifling in themselves, these details open a way into the hearts
of these long-dead men, Linacre, Grocyn, Colet, Erasmus,
More, all bound together by friendship and their devotion to
the new learning. But the storms of the Reformation — that
age so like our own — swept down upon them, scattering the
friends, though not breaking the bonds of friendship, ruining
their hopes like ours. These last letters of Erasmus, which the
Bodleian was so fortunate to obtain just before the last war, are
full of the disasters of the time, particularly of the ruin in
England. He writes in June 1535 to his confidant Erasmus
Schets, of the imprisonment of More and Fisher, that the latter
has lost his sight, while he fears More will lose his head. " I
wonder whither this savagery of the King will lead ", he writes.
Henry's accession in his golden youth had seemed to offer such
hopes to them all. Mountjoy had died, but of a natural death,
he says ; it is a sufficient comment upon the drift of the time.
Next year, in June again — it is his last letter — he scribbles a
brief note to Schets : " *Prodigiosa scribis de Anglia.* Would that
these things had been stopped before the death of those good
men." (More and Fisher had been brought to death upon the
block the year before.) Erasmus subscribes himself, for the
last time, " *aegra manu* ". A month more, and he too was dead,
working in the house at Basel right up to the end.

There are a few portraits of no particular consequence, yet
appropriately brought together ; a copy of a Holbein portrait
of Erasmus, a book open before him (his life was books) ; a
late copy of a portrait of the printer Froben, an honest, ugly
face, blunt and deeply lined. Higher up on the wall hangs the
sardonic genius who scattered them all, Thomas Cromwell.
And across the intervening space and the show-cases, high up
on the opposite side, a gay and unconvincingly youthful
portrait of Elizabeth, flanked by two bilious-looking Elizabethans, Thomas Sackville and Lord Chancellor Ellesmere,
confronts the Laszlo portrait of Pope Pius XI.

(iii) The Personality of Erasmus

Erasmus is one of the great names of Europe ; but it is doubtful whether he is much more than a name to us today. There upon the library shelves stand the dozen or more great folios of the Louvain edition of his works ; there are the eight volumes of his *Letters*, two more still to come ; and in addition, his editions of the Fathers, Chrysostom, Cyprian, Jerome, Ambrose, Augustine, together with his life's crowning glory, the edition of the New Testament. Is it any wonder that the man should be so buried under such a mountain of Latin and Greek ?

And yet, in spite of all, he is a singularly modern personality ; he comes down to us as a very vivid, vibrant, sensitive human being. His problems were very much ours ; he was agonised by the same issues, extraordinarily contemporary in character ; living as he did in that disturbed and disillusioning period when the Renaissance passed over into the Reformation and the Wars of Religion, he was at a very significant turning of the ways in Europe, much as we are in our time. It is fitting that we should call him to mind, not only because he was a very great man, but because his life holds a special significance for us and our age.

Let us begin by calling up his physical appearance. He was so famous in his lifetime and so much painted, that his features at least are familiar to us. We see him then, as he was so often painted, seated at a desk, for ever writing, writing, writing. There are usually books in the background, an open book before him. The face is wonderfully expressive : sensitiveness, refinement, delicacy in every line of it. It is the face of a very clever man, who is also a valetudinarian ; something of an invalid, who is perpetually over-working, nervous, and alert ; there is a querulousness in the brow, the tight repressed lips. And then one remembers the extraordinary life of devotion and persistent labour this man lived ; beneath the surface appearances, the sparse greying hair, the thin worn cheeks, the mobile hands heavy with rings, there is the unmistakable purpose of that life, the ardent, eager spirit. The expression of the face has something incalculable about it : it is at once grave, and yet for ever on the verge of a smile ; half tender, half querulous : evidently in life a fascinating man — all the more fascinating because there is something that for ever eludes one in all his changes of mood. One of those subtle and brilliant personalities who redeem our race, having genius.

All this mirrors the man we know him to have been. He was first and foremost the scholar, the prince among the scholars of the Renaissance. He won this position after a long and hardly endured apprenticeship over years, at school at Gouda and Deventer, at the Augustinian monastery of Steyn of which he was a canon, in Paris teaching himself Greek, at Oxford where Colet inspired him with a sense of his vocation, at Cambridge where he lectured and taught and studied : it was not until he was a man of thirty that he began to reap the rewards of his industry and genius in a growing fame. But in addition to his scholarship he was a brilliant original writer. No one had handled the Latin language as he did since the Dark Ages closed down upon Europe — in his hands it became almost a living language again. At least it was a living language to Erasmus, who took pains not to speak his native Dutch and as far as possible to converse in Latin only, so as not to spoil his natural style in it.

And no one had more arresting or more original things to say : he was a preternaturally sharp observer of events and opinions and persons, essentially a moralist and critic, with a biting wit. He belongs to the small and distinguished class of writers to which Voltaire and Swift and Shaw belong. But not even Voltaire's European reputation equalled Erasmus' position in his lifetime. He was the admired of all scholars, churchmen, and princes, sought after by Charles V, Francis I, Henry VIII, and successive Popes, the friend of Sir Thomas More and Colet, Fisher and Archbishop Warham ; different countries competed for the honour of his presence and their notabilities loaded him with presents and kindnesses. To get an idea of his position in contemporary terms, one would have to add together the work and the reputations of, say, Bernard Shaw, Professor Gilbert Murray, and Cardinal Szeredi.

Of the works that went to justify this immense reputation,

we cannot now deal with those of pure scholarship ; let us take his own original writings. I suppose the *Moriae Encomium* (*The Praise of Folly*) to be his most characteristic work, in some sense a real clue to the man. The idea of the book occurred to him while journeying back over the mountains from Italy to Northern Europe, on his way to England in 1509 ; arrived in London, he wrote it in the space of a few days in More's house in Bucklersbury — a characteristic play upon More's name gives it its title. The subject of the book is the foolery of mankind, the tragedy that lies at the root of human nature. Why is it that immortal man, the one animal gifted with reason, should choose the irrational, the inane, the senseless ? You will see that the book belongs to the same class, the very select class, as *Gulliver's Travels*, Voltaire's *Candide*, and Grimmelshausen's *Simplicissimus*. Why the Renaissance should have been so concerned with this subject of human folly one can hardly say ; but there is a large Fool-literature of that time, of which the famous *Ship of Fools* and Rabelais are examples. The perfect expression of all that literature is, however, Erasmus' *Moriae*.

The treatment of the subject, as the title shows, is ironical ; but the irony is so subtle, perhaps one should say so successful, that the average reader can hardly distinguish between what is seriously and what is frivolously intended. Perhaps it was just as well, for there is hardly any form of human folly that is not touched upon, sometimes with a mock serious approval, sometimes with downright castigation. The latter is employed for all the fooleries of the Church, the attention to forms instead of to things of the spirit, the concern with property and pomp (think of Wolsey, for example) instead of preaching the gospel, the character of secular priests who justify their name by being so much better acquainted with the affairs of this world than of the next. Let us take an example from the book :

" To work miracles is old and antiquated, and not in fashion now ; to instruct the people, troublesome ; to interpret the Scripture, pedantic ; to pray, a sign one has little else to do ; to shed tears, silly and womanish ; to be poor, base ; to be vanquisht, dishonourable, and little becoming him that scarce admits even kings to kiss his slipper [*i.e.* the Pope] ; and

lastly, to die, uncouth ; and to be stretcht on a Cross, in-
famous."

The reforming ardour is obvious in such passages ; but
more remarkable is such a thought as this :

" In a word, this Folly is that that laid the foundation of
Cities ; and by it, Empire, Authority, Religion, Policy and
public Actions are preserved : neither is there any thing in
Human Life that is not a kind of pastime of Folly."

Nothing could be more far-reaching than the scepticism
implied by that : human folly is the foundation of all politics,
that is what it means : if only men were reasonable there would
be no need for empires, states, authority. These two tendencies
in Erasmus, the reforming and evangelistic ardour, and a
profound scepticism regarding life and men, were held together
in a delicate equipoise which gives the whole character to
his mind. The equipoise was broken by the irruption of
Luther into the European scene. The conflict between these
two sides to his nature was tragically and vividly revealed to
all the world, as by a lightning flash in a thunderstorm.

Up to 1518–19 all had gone well with Erasmus : he stood
at the apex of his European reputation : there had been nothing like it since Virgil. Himself a humanist and a reformer,
he stood at the head of the movement for Reform within the
Church ; all men looked to him, yet he retained the golden
opinions of kings, Emperor, and Pope. The revolutionary
upheaval which Luther set in train destroyed all this. It is
usual to consider that the fundamental weakness of Erasmus'
position was revealed by Luther, that he was but a Laodicean,
as certainly he confessed that he was not of the stuff that
martyrs are made. But the tragedy went deeper than this :
Erasmus was not wrong in the stand he took up — *he was right,
but rendered totally ineffective by the course of events and the madness
of men.*

This not infrequently happens in human history. The
essential point of Erasmus' position was that he was a ration-
alist, he wanted men to be guided by reason. He had been not
unsympathetic to Luther in the beginnings of his movement for
reform ; but he foresaw as Luther went further and further in

his challenge against the Church, that new dogmas were being set up against the old and that this would lead on to disastrous conflicts and wars, leaving the world in a worse state than before. Erasmus, alas, was right, but could do nothing ; his own views about the idiocy of human beings were being only too exactly justified in the destruction they were bringing on themselves and in the ruin of all his hopes of concord and agreed reform in a spirit of charity. Erasmus was caught by the whirlwind out of the interior depths of barbaric Germany, in much the same way as the Girondins were caught by the French Revolution, or the Mensheviks by the Russian. The contemporary parallel is obvious. It is a pity that human beings are unable to bring about necessary change except in a storm of blood and anger. There is a fine, discerning phrase of Froude's in his book on Erasmus, to the effect that two centuries of religious wars were to vindicate the rightness of Erasmus' judgment.

It was not otherwise with Erasmus' views as to internationalism and peace. He had a horror of war and killing which was a dominant strain in his sensitive temperament. A modern German scholar has called him " the first of pacifists " ; and some of his finest writings are denunciations of war and war-mongers, the preaching of peace. There is the most brilliant and incisive of all, the *Julius Exclusus*, the dialogue concerning the bellicose Julius II, author of a general European war (whom Erasmus had seen entering Bologna in triumph and never forgot the spectacle), clamouring for admission at the gate of Heaven ; there is the *Querela Pacis* (The Complaint of Peace), the *Dulce bellum inexpertis* (Sweet is War to those who know it not).

He was above all a European, equally at home in the Netherlands, Paris, England, Italy, Basel, or Freiburg ; perhaps in the end equally homeless, for the city of the mind in which he dwelt was that Europe of which he was such a good citizen, but which has not even yet come to be.

G

XII

THE TUDOR CHARACTER

It is amusing to reflect, in walking through a portrait gallery, how different historical periods produce their corresponding types of face and appearance. There is, for example, that earlier Tudor type of the Court of Henry VIII, clean-shaven and heavy-jowled, which the genius of Holbein has made familiar to us upon the walls of all the picture galleries of Europe, though nowhere more richly than at Windsor. Or, again, even more familiar, more intimate, is the Stuart type : there is none so charming as this, with its vein of mingled melancholy and a refined distinction, making an irresistible appeal to the heart. The eighteenth century produced a dominant type, more placid and contented, as well it might : it was a good world for them, and they were by no means meek who inherited it. As the century went on they became even more at ease in Zion ; the type loosens, becomes more florid and well-liking, until it moves into the romantic *bravura* of the Regency.

Something of these changes of type and appearance may be put down to fashion ; with the men to different styles in the cut of the beard, from the full spade-beard fashionable in the later years of Elizabeth to the small pointed beard of Charles I's time or to the imperial of the mid-nineteenth century. But these changes in external appearance may reflect, more deeply, differences in type and character. Character must always be in part a function of social environment, since it is built up so largely out of responses to its surroundings. And this being so, it must be particularly marked in the leading figures of an age, who are more significantly and more conspicuously in contact with the main currents of thought and action in their time than any others. It is this that enables us with advantage to take such a figure, a Thomas Cromwell or an Oliver, a Strafford or a Ralegh, and to illuminate the age through the currents that flow through him.

A recent book on the " Great Tudors ", containing essays on some forty prominent Englishmen of the sixteenth century, from Henry VII and Bishop Fisher to Essex and Francis Bacon, enabled us to watch in quick succession the variations in type and character called forth by the changing circumstances within the confines of that period. Two new biographies, one of Ralegh, the other of Sir Edward Dyer, help us to continue the process with more closeness and in greater detail.[1] The earliest years of the Tudor period, the reign of Henry VII, have something of the impersonality of the Middle Ages about them still ; so that we do not know much about Cardinal Morton or Foxe, or even Henry himself, as men. We cannot penetrate beneath the mask, beyond that silence. With the accession of a young prince of such promise as Henry VIII there came a release ; those were joyous years ; Erasmus called it " a golden age indeed ". Youth and merry-making were to the fore ; in the background, though by no means in obscurity, was the charming circle around More, More's family, Colet and Linacre, and Erasmus coming and going. The foreground was taken up by heartier and lustier characters : the young King — we all remember Giustiniani's description of him coming from tennis, or the atmosphere of enjoyment in many of Skelton's and Wyatt's Court poems. There was Wolsey with his moods and emotions, his feasts and his tears, his gluttony for work and play — a genial type, when all is said ; or the Duke of Norfolk, who thought that " England was merry England, before all this New Learning came in ", and the Marquis of Exeter, Henry's companion from boyhood — but with them the shadows begin to fall.

The men who were thrown up in the upheaval of the Reformation, or who survived it, were a different type again ; since the times were harsh and treacherous, they were harsh and treacherous. In thinking of them one is reminded of a contemporary's famous description of the Parliament of 1918 : " hard-faced men who looked as if they had done well out of the War ". Since it was a time of social and religious revolution, those who survived were necessarily tenacious and

<hr>

[1] Edward Thompson, *Sir Walter Ralegh : The Last of the Elizabethans* ; Ralph M. Sargent, *At the Court of Queen Elizabeth : The Life and Lyrics of Sir Edward Dyer.*

adaptable ; and perhaps it was better to be adaptable than tenacious, for the mortality in those close and eager front ranks was very high. One has only to think of that little area within the communion rails of the chapel of St. Peter-ad-Vincula within the Tower — " the saddest spot in Christendom ". Those came off best with whom principle sat very lightly indeed, and who moved (and conformed) with the times : the Russells, for instance, whose loyalty to the existing order (whatever it was) and to their own fortunes deserved the success they obtained. Catholic in doctrine under Henry, they yet more devoutly upheld the Royal supremacy ; Protestant under Edward VI, they found no difficulty in accepting the Mass again under Mary. Sir William Cecil at the same time received a priest into his household " for the better direction of his spiritual affairs ". Or there was that incredible old Marquis of Winchester who held office in all four reigns, under Henry VIII, Edward, Mary, and Elizabeth, and was Lord Treasurer from about 1550 until well on into Elizabeth's reign, when he died near ninety, in 1572. They were a tough lot. A recent archbishop is said to have observed, on entering into possession of Bishopthorpe, that the early post-Reformation Archbishops of York whose portraits hang upon the walls looked a rare collection of rascals.

The constraint, the watchfulness, the latent savagery of the time are depicted for all to see in the portrait that Holbein painted of Cromwell — the immense capacity of the face, the cunning, clever eyes, the fat hands — no less than in the famous note among his Remembrances, " This day the Abbot of Glaston to be tried and condemned ", or in his last piteous letter to Henry crying for mercy. But with the country's emergence from the years of internal crisis, the scene is less dominated by the harshest, most fox-like types — it is significant how frequently particular statesmen in the literature of the time are compared to the fox : " the foxy Gardiner ", " Bonner the fox ", " the old fox Burghley ". We move from these, and from others like them, Northumberland, Walsingham, to the more settled assurance of Elizabeth's later years and to a new type, the young men, more brilliant and dashing, unrestrained by the fears of their fathers, more gallant and venturesome, no less unfortunate. Of these Ralegh and Essex were the types, to many of them rival inspirations.

Magnificence was the keynote, the foible of this later generation ; not only in the externals of life, in their dress and appointments — Cromwell was magnificent enough in this respect, a great collector of Venetian glass, of carpets, tapestries, and books — but in their behaviour and bearing, in the way they thought of themselves. (It was this last that gave them a certain unreality in their judgment of the external world, that led some of them, Essex and Ralegh notably, to their undoing.) No one expressed this spirit better — that of possessions, pride of knowledge, and power — than Marlowe : the first is the real subject of *Tamburlaine the Great*, as the second is of *Faustus* :

> " How am I glutted with conceit of this !
> Shall I make spirits fetch me what I please,
> Resolve me of all ambiguities,
> Perform what desperate enterprise I will ?
> I'll have them fly to India for gold,
> Ransack the ocean for orient pearl,
> And search all corners of the new-found world
> For pleasant fruits and princely delicates."

The men of action and the politicians fell hardly at all behind the words of the poets. The cautious Cecils built sumptuously. The elder had his houses at Wimbledon and Theobalds and the great house that remains at Burghley ; the younger built Cecil House in the Strand ; he filled it full with rare and precious things, of which the inventories remain, and himself designed his palace at Hatfield, employing an architect merely to advise. With this magnificence there ran a spirit of bravado, which is perhaps the quality most alien to us in the Elizabethans, and which reduces contemporary writers, Mr. Thompson no less than Mr. Strachey, to regarding them as brilliantly gifted, incomprehensible children. But the gesture was often inspired, and entered into the tradition of the English people : Drake before the Armada promising the Queen to send the Duke of Medina Sidonia back to " St. Mary Port, among his orange-trees " ; or Essex, throwing his hat into the sea before the assault on Cadiz. With Ralegh, in his contempt of the people, the gesture was apt to be more sinister, like his words :

" Say to the Court it glowes
And shines like rotten wood,
Say to the Church it showes
What's good, and doth no good.
If Church and Court reply,
Then give them both the lie. . . .

Tell zeale it wants devotion,
Tell love it is but lust,
Tell time it meets but motion,
Tell flesh it is but dust,
And wish them not replie
For thou must give them the lie."

Magnificence, with a man of such gifts of intellect as Ralegh, ran to intellectual pride : that, more than anything else, more than mere ambition, which was but one expression of it, was the root of his being. Mr. Thompson quotes Poe's phrase, " the mad pride of intellectuality ", and it certainly describes the very quality which made Ralegh impossible as a statesman. It was a characteristic frequent enough among the Elizabethans — Essex had more than a touch of it, perhaps also Bacon ; Northumberland and Cobham were ruined by it ; among the poets, it was the mainspring of Marlowe's genius. With us, it seems to be entirely absent from our public figures, with whom more pains are taken to disguise any tincture of intellectuality behind a decent exterior of commonplaceness than the Elizabethans took to display all their brilliance.[1] But, then, this is a democratic age, as the Elizabethan certainly was not. It was essentially aristocratic, even if showy and not altogether what we understand by the term. And its *arrivisme* can be exaggerated : people did not rise, under Elizabeth, from the bottom of the social scale. Sir Robert Naunton observed, " It is a certain note of the times, that the Queen in her choice, never took into her favour a meer new man, or a Mechanick ", and he says of her attitude to the Howards, " it was part of her naturall propension, to grace and support ancient Nobility,

---

[1] Written in 1935. Things have undergone a fortunate change since, though not until a great war made it necessary.

where it did not intrench, neither invade her interest ".
Ralegh, for all his unpopularity as an upstart, and in spite
of the insufferable airs of the Earl of Oxford, came from an
old family of long standing in the west country.

Ralegh's practical career was fragmentary, baffled, and in
the end shattered. But was his life, as Mr. Thompson reiterates,
a failure ? " To a smaller, but considerable, public, that of
historical students," he says, " he is the supremely unsuccessful
man." There is not much advantage in these summary
judgments of such complex lives. Moreover, it is precisely this
smaller public which is capable of looking beyond the ill-
success, the tragic reverses, to the fundamental (and astonishing)
achievement. To have been so fine a poet, so philosophical an
intelligence, so fertile in expedients for colonising and planting,
in setting on foot voyages of exploration and discovery, in the
art of chemistry, in the sciences of navigation and war ; to
have founded Virginia, to have risen from " poor beginnings "
by his wits to a leading place among the constellation of talents
that Elizabeth drew around her, to have written the *History of
the World* is failure the word to describe so fruitful, so crowded
a life ? No : rather his career — and in this he is more typically
an Elizabethan, since failure was not characteristic of that age
— lights up the fortuitousness, the hazards of the time. As
Naunton wrote of him :

" Sir Walter Rawleigh was one, that (it seems) Fortune had
pickt out of purpose, of whom to make an example, or to use as
her Tennis-Ball, thereby to shew what she could doe ; for she
tost him up of nothing, and too and fro to greatnesse, and from
thence down to little more than to that wherein she found him
(a bare Gentleman)."

Or again, as a universal intelligence wrote of the case in
general, and of the times :

" Great Princes' favorites their faire leaves spread,
But as the Marygold at the suns eye,
And in themselves their pride lies buried,
For at a frowne they in their glory die."

His career may stand as an example of that, of a tragic
fortuitousness ; not of failure. The one implies that though

the man suffered, the work remained; the other that both alike went down to common oblivion and fruitlessness. But it is not so ; for think what remains. There are the poems — and he is one of the loftiest and most enduring of Elizabethan poets. There is the prose — and after Bacon he is perhaps the finest of that age of native prose-writers. It is hard to say, there are so many of them. But Mr. Thompson falls into the error — which has enticed even so subtle a critic as Virginia Woolf — of speaking of "the lumbering Elizabethan prose". That comes from too much regarding a few artificial flowers of self-conscious literary composition, Sidney's *Arcadia*, or Lyly's *Euphues*, or Lodge. If one reads their letters — and Essex wrote letters as fine as Ralegh's, and Drake and Howard of Effingham and Robert Cecil come not far behind — or if one reads the reports of the seamen, the voyages of discovery gathered together in Hakluyt or Purchas, there never was writing more direct, vigorous, and eloquent. After all, these were the years when the Authorised Version of the Bible was made. Then, too, Ralegh was, though not the first, yet the centre of the whole group which carried out the most persistent attack upon the great colonial question — England's share in the opening-up of the New World. Oxford in our time was right to name its first Empire club after Ralegh, for he was the most conscious and determined of the makers of Empire. To have destined North America for the dominion of English-speaking people can hardly be regarded as the work of one whose career was a failure.

Mr. Sargent's life of Sir Edward Dyer is unpretentious, scholarly, and exact ; moreover, except for a lamentable partiality for the unattractive phrase " aside from ", it is singularly well written. " The proud fantastic community known as the Court formed the matrix of Elizabethan society " : it is both true and well said. Since Dyer's life had not been written before, it is a useful piece of work to have investigated it with such care — Mr. Sargent has pursued his researches into all the repositories of likely material, both public and private, and has brought the results of his research into the life and the poems conveniently into one volume, printing them together. Sir Edward Dyer was purely a Court figure, in his time a

brilliant one, though now forgotten or remembered only as
the name attached to the lines

> " My mynde to me a kyngdome is,
> Suche perfect joy therin I fynde,
> That it excells all other blisse
> That worlde afords or growes by kynde :
> Though muche I wante which moste would have,
> Yet still my mynde forbides to crave. . . .
>
> I laugh not at an others loss,
> I grudge not at an others gaine :
> No worldly waves my mynde can toss,
> My state at one dothe still remayne :
> I feare no foe, I fawne no freende,
> I lothe not lyfe, nor dread no ende."

That gives something of the man's temper, the undertone of
melancholy which so many Elizabethans had (none more than
Ralegh) by way of reaction perhaps from so much pushing and
striving for place. and power ; in addition, there is a certain
detachment of mind, which not all of them possessed, a spirit
of independence, which may in part have accounted for Dyer's
lack of success in life. For he was, though his biographer does
not insist upon it, a failure. It was not, at first, for lack of
trying. Born in the same class as Ralegh, the lesser gentry
who had done well out of the spoils of the Church — the Dyers
obtained several of the Somersetshire manors of Glastonbury —
he began early at Court, lost the Queen's favour by some youthful prank, recovered it again by a skilfully devised entertainment
at Woodstock such as Elizabeth loved, and spent the rest of
his life at Court and with it all his patrimony and fortune. He
belonged to the generation before Ralegh : this was his import-.
ance poetically, as a link between Wyatt and Surrey and the
full blossoming towards the end of the reign. He was educated,
like Ralegh, at Oxford, where, according to Anthony Wood,
" his natural inclination to poetry and other polite learning,
as also his excellency in bewailing and bemoaning the perplexities of love, were observed by his contemporaries ". He had a
good singing voice and sang his own songs to the lute.

At Court he became an especial friend of Philip Sidney's,

accompanied him to Penshurst, where they versified together, and was a chief mourner at his funeral. This was the chief friendship of his life, and afterwards he made no other, though Essex was attached to him and sought his advice with respect, and Cecil had a friendly regard for him. We find him engaged in the ordinary pursuits of the Court, giving and receiving splendid presents from the Queen, which he could ill afford, subscribing to Frobisher's voyages, being used on a few unimportant diplomatic missions, where he acquitted himself well ; at one time talked of as Secretary of State, he was in the end promoted to be Chancellor of the Order of the Garter, a post more honorific than important. His name was chiefly known, outside the Court circle, to poets, particularly to those of the next generation, who looked up to him as a father in the art. And certainly his poetry is technically skilled, while in adhering to the native accented measures in spite of his quantitative experiments with Sidney, he showed his instinctive sense of the language. But most of it is lost, like Ralegh's : with these courtiers it seems to have been a point of honour not to set much store by their verse ; and neither made any effort to preserve it.

There is a further similarity between the two : the melancholy, the tart, strung rhythms. The old foundations of faith had gone and nothing had arisen yet to take their place. These men were thrown back upon their own resources, Dyer no less than Ralegh, Spenser no less than Marlowe, Shakespeare no less than Bacon or Donne. One thing reveals this little-known courtier and poet in a much stranger and more searching light than anything that remains of him — his passionate interest in the semi-scientific, semi-magical arts of Dr. Dee and his associate, the extraordinary charlatan Kelly. Dyer journeyed twice across Europe to the Court of the Emperor Rudolph II at Prague, once to find out for himself if Kelly really had found the way to transmute into gold, and once (in vain) to bring him home at Burghley's orders. It is this queer fascination — for the rest of his life seems unimpassioned enough — that brings him close to the restless and various imagination of Ralegh. They were both types, in this time, of " the searching and unsatisfied spirits of the English ".

XIII

THE ELIZABETHAN EXHIBITION

It is curious to think how little of Elizabethan London, or even of the London that Elizabethans knew, is left to us. The age was not a time of much building in the capital — the aim of the government seems to have been to prevent London from growing rather than to add to it ; and even that much of London which we have in common with them, buildings which an Elizabethan would know if he were to return to a strangely unrecognisable city, has mostly come down from a time earlier than theirs. And these are but a few fragments ; in the west, the Abbey, Westminster Hall, and St. James's ; in the east, the Tower, and some remains of older churches — St. Bartholomew's and St. Saviour's, Southwark ; and with only a suggestion of a connecting link in some of the Inns of Court and in a few old houses in Holborn. Only the river remains the same — yet hardly the same. For London has become, is now, an unrepentantly Georgian town : all the best of it the creation of the eighteenth and early nineteenth centuries.

And yet, on a smaller scale, there are innumerable relics — pictures, books, armour, tapestry, furniture, jewels, ornaments — out of which it is not difficult to construct something of that vanished age. Indeed the Elizabethan Exhibition does succeed in creating within a few rooms the illusion of the crowded life of that glorious reign. It does more than bring together a number of interesting historical objects ; in paying a visit to it, you find yourself taking a step back through three centuries, to another world where the great names were Elizabeth and Burghley and Drake, where the Armada had still to be fought, and then was vanquished (" God blew with his breath and his enemies were scattered ").

If you care, you may reflect what a singular thing it is that here are these men and women, vanished from the earth three hundred years and more, whose bodies are but dust, and yet whose little cherished objects — a ring, a crucifix that Mary

97

Queen of Scots wore to her execution, an ivory walking-stick made for the hand of Elizabeth — remain to tell something of the lives and secrets of their owners, when everything else has gone.

The Exhibition naturally centres upon the figure of the Queen. There are perhaps half a dozen portraits of her and more, besides miniatures ; from the time when she was a young woman of twenty, in the Tower, in danger of her life, and gave this portrait of herself to Sir John Harrington, a fellow prisoner with her, to the time when she had become a figure of legend and it was highly indelicate to remember her age. It was not to be expected that the portraits from private possession should rival the famous ones in the National Gallery : particularly those two magnificent pictures of her, the one (which Lytton Strachey chose for the frontispiece of his book) where she has a pearl-spangled veil and holds up a flower in her hand, the other with a string of pearls twisted on one side and with a plume of feathers held in front. Nor are all the portraits here of equal merit ; indeed, one or two of the school of Mark Gerhaerdts give one very little impression of the person they are portraying, they are so conventional and stiff.

It is well known how difficult a person Elizabeth was to render ; there was so little chance given of getting at the character of the person behind such a barrage of ornament, at the woman behind the mask of the Queen. The public was used to a certain idea of her — and any other than the official image would be confusing, to say the least. Hence the extraordinary impersonality, the mask-like image, the unsatisfactoriness of so many of Elizabeth's portraits. She had a certain idea of herself, and of what was due to her, and her life was one magnificent piece of acting the part. Hence the pageantry she kept up around her, the astonishing wardrobe, the inscrutable behaviour, the incomprehensible style of writing in which she enveloped what she wished to say. It was all a superb defence against the world — and at the same time a way of imposing herself upon the world.

But there was a pathetic side to it all — to anyone who has the clue. And the Exhibition gives it. The place of honour is given in the main room to the best portrait of her here, a fine one by Zucchero. This, the *Rainbow* portrait from Hatfield, is in a sense the most official : there is the Queen, with an enormous head-dress, the arch of a rainbow in her hand, and with the motto *Non sine sole Iris*. Perhaps it is fanciful, but it seems to me that he has painted a certain awareness in the eyes, as if a really good painter saw, what the others had missed, the magnificence to be but a defence. Next to her hangs the superb Leicester, painted rather late in life when beard and hair were grey ; but his black cap is set at a tilt all the same, and he is still handsome and swash-buckling as ever. Elizabeth was for years in love with him ; and of all the flatterers that surrounded her, he seems alone to have had a place for her in his heart. But indeed, their love could have had no consummation. Elizabeth, unlike Mary Queen of Scots, sacrificed her private happiness for the sake of politics, that she might be a great ruler. Her heart withered in the process, and Leicester died in the year of the Armada, fifteen years before the end of her course. Now here at last they hang together, with a bowl of spring tulips between them.

In some ways the simplest and most impressive portrait of the Queen is the lead head, attributed to Nicholas Hilliard, that confronts the visitor on entering the first room. It is so simple and regular in its lines — doubtless the medium dictated that — that it brings out better than any picture the fine structure of the head, with a suggestion of the Italian in it (was there not Visconti blood in her veins ?) : the small and bony oval with its low wide forehead and high cheek-bones, the hawk-nose, downward-pointing ; the oval eyes slightly slanted, the small regular mouth, with the tight lips so impossible to extract any secrets either of life or State from. There she lies, pillowed in her great ruff, a string of pearls with a great pendant at her throat, and long pearl drops at her ears. No wonder her people took pride in her. The leaden effigy, resplendent upon its purple velvet, recalls the scene at her funeral :

" The city of Westminster surcharged with multitudes of all sorts of people in their streets, houses, windows, leads, and gutters, that came to see the obsequy ; and when they beheld her statue or picture lying upon the coffin set forth in royal robes, having a crown upon the head thereof, and a ball and sceptre in either hand, there was such a general sighing, groaning, and weeping, as the like hath not been seen or known in the memory of man, neither doth any history mention any people, time, or State, to make like lamentation for the death of their Sovereign."

A more usual vision of the Queen — though indifferent from a pictorial point of view — is that recalling her many processions by water up and down the Thames, and garnished with the sort of quaint conceit that the age loved and Elizabeth fed on :

> " The Queen was bro't by water to Whitehall
> At ev'ry stroke the oars did Tears let fall ;
> More clung about ye Barge, Fish under water
> Wept out yr eyes of pearl and swome blind a'ter.
> I think ye Bargeman might with easier sighs
> Have rowed her thither in her people's eyes
> For, howsoe'er my thoughts have ever scann'd
> Sh'ad come by water had she come by land."

For all that, I cannot help feeling that there is a certain posthumous, seventeenth-century flavour about the rhyme ; as if expressive of her people's regret for her and her splendour, when compared with her successor, James, spindle-legged, snuff-stained, undignified.

In the next place of honour come, as is only right and proper, the Cecils, the brains of the régime. The *Rainbow* portrait of the Queen has Leicester on one side, but on the other — the right hand — it has Burghley : on one side her affections, on the other her political judgment, her will. It is a well-known picture of Burghley as Lord Treasurer, holding the white staff in his hand, and wearing the large black cap with ear-flaps that lend a slightly comic touch to an otherwise sedate and mournful countenance. Why should the Cecils look so melancholy in their portraits ? The weight of affairs of State ? But they had pretty much their own way in politics ; and if they hadn't positively the last word — Elizabeth saw to that herself — then they had the next to the last word. Up the staircase there is a double portrait of them, old

Burghley and his favourite son Robert Cecil together, that throws some light on the question. There is a common look of sickliness in the pale, watchful faces with the candid brows. Robert Cecil's is definitely that of an invalid — he was a hunchback — with long sunken cheeks and deep shadows under the eyes ; but the eyes themselves very wide open and coldly taking everything in. That was like his character ; what Lytton Strachey says of him is very true :

" A discerning eye might have detected melancholy and resignation in that patient face. The spectacle of the world's ineptitude and brutality made him, not cynical — he was not aloof enough for that — but sad — was he not a creature of the world himself ? "

There he is ; the most exquisite speaker of the age, the most astute political intelligence, the most philosophically-minded. Yet all this omits something of him. As a young man, he was like Pitt in his youth — before the responsibilities of office grew thick upon them and made them both older than their years — a creature of extraordinary high spirits and gaiety. In an age of brilliant letter-writers, his were the best ; in a court full of wits and merry-makers, he was the wittiest and the most full of merriment.

In close propinquity to these stand, or rather hang, Essex and Southampton : the tragic Essex, the secret of whose undoubted attractiveness to the age is now difficult to appreciate ; and Southampton, who in spite of youth and beauty, always makes a bad impression. The portrait of him here shows him as a prisoner in the Tower for his part in the Essex conspiracy ; he is surrounded with all the trappings of melancholy, dressed in black as if in mourning, and with his long auburn hair falling below his shoulders. It seems hard to think, though probably true, that it is of him the divine poet wrote :

" Nor did I wonder at the lily's white,
Nor praise the deep vermilion in the rose ;
They were but sweet, but figures of delight,
Drawn after you, you pattern of all those."

It is perhaps a mitigating circumstance that the picture affords

considerable evidence of the comfort obtainable in the Tower.
From what we can see, Southampton has a charming room, with
a window open behind him, and a comfortable oak window-
seat ; he has his book and he has his cat, a black-and-white
one looking very knowing out of the canvas. And then there
is Bacon — there is always Bacon — so impossible to like, so
hard to explain ; yet a great genius, along with Shakespeare —
with whose name his own has become curiously knit — a twin
peak of the age.

Around these greater figures, there is a crowd of lesser ones
who decorated the Court or Elizabeth's service. There is
Hunsdon, her cousin, her only near relative surviving in her
latter years, of whom she was very fond. " My Harry ", she
would write to him and sign herself, " Your loving kinswoman,
Elizabeth R." How well one remembers his signature, the
large clear fist all of a quaver, as if he drank not wisely but too
well ; and indeed, there is a suspiciously good complexion on
him compared with all these sallow ones. Then there is the
young Edward de Vere, Earl of Oxford, whom the age thought
not much of ; and Sir Edward Hoby at the age of eighteen, a
very foppish-looking youth with a tall Charles IX hat and a
white slashed tunic ; he looks very anaemic and puffy about
the eyes, his head propped up by an incredibly intricate lace
ruff — but he survived to go on the Cadiz expedition with
Essex and well into the reign of James I. And all around are
the fine young men who filled Elizabeth's Court. There is Sir
John Pakington, whom she called " Lusty Pakington " for his
feats of strength and athletic skill. He once laid a wager with
three other courtiers to swim from Westminster to London
Bridge, but for some reason the Queen would not allow the
match. Here he is, long-limbed and athletic-looking, a gawky
rough ; but — and this is indicative of the age — he has the
long fine hands of an artist. The ladies of the Court are much
less in evidence ; one remembers only the Lady Catherine
Howard, an old-fashioned dame with a complicated head-gear,
and her eyes wide open with surprise, as if in alarm at finding
herself here. And so we come to the two Somerset brothers,
very much of a type, both of them extremely handsome ; Sir
George in a glittering suit of armour with an arabesque

pattern ; and his brother Sir Charles, Captain of the Rysebank at Calais, in the famous black-and-gold armour now in the Tower. In the former, a certain arrogance of pose goes curiously with a shifty look in the insolent eyes ; but the latter, painted in 1566 when he was thirty, needs no qualifying. It is a picture of the handsomest Elizabethan type ; a swarthy complexion, long beard and high forehead, with wide-apart dark eyes and beautifully curved brows. Such were the men Elizabeth delighted in.

So let us pass into the room given up to the men who in the end brought more glory to the reign than even all these : the great seamen. Here is Drake to the life, down to the wart on his nose ; the small slanting head compact with furious energy stands out from the canvas darkened with age. On a table by him is a globe, with the map of the world ; and he has at his belt the large pendant jewel the Queen gave him. Near him there are the maps his voyages produced, contemporary accounts of them, written and published, and the astrolabe that Humphrey Cole made for his aid in navigation. He seems somehow so alive, in spite of the years, that, looking at the flesh-coloured cheeks of the seaman (or is it of the Devonshireman ?), I cannot but remember the superb force of the man, as revealed in his letters to Elizabeth when keeping watch night and day in the Channel for the Armada. " The Lord of all strengths is with you ", he writes to her ; and then, " I surely think there was never any force so strong as there is now ready and making ready against your Majesty, but that the Lord of all strengths is stronger ". There is something so English about Drake ; and yet, it is touching to think that of all English heroes, no English soil holds, or has ever held his body. Even Nelson lies in St. Paul's ; but Drake lies buried at sea off Porto Bello in the Spanish Main.

So too with his neighbour, Humphrey Gilbert. His picture reveals a similar slant head to Drake's ; only whereas Drake had a fresh colour, blue eyes, and brown hair, Gilbert was sallow and dark like a Spaniard (or shall we say like a Cornishman ?). He too has the same bravado, this time expressed in a motto, *Quid Non* : what not, indeed ! What would they not do, these makers of an empire, these explorers of unknown seas ;

H

what dangers were they not prepared to face, what deaths to invite ? The end with Gilbert is inscribed upon the canvas, " Drowned in the discovery of Virginia, anno 1584 ". We all know the story of the little 10-ton bark, the *Squirrel*, in which he foundered, the dark night, the light at her mast which suddenly disappeared and was seen no more ; and how when his companion ship last saw him, Gilbert was sitting in the stern with a book in his hand, and refused to change ships, calling out, " We are as near to heaven by sea as by land."

Last of them, and not unworthy, comes the Lord Admiral, Howard of Effingham. It is a noble portrait of a noble man. He is painted on a large scale, life-size or more, in his robes as a peer, red velvet and grey-tawny satin. His face is an old man's, with grizzled beard and large nose, and with a turban close-fitting on his head ; it reveals all that he was — a great public servant, and of absolute integrity. As is fitting for so grand a sea-dog, the painter with the romantic touch of the Flemish school has painted in a sea-scape beyond the rich hangings, with dim shapes of ships tossing on the grey waves. Does he not intend us to think of the storms of 1588, when the fleet lay tossing in Plymouth Sound, and the Lord Admiral was writing to Walsingham ? — " Myself and my ships do continually tarry and lie aboard in all the storm, where we may compare that we have danced as lustily as the gallantest dancers in the Court ". Waiting, waiting for Philip's Armada ; and meanwhile provisions were running short and no more had come ; " and if it do not come," he writes, " yet assure yourself we will not lose any opportunity nor we will not lack, there is good fishing in the seas ". This was the spirit of 1588 — of Howard, of Drake, of Hawkins, of them all.

So, passing hurriedly through the remaining rooms, we will not linger long over the soldiers, the warriors, but come to a quieter, a more peaceful side of the reign. But, in passing, a charming little picture catches one's eye — of an Elizabethan captain, looking very young, rather silly and frightened — but all the same looking out of his frame as if he were alive. The date is 1587, the year before the Armada ; and it has a typical inscription, just the kind of sentiment that would commend itself to his heart :

> " Only · death · makes ·
> Captains · quayle ·
> And lusti · souldiers
> for · to · fayle . "

How many such young men, captains of their troops, there must
have been, who left their bones on the plains of the Netherlands, fighting under Norris or Leicester against Don John,
or the redoubtable Parma ? Sir Nicholas Parker, whose
portrait by Custodis has been lent by the King, served as a
young captain in the Low Countries and in France ; but he
came home again to marry into a Cornish family and live to a
hale old age as Governor of Pendennis Castle. He appears in
gorget and black tunic, a lean, narrow-faced man with narrow
temples and steel-grey eyes ; while he brandishes above his
head a heavy broad-sword, with the inscription *Pro Fide et
Patria*.

One does not think somehow of Sir Philip Sidney as a
warrior, he seems to belong to that earlier, more idyllic time
before the great storms gathered. Half the pathos of his end
lies in that — that the most chivalrous man of his time, the
pattern of perfect courtesy, one of those men like Lord Falkland
who had no belief in fighting, should have come upon his death
in battle. He was mortally wounded (" Thy necessity is yet
greater than mine ") outside Zutphen in the Low Countries,
lingered a while and died. When he died, his contemporaries
felt that something had finished in them, that spring had gone
out of the morning. There is here a print of his funeral procession, with his friends about him carrying the pall and bearing
his standards : Fulke Greville, Edmund Pakenham, Henry
Sidney, Edmund Walsingham, Will Sidney, Edward Wootton,
Edward Dyer ; and not far away there is — curious memento
— one of the mourning hoods worn by the heralds.

But the portraits of him that hang in the Music Room show
him bright and happy in his young years ; one of them is
taken with his brother Robert, two boys arm-in-arm in their
white doublets and stockings and plum-coloured breeches ;
the other shows him as a young man, with his fair hair and light
hazel eyes. On the other side is his sister the Countess of
Pembroke, for whom he wove the long dream-like tale of the

Arcadia in the groves of Wilton. Wilton was their Arcadia ; and the thought of Sir Philip Sidney and his sister (" the subject of all verse ") seems ever to be associated (in the picture she is holding a lute) with music and gardens.

Gardens and music — they were both such strong passions with the Elizabethans. It was Bacon who said, " God Almighty first planted a garden " ; and Bacon himself, in friendly philosophic rivalry, was a great gardener : he made the garden at Gray's Inn, and spent years over the gardens of Gorhambury. And when one thinks of how Elizabeth spent her time, one has the impression of much walking and talking in gardens ; as often as not, her conversations with foreign envoys, no less than with her courtiers, took place while walking up and down the gardens of the palace. From a tapestry in the Exhibition, one may gather something of how they conceived of a garden ; needless to say, it is of a very romantic character with an Eastern potentate reclining in a corner, and a large number of ladies and gentlemen crowded among the formal walks, the box-hedges, and the roses. But in the background there is a carriage going by, a gaily-curtained affair on springless wheels, drawn by two diminutive ponies. And this is realistic enough. It reminds one of the state in which Elizabeth and the Court went, always trundling from Richmond to Whitehall, from Nonsuch to Oatlands and Greenwich and then back again.

As for music, it is well known that English music reached a height of achievement in Elizabeth's reign which it has never since attained ; that William Byrd was to Elizabethan music what Shakespeare was to poetry. There are few, all too few, relics of him here, a manuscript of some songs and a signature on a document — not much to suggest the depth and range of his genius. It is some consolation that there is a pleasant little portrait of the handsome (and libidinous) Dr. Bull, organist of the Chapel Royal and most popular of musicians : all in black satin, very clear in texture like a Hals, with white ruff and wristbands by way of contrast, and his spruce moustaches waxed out to a fine point. It is a taking portrait, though nothing like so striking as the brilliant one of him at Oxford. Various other relics in this room exhibit the musical skill of the time : there is a viola da gamba, of exquisite workmanship, made by John

Rose in the old palace of Bridewell, a virginal of 1570 still in perfect playing condition and several pieces of music, the funeral Psalms of Mr. Henry Noell, with music by John Dowland, and Thomas Morley's *Plain and Easy Introduction to Music.*

But there is a fuller and more representative collection of documents, as is only reasonable, in the section devoted to literature. Among many first editions of Spenser and Sidney, Peele and Kyd and Dekker (no Marlowe, however !), there is a first quarto of *A Midsummer Night's Dream* " as it hath been sundry times publicly acted by the Right Honourable, the Lord Chamberlaine his servants " ; and John Lyly's *Sapho and Phao,* " Played before the Queenes Majestie on Shrove Tuesday by her Majesties' children and the boyes of Paules ". And one remembers the jollifications at Court always when Shrove-tide came round, and the payments to the players that regularly appear in Elizabeth's Household accounts. Throwing no less light on the minds of men then is the translation of a book published in 1572 : *Of ghostes and spirites walking by nyght and of strange noyces, cracks and sundry fore-warnyngs, whiche commonly happen before the death of menne, great slaughters and alterations of kyng-domes.* We remember :

> " And yesterday the bird of night did sit
> Even at noon-day upon the market-place,
> Hooting and shrieking. When these prodigies
> Do so conjointly meet, let not men say,
> ' These are their reasons, — they are natural ' ;
> For I believe they are portentous things
> Unto the climate that they point upon.
> . . . . . .
> It is the part of men to fear and tremble,
> When the most mighty gods, by tokens, send
> Such dreadful heralds to astonish us."

How often in reading Shakespeare are we reminded of this tremulous apprehension of signs and portents, and how much in this respect he was a child of the age.

To our lasting loss, very few portraits of the poets and dramatists have come down to us — perhaps not many were even painted. But Spenser is represented to us in Thomas

Wilson's copy of a contemporary portrait that is now lost. It is just what one would expect, a massive though delicate head, with a very notably high forehead and of melancholy dignity; the eyes are large and blue and heavy-lidded — the whole thing dreamy and a little weak.

Among the other documents nearly all the well-known signatures appear ; the crabbed spidery scrawl of Burghley (the old Polonius), the lovely fluent Italian hands of the young men at Court, Robert Cecil, Essex, Bacon. There are letters of Mary Queen of Scots, and a number, as there are a few portraits, of the French Court, Catherine de Medici, Charles IX and Henry III. Last, there is Elizabeth herself, from the lovely, self-confident, baroque signature of the early years of the reign, to the loose and ugly scrawl of her last years in which one seems to see reflected all the storms of State that have passed over her in the intervening time, all the anxieties of heart and mind. "Je prieray", she writes to the young Charles IX on the eve of the Massacre of St. Bartholomew, "Je prieray le Seigneur Dieu vous garder de tout mall et vous donner bonne vie et longue."

If it is not ungrateful, one might specify one conspicuous lacuna here : the virtual absence of Ralegh from the Exhibition. True, we are given his pipe, and a very formidable object it is ; but it is not as the populariser of smoking that the Elizabethans knew him. After all, in the last years of the reign, that " superb, dangerous man ", as Strachey calls him, was one of the three most powerful persons in England, and he was certainly the best hated. It may be that owing to the ill-fortune that overtook him and wrecked his family, little enough of the evidences of his splendour remains in private hands — even at Sherborne which he made what it now is. And one might suggest that more space should have been given to what may be called the Opposition — the Catholic circles which could not accept the new régime and formed and re-formed a hostile party throughout these years ; to that body of opinion whose view of things is pathetically expressed in scarlet needle-work on a nightdress of Mary Queen of Scots : *Camisia sanctis-simae martyris Mariae Scotorum Reginae quae passa est sub Elizabetha Regina Angliae 1587 Feb. 18.* There are a number of great families, the Norfolks, the Arundells of Wardour, whose treasures it would have been a privilege to see — such things, for instance, as the fine portrait of the Venerable Philip, Earl of Arundel, in the possession of the Jerninghams, or a relic of Cardinal Allen's.

But perhaps these things would have struck a discordant note amid the unanimity of glory. And anyhow, there is a sufficiently curious reminder in the shrivelled hand of Sir John Heydon, cut off in a duel in 1600, yet still in perfect preservation to the nails, of the more gruesome, the no less characteristic side of the Elizabethans : the dangers that attended life on all sides, the executions, the punishments, the rackings, the heads on the gateways of towns, the gibbets at cross-roads.

In spite of the intensely English character of the age, the truth is that there seems something alien to us in its spirit, something ingrained that gave it a twist of magnificence and cruelty, a streak of the Italian, Italy of the Medici and of Machiavelli. You can see it looking out of the face of Elizabeth herself, and her whole environment was no less marked by Italian refinements ; when the musicians at Court were mostly Italian, when Italian was spoken by courtiers in preference to French, when translations from Italian were all the vogue with the dramatists and poets. It is the Renaissance in full blow on English soil, though a little late, that is the explanation of it all : the common spirit giving common form to these innumerable diverse objects here brought together. Look at this great chimney-piece from Madingley, with its noble proportions. If you half-shut your eyes, you can see the dominant classical structure of it as pure as the purest Georgian ; yet here it is bedizened and bulging with decorated caryatids and figures and fruits. And the same is true of all these things, the full-blown suits of armour and the flagons and silver bowls, the great chairs and flowing gowns no less than of the humbler vessels of green glaze ware.

It may be fanciful to see a common spirit in the inflated pantaloon-like breeches of the men, the farthingales of the women, and the great bulbous legs of the tables — an expansiveness, a generosity of line, unrestrained by the maturer taste of a more sophisticated age. They were children ; they rioted

in extremes of opulence, ardour, joy ; they must even have
derived pleasure from their exaggerated griefs. The Lord
Treasurer, Burghley, when he could not persuade the Queen
to what he wanted, used to give way to floods of tears. A sober
statesman overeats at a feast, and having to take physic, has to
absent himself from important affairs of State for days or weeks.
The same unrestraint, the same bravado that led a sea-captain
to sail his ship up the Thames with sails of damask, that led
Ralegh when there was a rumour of his disgrace to show himself
to the people who hated him, clad in silver from top to toe,
inspired the ladies to their gigantic ruffs which the Puritans
so disapproved of, and the dramatists to pile the stage with
corpses in their final acts. In a word, the Elizabethans were
unrestrained, because creative.

It is impossible to speak of all the ornaments, the jewels, the
tapestries, the plate that garnish these rooms : the same breath
of creation is in them all, as in the men and women whose
images hang upon the walls ; in them, as in a pair of shoes or
a faded bodice once worn by Elizabeth.

(Written 1933.)

XIV

ELIZABETH AT RYCOTE

Now it is afternoon over the rolling Oxfordshire country between Shotover and Brill and Thame — much of it part of the old Royal Forest of Shotover. Bruce and I, having come by Waterperry and Waterstock and round by Shabbington, where in front of " The Old Fisherman " a duck-board conducts the villagers along the low-lying road, so liable to be flooded by the sudden and uncertain Thame, and from there across the fields to Rycote, having scrambled down and up the narrow moat and through the little nineteenth-century plantation gone wild, full of lilacs and rhododendrons among the bushes and small sycamores, now sit by the lake-side, tired with long walking, Bruce on a branch out over the lake where he plays with the water, making the ripples widen into the still unbroken surface, while I turn back to see the chestnuts holding their candelabras low down upon the water, their great flowers reflected as in a mirror. It is the sleepy hour of the afternoon, lovely and willing ; but it being Sunday, the angry rooks are restless and disturbed above the tree-tops, cawing for minutes together and then falling silent. Everything leans towards quiet and sleep-in-the-sun ; the cry of a moorhen out on the water, a lonely liquid " qurr ", only deepens the silence. Above, as always nowadays over this country, there is the drone of an aeroplane, enticing to sleep, with some afterthoughts.

Then, looking up the lake, between the trees, I first catch sight of the house and remember Elizabeth. Here, then, she was happy once with Leicester ; here she came often enough to see the Norrises, coming from Woodstock or from Oxford over Shotover, or in earlier, more difficult days, from Brentford, being conducted to the half retirement, half confinement of Woodstock while Mary reigned. Not much of the house remains as it was then ; only a wing, and the chapel in the grounds. In the orchard below the house there is a detached octagonal turret of the Elizabethan house still standing, of

diapered red brick, upon the line of the old front ; and behind
the walled garden, in the open field there are humps which
may indicate a ruined gate-house or stables. And all around
in the fields are scattered oaks and beeches, a few of the oldest
oaks the remains of the medieval forest : one of them standing
not far from the house, very old and wide and dying at the top,
must surely have seen Elizabeth ? It is chastening to think that
some natural or inanimate object, a house, a tree, has looked
upon Elizabeth, or all the Henrys and Edwards before her, that
long procession of time which, a human being, one can never
know : some reminder to irk one, of the shortness, the fragile
uncertainty which is our lot in comparison.

What remains of the house is singularly satisfying, with its
pleached and patterned brick, its end-wall rising to a fair
Flemish gable, stepped and parapeted, as was then much the
fashion, its sunken flower-garden below the balustrade of the
terrace. One can almost see those formal figures, the pleated
farthingales, the ruffs, the heads held high, moving stiffly, so
many figures on a chess-board, among the vanished box-hedges
and trimmed yews. One great yew still stands that outdoes
them all, even those shadows, in time, standing sentinel by the
tower of the chapel among the graves ; the tree, this little stone
building with its western niche for the saint, remember days,
years, centuries before Elizabeth and Leicester came and were
together here ; the chapel of St. Michael and All Angels
founded in the year 1449 by Richard Quatremains and Sybilla
his wife, the sentinel yew going back perhaps to Edward III
and his order to plant yews in the churchyard of every parish,
in the time of the French wars, the seasons and the wars abroad
passing them by and leaving them quiet at last on the shoulder
of this hill, this summer afternoon.

To this pleasant house in a fold of the hill, looking to the
east and the south, Elizabeth came first in 1554 on her way to
Woodstock, when Mary was Queen. Here she was entertained
by Lord Williams of Thame, to whom Henry Norris, her kindly
keeper at Woodstock, succeeded in the first year of her reign.
Her time at Woodstock must have been not unpleasant : it
ministered to wounded pride to nag even at Bedingfield ;
perhaps it was all a game to her, practising the part of injured

innocence that was so useful in later years, sharpening her talons upon an old, blunt, fanatic knight. At any rate, Norris was all kindness, and she grew to like him and his dear dark wife, her " black crow " she called her, having names for everybody. And when she came to be Queen, she remembered them as she remembered all who had been kind to her and to the mother she never spoke of : Norris became Sheriff of Oxfordshire, was made Ambassador to France, became Lord Norris of Rycote, and better still, was graced by the Queen herself coming to visit him.

She came again, this time with Leicester, in 1566, after the extraordinary festivities of her reception at Oxford, the interminable orations in Latin and Greek (Her Highness throwing in a word here and there in witness of her scholarship), the disputations in the Schools, the sermons, the verses, the plays in Christ Church Hall — one of them in English, Richard Edwards' *Palaemon and Arcyte*, a sprig from which grew the mighty tree of the Elizabethan drama ; another in Latin, called *Progne*, by a Canon of Christ Church — " But it did not take half so well as the much-admired play of Palaemon and Arcyte ". All which over, she rode away to Shotover, the Masters and Scholars of the University accompanying her ; and turning back to the city, said farewell : " Farewell the worthy University of Oxford ; farewell my good subjects there ; farewell my dear scholars, and may God prosper your studies : farewell — farewell ". " And so she rode that night to Ricot, to Mr. Norris's house, eight miles from Oxford."

It was early September — Leicester was with her — and the height of their intimacy : she a woman now in her early thirties ; he handsome, rakish, cap set on one side, well educated. He had shared the prison of the Tower when she was there : a memory that perhaps held her more constantly to him than all his physical attraction. Who knows now what whisperings there were, those late summer evenings, what smiles, what intimate pressure upon the hand given to be kissed, beneath the yew ?

The years passed on and over ; she was here again in 1568, and in 1570, always at the same time of year, late August, early September. Then for many years she came not at all. The

Norris children, six fine strapping lads, grew up about these fields. In 1582 it was rumoured that she was coming ; but the Norrises could not have been so pleased when Leicester, magnificent deputy, arrived instead. However, his Lordship found them " a hearty noble couple as ever I saw towards her highness ".

Great storms of State were gathering, and Elizabeth did not move far into the country. Then at the end of August 1588, that memorable month, Leicester was here once more, straight from the camp at Tilbury. It was the time when he and Elizabeth had been there together, the high, late summer ; now the remnants of the King of Spain's fleet were labouring their way through the northern seas around Scotland homeward. Remembering the earlier years, he took up pen and wrote to her, inquiring after her health, " the chiefest thing in this world I pray for " ; and then, dated his letter, " From your old lodging at Rycott ". There was constancy in that and true affection. Five days later he was dead. When the news came, Elizabeth took the letter and, writing upon it in her own hand " His last letter ", folded it up and put it away.

Four years later, at the end of September 1592, she came here for the last time, on her way from Oxford. There were the usual jubilations, the usual speeches. But somehow it did not go with a swing as of old ; there was no Leicester there ; the shadows were deepening around her. On Thursday, 28 September,

" Her Highness departed from the University this day, about eleven of the clock in the forenoon, in hir open and princely carriadge. And heard, lastly, a long tedious oration made unto hir by the Junior Proctor of the University, about a mile from the city, in the very edge of their bounds or liberties towards Shotover."

Arrived at Rycote, she was received with a curious little ceremonial set-piece such as the time and she delighted in : " an olde gentleman, sometime a souldier " delivered a speech :

" I meane not to recount my service," he said, " but to tell your Majesty that I am past al service, save only devotion. My horse, mine armour, my shielde, my sworde, the riches of a young souldier, and an olde souldier's reliques, I should here offer to your Highnesse ; but my foure boies have stollen them from me, vowing themselves to armes, and leaving mee to my prayers. This is their resolution, and my desire, that their lives maye be imployed wholy in your service, and their deathes bee their vowes sacrifice. Their deathes, the rumour of which hath so often affrighted the Crowe my wife, that her hart hath bene as blacke as her feathers. I know not whether it be affection or fondness, but the Crowe thinketh her owne birds the fairest, because to her they are dearest, and although nothing be more unfit to lodge your Majestye than a Crowes neste, yet shall it be most happy to us, that it is by your Highnesse made a Phoenix neste."

It was Norris, protesting his devotion and his sons', serving abroad for the Queen. Twenty years had gone by since Elizabeth was here last, and the six lads were grown into stalwart men, two of them, John and Henry, the best soldiers of their time. The wars now continuing, and to continue for the rest of her life, they were serving in Ireland (where one of them, William, had already died : no wonder the dear Crow was so fearful for her brood), in the Netherlands, in Brittany, the various theatres of the war. On the Sunday, " her Majesty going to the garden, was received with sweete Musicke of sundry sorts ". There letters were brought to her from different directions ; one delivered by an Irish lackey, in which was enclosed a dart of gold, set with diamonds, with this motto in Irish, " I flye onely for my Soveraigne ". A second brought a skipper from Flanders, with a key of gold and a motto in Dutch ; the third and fourth brought a sword of gold, and a truncheon set with diamonds, and with mottoes in French and Spanish. These last were from the brothers waiting to take shipping into Brittany : " the same time that I received letters that her Majesty would be at Ricot, the winde served for Britaigne : I was overjoyed with both ; yet stoode in a mammering whether I should take the opportunity of the winde, which I long expected ; or ride poste to do my duetie, which I most desired ". The letters read and the presents delivered, in this little garden scene, " the olde man kneeling downe, ended thus " : " That my sonnes have remembered their dueties, it is my harts comfort ; that your Majestie accepteth them, their harts heaven. . . ." This being done, " there was sweete musicke and two sonnets ; which ended, her Majesty went in ". Next day she took horse and left, to come again no more.

A few more years and the shadows thicken round the faithful house. The pigeons wheel in and out and around the dovecote ; the yew darkens by the chapel tower ; the house grows emptier than it was ; old age steals perceptibly on and there are youthful images that linger in the dark corners of the rooms, or where a turning comes in the passages (who is it that passed soundlessly upon the stairs ?) or in the garden walks on late summer evenings, in August or early September. One day in 1593, word comes that Maximilian the youngest had been slain in Brittany, fighting under his famous brother, Sir John. Then another day, in 1597, John died, worn out with service and war wounds, in Ireland. The Queen, grown old now, called her secretary, and wrote by him a letter of proud consolation to the Lady Norris :

" Althoughe wee have deferred long to represent unto you our grieved thoughtes, because we liked full ill to yielde you the first reflection of misfortune, whom we have always sought to cherishe and comfort, yet, knowing now that necessitie must bring it to yor cares, and nature consequently must move both griefe and passions in your harte, we resolved no longer to smother either our care for yor sorrowe, or the sympathy of our griefe for his love, whearin, yf it be true that society in sorrowe workes diminution, wee doe assure you, by this true messenger of our minde, that nature can have stirred no more dolorous affection in you as a mother for a deare son, than gratefulness and memory of his services past hath wrought in us his Soveraigne aprehension of our misse of so worthy a servant."

It was the Queen that spoke, in her royal style, words of a formal, a majestic consolation. Then the woman in her was moved, and taking up the pen, she wrote a few words in her own scrawling hand — the hand that was so neat and beautiful once — now witnessing in itself what storms had passed over her, what strains of state : " Myne owne Crowe, harme not thyselfe for booteles healpe ; but shewe a good example, to comfort yor dolorous yokefellow ".

Not long now, and Norris and his dear Crow were dead and buried in the vault beneath the altar of the little chapel, the stately monument to them both, supported by their six sons, rising in the Abbey at Westminster.

So remembering, we go over the hill, the house sinking below its shoulder. The sun comes out over Brill and Muswell Hill ; the sky that was grey is now blue ; a cuckoo flutes across the fields. There is a silvery quality in the tufts of grass in this field, I notice ; my feet find a ridge-way running through it : under the turf, between two banks is the old carriage-way going due west to Shotover. A haze of memories surrounds that house below the hill ; I seem to see an old triumphant woman in her carriage coming this way from the west. What, I wonder, was the reason for her constancy, her fidelity to this house ? That memory of Leicester ; her affection for her dear Crow ? And then I remember yet another shadow, a man she never knew — Henry's friend, the gallant victor of so many tournaments, the man who died for being her mother's lover : poor ghosts whose innocence she chose to vindicate so, keeping silence through all the years. For Norris was his son.

XV

ELIZABETHAN SUBJECTS

(i) ELIZABETH AND CATHERINE DE MEDICI

THESE two books provide an instructive contrast not only in subject but treatment : the one an example of how history may be written, the other of how it should not.[1] Professor Neale's little book consists of four lectures, very concise and beautifully clear, dealing with the complicated story of the French Wars of Religion, in which Catherine de Medici played a tortuous, Italianate, and, on the whole, ineffectual part. Mr. Neale treats the subject and its leading characters fairly and dispassionately — he even finds something reasonable to say in defence of Henri III and his *mignons* ; he reduces a desperately intricate plot — a period of ideological warfare in many ways like our own — to its simple elements and gets the whole thing into proportion. Mr. Maynard is an American Catholic — not, I should say, very well acquainted with English history, or for that matter with the English background : Wimbledon appears as pronounced by some foreign agent, Vembleton.

Mr. Maynard's book is indeed full of mistakes ; though these do not matter so much as the way in which he gets his judgments of people, and the whole proportions of the story, wrong. William Cecil is described as perfidious and cruel. In fact, he was a temperate man, very wise and prudent, and a great deal more scrupulous and humane than most in that age. Leicester's " whole career is a tissue of treachery and lack of principle ". The truth is that he was always loyal to Elizabeth, and his consistent aim was to advance his country's interests. There is far too much of the popular nonsense about the Tudor oligarchy " stealing " the lands of the Church. They were for the most part bought and paid for, as anyone who has been into the detailed figures knows. We are told that the mass of the people in the Elizabethan period became more and more

[1] Theodore Maynard, *Queen Elizabeth* ; J. E. Neale, *The Age of Catherine de Medici*.

impoverished. The direct evidence is to the contrary. They were better off, and, as wealth increased, it is not surprising that the rich became richer too. When Mr. Maynard writes of Henry VIII as a " hopelessly immature " character we do not respect his judgment.

On the whole he gets Elizabeth better than he does his other characters (Drake is described as " not far removed from insanity "). Mr. Maynard, in spite of his *parti pris*, does not subscribe to the nonsense which Mr. Belloc has spent half a lifetime in propagating about Elizabeth having been entirely run by Cecil. (Cecil, indeed, knew better !) But he does write a lot of rubbish about Elizabeth's " abnormality ", her " neurosis ", and " ill-health ". " What was wrong with Elizabeth's health — both of mind and body — was a sexual abnormality aggravated by syphilis." This strikes me as little short of wicked — if it were not such obvious nonsense. Elizabeth was, of course, highly strung, as anyone so intelligent would be. But she had astonishing spirits and vitality, when an old woman was capable of dancing with the best at Court ; she had a long run of good health on the whole and lived to be older than any of her predecessors. She had an immense gusto for life ; there is nothing tortured about her. Even her attitude to marriage, with all the complex negotiations it led to, is explicable enough in terms of politics and her own personal position. She was determined to rule the roost — that was one difficulty ; she was a first-class politician and bent on drawing all the advantages she could out of her eligibility ; and then, she was exceedingly vain and rightly proud of her own abilities : " I am your anointed Queen," she told Parliament. " I will never by violence be constrained to anything. I thank God that I am endowed with such qualities that if I were turned out of the realm in my petticoat I am able to live in any place in Christendom." That she was a great woman there can be no shadow of doubt.

But the moral is that lives of her ought only to be written by trained historians who know the background and the time. The paper that has gone into this book might well have been saved.

The historian may well ask why Elizabeth's career was such

I

a triumph and that of Catherine de Medici a failure. Professor Neale has some illuminating suggestions to offer. He recognises Catherine's good qualities, her ability and tireless industry, her charm and the cheerful optimism of her temperament. He sees the weakness of her position compared with Elizabeth's : Catherine was not a queen reigning in her own right, she was merely a Queen-mother and a stranger to the country to boot. " What more could one poor woman, with a handful of small children, and torn between our family and the Guises, have done ? " said Henri IV in his good-natured way.

For one thing she could have built up a middle party, given all her support to the Politiques instead of turning first to the Huguenots and then to the Guises and back again. Catherine was too clever by half — and, like all such people, not quite clever enough. Like Mary Queen of Scots she was incapable of realising that it pays better to be straightforward — especially when you are the weaker side. When you are the stronger, you can, of course, afford to be straight. The clue to Elizabeth's success was her maintenance of national unity : she did build up a following, neither Catholic nor Puritan, but which consisted of the bulk of the nation. Catherine, a Florentine doing her best manfully to cope with the welter of French politics in her time, had not Elizabeth's instinct for national unity and her people. The moral of the two tales is that the Middle course is always Right.

Then Professor Neale attaches great importance to the fact that " Elizabeth had a trained intellect. Behind her bewildering opportunism there was a firm grasp of principle. She was a statesman, and Burghley in his old age paid tribute to her greatness as such." That is no more than the truth.

(ii) Queen Elizabeth as Letter-Writer

The danger of this sort of book, a collection of letters, particularly of royal letters, is that it may not make a book at all.[1] It is a danger that Dr. Harrison — or is it Queen Elizabeth ? — has triumphantly surmounted. Perhaps both have contributed to this result, for if Dr. Harrison is modest in his

[1] *The Letters of Queen Elizabeth*, edited by G. B. Harrison.

claims for the Queen as a letter-writer (she was " not an easy correspondent in any language "), so well has he chosen and so sensibly has he done his work, that the book that has emerged from their joint efforts is one of the best in the series.

One can hardly expect royal persons to make good letter-writers : there is so much in their position that must militate against intimacy. Particularly was this the case with Elizabeth. In the nature of things there were no gay little notes such as Robert Cecil, her Secretary, used to indite to his friend Master Hicks of the Temple, or Lady Ralegh to Lord Cobham inviting him to partake of their oysters and partridges. The intimate note is here conspicuously lacking. Perhaps Charles II makes up for it in his letters ; for he was an unbuttoned monarch if ever there was one. Whereas Elizabeth was not only buttoned and knotted (except on one shameless occasion when the French Ambassador was reduced to blushing confusion), but tight-laced and corseted, stiff with pearls and a great ruff, painted to the eyes and a red wig to crown all. It was intended so that the world might not too familiarly gaze upon the human being beneath the sovereign. In her the two were one, more than with any other monarch of modern times — even Louis XIV ; for his dramatisation of himself was obvious, and the disjunction made for vulgarity.

Elizabeth thought of herself as Queen in every aspect of her life ; the effect may be seen in her letters. There is not one that is not in a sense official. Even the more private letters, or notes scribbled in her own hand, deal with affairs of State or matters of public business. The most intimate are letters of condolence or congratulation to personal friends ; but these are few in number and always upon occasion of public service. The note is even then one of public pride in achievement, or of majestic consolation in sorrow.

Nevertheless, if not intimate and confiding, her letters are revealing of the character behind them, not least in that very fact. They portray her reticence, her inability to give anything away, her courage and spirit, her lack of candour, her hesitation to make up her mind. All the rest is there and at her service ; cajolery, the arts of encouraging men to serve her and their country, finesse with concealed, and a royal wrath with discovered, enemies. The main dramatic interest of the book is in the letters to Mary Queen of Scots. They range from the tart exchanges and the sound, if straight-hitting advice of the earlier ones to the hatred breathed out against the " murderess " in the last. It was Mary and her son who gave her most worry throughout her life ; " I am in such a labyrinth that I do not know how to answer the Queen of Scotland after so long delay ", she wrote appealingly to Cecil in 1564. And at the end of her life she was writing mostly to James. She can never have liked him, the child of Mary and Darnley, and her inevitable successor. He was so little of a man, and so apt to deal with something of her own tortuousness, only permissible in her, a woman. She had early given him warning : " And if you suppose that Princes' causes be veiled so covertly that no intelligence may bewray them, deceive not yourself : we old foxes can find shifts to save ourselves by others' malice, and come by knowledge of greatest secret, specially if it touch our freehold ". The other main subject of the letters is the projected Anjou marriage, an extraordinary affair which was drawn out over years and led to a large correspondence, mostly formal and unreadable unless regarded from its comic personal side. Through all her official correspondence the Queen's acute political sense emerges luminous and clear.

This selection then gives an admirable index to her mind. There is no letter of interest that I know of which is omitted, and many are given here which are not easy to come by elsewhere. On the other hand, with a little more care, the text of a number of the letters could have been rendered more accurate. And Dr. Harrison has stretched a point to admit the " Proud Prelate " letter supposed to be addressed to Cox, Bishop of Ely. As a letter it could never have been written by Elizabeth, yet there is something authentic about its note. Its place would seem to be among a collection of sayings of the Queen.

(iii) The Elizabethan Mind

This is a very odd and curiously interesting work.[1] It is also difficult to appreciate, still more to estimate. The difficulty is

[1] Hardin Craig, *The Enchanted Glass : The Elizabethan Mind in Literature*.

that it is so singularly ill-written, in that worst of American academic styles, abstract, repetitive, allusive, pretentious, unsimple, in which a spade is never by any chance called a spade, and one word is never allowed to make do if a dozen (all long ones) may be employed instead. One can hardly read the book for the blessed words " instrumentation ", " methodology " (so beloved of the London School of Economics), such phrases as " the fundamental cohesive principle of the cosmological system ", " the world-wide disputational inconclusiveness ", or such sentences as, " Thus correspondences, all exemplifications of the cohesive principle of orderliness (resting upon the two poles of authority and obedience), are permeative and innumerable, to be sought for in the fields of religion, natural science, ethics, politics, psychology — throughout the whole field of rationalisation ".

It might be supposed that anyone capable of such *bêtises* would have nothing of any value to say at all. But not so — they must be put down to the lack of literary standards in American universities. For in spite of everything, Mr. Craig has much, I found, that is actually interesting, and still more that is suggestive. He has, what is above all important, thought of a first-class subject, which is infrequent enough among English scholars better equipped to tackle it, who, owing to some academic inhibition or other, more often fail to do so. Two years ago, Mr. Basil Willey published an excellent and scholarly book on *The Seventeenth-Century Background* ; now with this, Mr. Craig attempts much the same kind of thing for the Elizabethans.

He is engaged in depicting the intellectual background, the structure of belief and thought which expresses itself — or as Mr. Craig says, " finds literary exemplification and emphasis " — in Elizabethan literature. It is a task which demands considerable learning and wide reading, and Mr. Craig has addressed himself to it manfully. Whether he possesses the qualifications for so magnificent a subject is another matter ; for the first reflection that occurs to the reader is that one cannot fully appreciate the intellectual background of the Elizabethans without a knowledge of medieval thought (think of Hooker and Donne, for example), or the Renaissance mind without a knowledge of classical antiquity.

Mr. Craig, however, makes a brave attempt at a thorough survey of the beliefs held by the Elizabethans as to the nature of the universe and man's place in it ; their scientific and pseudo-scientific views — it is hard to draw a line between one and the other, and Mr. Craig is right when he says that the history of error is from this point of view as important as that of truth. He goes on to sketch their views on astrology, religion, the possibility of the existence of spirits — which has an obvious bearing on *Hamlet* — on ethics, politics, psychology, and aesthetics. Mr. Craig insists that Elizabethan science has been much under-estimated for lack of seeing it in historical perspective, and says, roundly, that from some points of view it was as good as our own. Indeed he makes the interesting point that " since the Elizabethan man had to rely solely on his own powers [*i.e.* without the help of powerful instruments], the limitation bred in him a habit of observation and an intimacy with detail which the modern man has often turned over to somebody else ". Vast as is the progress that has been made in the physical sciences since then, no such advance has been made in the social sciences. " The social data on which Plato and Aristotle worked remain relatively unchanged . . . As moral philosophers, ancient thinkers have not been superseded." It needed an American to say that : a truth to which Oxford has fortunately remained faithful, though it is salutary to be reminded of it from across the Atlantic : we take it so much for granted that we sometimes are in danger of forgetting it.

The Elizabethans, Mr. Craig holds, thought and knew more about conduct than we do ; they certainly appear to have been more interested in such questions. Nor is it unlikely that their psychology was far nearer being a true account of men's nature than the illusory idealism characteristic of the nineteenth century. When one reads Bacon on " the nature and condition of men ; who are full of savage and unreclaimed desires, of profit, of lust, of revenge ", one realises how much more a knowledge of the sixteenth century is in keeping with twentieth-century experience !

Certainly Mr. Craig carries his main point — " how greatly the aggressive nature of man's environment was enhanced in the realm of the fanatical and the superstitious. . . . These often more alarming voices could not but create in man an impression that he lived in an environment which demanded courage, caution and eternal vigilance."

(iv) A Conventional Elizabethan

There is little enough in Sir Henry Lee's life to excite, or perhaps even to interest.[1] A good-looking young man, much addicted to physical exercise, an excellent tilter, a minor figure at Court, Ranger of Woodstock Forest and Master of the Armoury, he was a very typical Elizabethan figure. He sprang from one of the new families that the fifteenth century brought up, the Lees of Quarrendon in Buckinghamshire, who made their fortune out of sheep-farming, amassed properties in that county and in Oxfordshire, and on that substantial basis pushed into minor positions at the Tudor Court. Lee's grandfather was a Gentleman Usher of the Chamber, and both son and grandson were bred up to Court life. There is an interesting parallel here to the Cecils : two generations of Cecils before paved the way for Burghley's career at Court.

Lee was a perfect courtier. He seems never to have got into serious trouble, which in itself was something of an achievement in the vibrant *entourage* of the Queen. It was so easy to fall, over women, or politics, or one's relations, or through an excessive attachment to religion, or simply by losing one's looks. It was a difficult, competitive world. But Lee had much to recommend him. In addition to being a fine figure of a man — Aubrey says that he was " a strong and valiant person " — he obviously had a nice nature, not too much ability, a sense of his own limitations and no pretensions, great tact, and an honest disposition which stood him in good stead. He managed to keep in with both Leicester and Burghley ; an honest broker, he took on the thankless task of mediating between the extravagant Shrewsbury and his still more extravagant son.

One writes about Lee mainly in negatives. His was an ordinary enough course. A young man, he had been present at the burning of Ridley at Oxford, when, Foxe relates, the

[1] Sir E. K. Chambers, *Sir Henry Lee.*

martyr " gave away divers small things to gentlemen standing by, and divers of them pitifully weeping, as to Sir Henry Lee he gave a new groat ". After that he went on the grand tour, to Cologne, Augsburg, Venice, Rome ; at Antwerp he had his portrait painted by Antony Mor — it provides a pleasant frontispiece to the book, revealing much charm. He returned at the height of the Anglo-Spanish crisis of 1569 ; " the desire I have to serve her Majesty as I am bound and my country maketh me desire rather to creep with the pismire than rest with the dormouse ". He established the annual tilt in honour of the Queen's accession ; from that time he was successful. He entertained Elizabeth at Woodstock with one of those curious, long-drawn-out, masque-like performances so appreciated by the Elizabethans and by the Queen herself. It is this aspect which drew Sir E. K. Chambers' attention to Lee. One wonders, however, whether in listening to those interminable lines, with all their allegories and tropes, there were not a few stifled yawns among the attendance. No doubt Elizabeth enjoyed them, or they could hardly have gone on.

Sir Henry seems always to have been successful with women, with the possible exception of his wife, who was a melancholy Paget and bore him no children. Other ladies responded more favourably ; indeed, the Lees seem to have been attractively prolific of illegitimate children — their genealogy is rendered so complex by them. Sir Henry was no exception : did not that old gossip Aubrey write (wrongly) :

" He was never married, but kept woemen to reade to him when he was a bed. One of his readers was parson Jones his wife of Wotton. I have heard her daughter (who had no more witt) glory what a brave reader her mother was and how Sir Harry's worship much delighted to heare her. But his dearest deare was Mris. Anne Vavasour."

This was the lady to whom Ralegh wrote, in vain :

" Many desire, but few or none deserve
   To cut the corn, not subject to the sickle.
Therefore take heed, let fancy never swerve
   But constant stand, for Mowers mindes are fickle.
For this be sure, the crop being once obtain'd
Farewell the rest, the soil will be distain'd."

In vain, for one fine day in 1581 she " was brought to bed of a son in the maidens' chamber " at Court ; and everybody held the Earl of Oxford to be the father. However, Mistress Vavasour comforted the declining years of Sir Henry at Ditchley, and in grateful recognition the old knight had her effigy carved at his feet upon his monument at Quarrendon, an interesting work which some miserable Bishop subsequently had removed, and now all has crumbled and decayed.

Sir Edmund Chambers makes a good point when he observes :

" Biography may complete the picture of an age, by its illumination of the lives of lesser men, who are themselves largely the product of the social forces at play, but reveal these from another angle, and by their reactions help to determine the resultant issue."

We have to be grateful for so complete and scholarly an investigation of the life of this lesser man, which went to make up the Elizabethan background.

(v) THE ENGLISH FAUST

Of all the astonishing and tragic careers of English writers that make the story of our literature so rich and exciting — Swift, Byron, Shelley, D. H. Lawrence — there is none perhaps more wonderful than Christopher Marlowe's. To have written what he wrote, to have made *his* contribution to Elizabethan drama and poetry, and to have died still under thirty! It is a chastening thought. Then there is his strange, enigmatic, powerful personality that so impressed itself upon friend and foe — one was apparently either one or the other to him — the mystery surrounding his end. What would one not give for a few letters of his, a diary, a note-book, to have survived? What would have come of him if he had lived, with his interests outside literature and the theatre, his passionate interest in religion, in thought, and politics ? (One can be pretty sure that he would have got into trouble.) But what might he not have written ; in what direction would the drama have developed if he had lived to write alongside of Shakespeare ?

These are fascinating, tantalising questions, fruitless almost

to ask ; and in the absence of diary, note-book, or even scrap
of handwriting, we have to be content with accumulating little
pellets of information, direct and indirect, concerning him.

It is pleasant to record that more of such information has
been accumulated in the past ten years than in any decade
before, and by both American and English scholars ; though
really they belong to one school, the Public Record Office
school, whence most of the valuable new contributions have
come. Dr. Boas, who has been at work on the subject over the
past forty years, is *au fait* with all the new research, and has
made contributions of his own, has now summed it up in a
critical and biographical study which is not likely to be bettered.[1]
Those of us who are at work in the splendid, and remunerative,
field of our sixteenth-century history and literature, expected
that this would be the standard work on Marlowe. It is.

Dr. Boas' particular contributions to Marlowe scholarship
have been mainly literary, and he exhibits admirably the
extent of the classical influences upon his work. He insists,
evidently quite rightly, on Marlowe's remarkable fidelity to
his sources ; more than any other dramatist his inspiration
was literary, other books. The image

> " Instead of music I will hear him speak ;
>   His looks shall be my only library,"

gains new force from this knowledge of the kind of man he was ;
he was very much an intellectual, like Ben Jonson, like Milton,
compared with " Nature's child ", Shakespeare. He was made
more strictly in the mould of the Italian Renaissance than any
other of our writers. Dr. Boas writes justly and well of his
Renaissance aspiration after the fullness of power and beauty
and knowledge, which inspires all his work and speaks magnifi-
cently out of his best passages :

> " Nature that framed us of four elements
>   Warring within our breasts for regiment,
>   Doth teach us all to have aspiring minds ;
>   Our souls, whose faculties can comprehend
>   The wondrous architecture of the world,
>   And measure every wandering planet's course,

[1] F. S. Boas, *Christopher Marlowe : A Biographical and Critical Study.*

Still climbing after knowledge infinite,
And always moving as the restless spheres,
Will us to wear ourselves and never rest."

He was the nearest thing to an English Faust, the " unsatiable speculator " : no wonder that character attracted him : he must have seen himself in the part, as Shakespeare in Prospero. The contrast between those two is most suggestively put by Dr. Boas ; he says that in their difference lies the measure of division between Marlowe and Shakespeare. He does not add, what is incredible but true, that Marlowe's Faust is a creation of a young man in his twenties, where Shakespeare's Prospero comes at the end of a lifetime of experience. The one was an intellectual poet, evidently fascinated by the problem of belief, full of contempt for human credulity : Dr. Boas points out that each of the three great religions, Christianity, Judaism, Mohammedanism, comes under his lash in turn :

" I count religion but a childish toy,
And hold there is no sin but ignorance."

" It was the combination of the ratiocinative and the imaginative faculties in Marlowe that was to be the distinctive note of his genius." Pride and contempt were the dominant notes of his temperament — Ralegh's was the nearest to him of all his contemporaries ; where Shakespeare was all gentleness, kindness, and courtesy, a nature full of pity and every human sympathy.

This being so, his life was according. Kyd described him as " intemperate and of a cruel heart ", spoke of his " rashness in attempting sudden privy injuries to men ". He was disputatious, and according to Baines " almost into every company he cometh he persuades men to atheism, willing them not to be afraid of bugbears and hobgoblins ", asserting that " the first beginning of religion was only to keep men in awe ". Like nearly all the poets, he could not abide Protestants : them he called " hypocritical asses ". He was, we must remember, very brilliant and very young ; a high-church, as opposed to a low-church, unbeliever. It would seem that what his intellectual position came to was a sort of Deism, like Ralegh's : paying tribute to a God

" that sits on high and never sleeps,
Nor in one place is circumscriptible,
But everywhere fills every continent
With strange infusion of his sacred vigour."

What made Marlowe's difference from ordinary men was his genius and his sexuality. Dr. Boas is as judicious on the latter as he is illuminating on the former ; and his sensible treatment of this subject is very creditable, particularly in one of his generation. He makes no bones about what it was that attracted Marlowe in the theme of Edward II — the relations of Edward and Gaveston — and draws our attention rightly to the parallels in *Dido, Queen of Carthage*, in the *Massacre at Paris*, and in Marlowe's treatment of Leander. He does not, however, discuss what light this may throw upon the attitude of mind of the Elizabethan public.

In the background of Marlowe's life, as in that of Babington to his great misfortune, there lurks the figure of Robert Poley, spy, informer, *agent provocateur*, a go-between the persecuted Catholics and the Government. From Babington's last despairing letter to him, he must have been a most fascinating, most plausible, false person : " Farewell sweet Robin, if as I take thee, true to me. If not, adieu *omnium bipedum nequissimus*." This man was present at Marlowe's death. Dr. Boas calls him " the very genius of the Elizabethan underworld ". But indeed there were many others like him in that astonishing age which Marlowe so well expressed.

(vi) Light on Shakespeare's Circle

Dr. Hotson has become a sort of fairy godmother from the other side of the Atlantic, who every year or two descends upon our public archives and, with the aid of his faithful accomplice Miss O'Farrell in the intervals, never fails to fish up something new or odd or, occasionally, exciting. What an apt phrase his is, " scouring the seven seas of the Public Records ", and how well have his optimism and industry been rewarded ! " When one considers the unexplored manuscript riches of England," he writes, " it is evident that now is no time to write *finis* to any Elizabethan subject, even to the most canvassed topic of all."

It was he who brought to light the depositions concerning the death of Christopher Marlowe, who revealed the background of Shakespeare's quarrel with Justice Gardiner, that rogue of a Surrey J.P., and found some of Shelley's letters to Harriet. A remarkable record : tribute to Dr. Hotson's imaginative combination of the detective with the scholar.

Now he has brought his powers to bear, following the clue in Shakespeare's will, upon Thomas Russell, esquire, overseer of the will and evidently a close friend of the poet's.[1] The result is what comes to a biography of this hitherto obscure person, detailed if necessarily discontinuous, together with various digressions and excursions into Russell's kith and kin, his friends and associations, by way of suggesting what must have been Shakespeare's circle, at least on this side. It makes a most interesting, if not altogether satisfying, book ; and Dr. Hotson is quite right to claim that " the importance of identifying Shakespeare's friends and exploring their lives and characters remains paramount ". It is, as a subject, about the most fascinating in the world. But it is also one of the most tantalising. For with certainly the best will in the world, and going through the records with a comb, one might almost say a toothpick, Dr. Hotson has not been able to gather more than here and there a nodule of significant information, and most of it suggestive, contingent, rather than establishing a direct contact with the poet. The silence from that quarter is as profound, as elusive as ever.

Thomas Russell was very much of a private person, like Shakespeare himself : hence the difficulty of tracking down information about him. If he had been a leading J.P., active in his county, we should know more. (Perhaps this, too, is significant of the sort of person Shakespeare would choose for an intimate.) Of a very good family — for one thing one can feel sure of about Shakespeare is that such things counted with him — a cadet of the Russells (Dr. Hotson might have made clear what his precise relationship to them was), Thomas Russell belonged to a family with large possessions near Stratford. He was born at Strensham, a little way down the Avon from the town ; and though brought up in the west country at Bruton, he lived later

---

[1] Leslie Hotson, *I, William Shakespeare, do Appoint Thomas Russell, Esquire* . . .

upon his manor at Alderminster just off the road from Stratford to Oxford and London. Dr. Hotson says roundly that this was " the place where Shakespeare was with him most frequently ". This is no more than a surmise, if a probable one, and Dr. Hotson should say so. He certainly has the art of making a little go a long way, and frequently drags in what is not relevant to the tale — for example, the well-known episode of Ralegh's atheistical discussion at Sir George Trenchard's supper-table. Again, Shakespeare did not need to draw upon the family quarrels between the Russells and the Sheldons — quarrels, moreover, very usual in Elizabethan society — for his picture of the Montague-Capulet feud, a theme drawn directly from his reading.

We are given an interesting chapter on *Willoughbie His Avisa*, which goes to strengthen the connection of that work with Shakespeare, for apart from the information it gives us about " W. S." being very consistent with what we know of Shakespeare's character, Dr. Hotson has found a link connecting Thomas Russell with Willoughby, the former's sister-in-law having married the latter's brother. Again, the full story of the quarrels between Russell's relatives, the Berkeleys, and the Herberts, increases the improbability of Pembroke's having been the " Mr. W. H." of the Sonnets. On the other hand, though Dr. Hotson has not found the link, it may have been that Shakespeare owed his introduction to the Southampton circle to Russell, who was connected with it. Russell's second marriage into the Digges family gives us the clue to the long and informative verses which Leonard Digges wrote for the First Folio.

(vii) ELIZABETHAN TOURIST

This is just the kind of book I like : [1] pleasant, agreeable reading about the Tudor age, when everything went right with us, unlike the present, when everything goes wrong and reading the daily paper is a daily torture.[2] Moreover, a work of scholarship and taste, in which the learning is not too heavy and is attractively presented ; a book, too, which adds something to

[1] *Thomas Platter's Travels in England*, translated and with an Introduction by Clare Williams. [2] Written in 1937.

our knowledge of the time, yields something new instead of rehashing, like so many contemporary books, what we knew before. For, I am glad to confess, Thomas Platter is a new figure to me, though I gather that he was not unknown to students of the Shakespearean drama, for he attended a performance of *Julius Caesar* and describes fairly fully the theatre, almost certainly the Globe, in which it took place. (If only to goodness he had made some effort to get into touch with the author of the play and described *him*! But Platter, appropriate name, missed his one chance of immortality.)

More than half the book is taken up by Mrs. Williams' introductory chapters on Elizabethan sightseeing, foreign tourists in England, the usual round they made while here, and the books they wrote about us when they went away. It is a learned and skilfully presented little survey, and one which is attractively written, save for a few touches of feminine overwriting here and there. She notes the difficulty of singling out what is original in each traveller's observations, because of their lamentable tendency to copy from each other, and what was common form in the guide-books. She certainly disentangles her Thomas skilfully from his borrowings, though at the same time she may be thought a little hard on him — she calls his tour the " Pedant's Progress " — though poor Platter had an eye of his own, reports interestingly what he saw, and to one reader at any rate does not convey the impression of a pedant. And isn't Mrs. Williams a trifle impatient with Queen Elizabeth ? — " performing her customary antics for public inspection ", indeed ! Queen Elizabeth would have been more than a little impatient with Mrs. Williams for a phrase like that ; would perhaps have awarded her the ducking-stool, or the pillory, or a box on the ear such as she was accustomed to administer with a scolding to her maids of honour (I am sure they needed it).

Thomas Platter — he was a member of a distinguished Swiss academic family, of Basel, himself a doctor — came here in the autumn of 1599 and made the usual round that the foreign tourist makes in and about London. It is odd, when one thinks of the distance of time since then, how little it has changed : first impressions of Dover, the Tower of London, the Lord Mayor, Westminster Abbey and St. Paul's, Hampton Court, Windsor and Eton, the Royal Family, the old Universities. As if in pursuance of the guide-book instruction, " If time presses, Cambridge may be omitted ", Platter went to Oxford but not to Cambridge : he found the way from Oxford to Cambridge impracticable, which not everybody has found since. Of these, little enough has changed since Platter saw them and Donne wrote of

> ". . . the man that keeps the Abbey tombs
> And for his price doth with whoever comes
> Of all our Harrys and our Edwards talk " ;

perhaps only St. Paul's and the Royal Family unrecognisably. Where Platter looked upon the tombs of Sir Christopher Hatton, very recent and magnificent, and of William Herbert, the later glories of Sir Christopher Wren, the tombs of Wellington and Nelson have taken their place. Then, too, the Royal Family consisted of one person, which very much increased the effect. Elizabeth, reigning in solitary splendour, had become the chief sight in her kingdom.

The useful Thomas was very fortunate in this respect ; he saw her twice, once at Nonsuch and again at Richmond, and his close-ups of her are very veracious, except that it seems to have been *de rigueur* to say that the Queen looked twenty when in fact she was nearing seventy. Platter came at a very interesting time, just when Essex threw up his Irish command, and, arriving unexpected, forced his way into the presence of the Queen at Nonsuch and was put under guard. But of all that, and of the anxieties of the magnificent old woman, the Swiss tourist knew nothing : he saw only the glittering exterior, the Queen " lavishly attired in a gown of pure white satin, gold-embroidered, with a whole bird of paradise for panache " and, of course, be-ringed and be-jewelled, attending service and listening to a short sermon at Nonsuch. (Sermons preached before her had to be short, or else they were cut short.) And again at Richmond he saw her looking down " from a window in the gallery on her people in the courtyard ; they all knelt and she spoke in English : ' God bless my people,' and they all cried in unison ' God save the Queen,' and they remained kneeling until she made them a sign with her hand to rise, which they did with the greatest possible reverence ". This was just after the Essex episode. What Platter goes on to say about the Queen's popularity is valuable historical evidence; and really how much more attractive were the ways of Tudor publicity and propaganda than contemporary ones !

(viii) THE ELIZABETHANS AT SEA

A new book by Dr. J. A. Williamson is a pleasure to look forward to, and one is never disappointed.[1] He has made himself the leading authority in our generation on Tudor sea history, the successor to Sir Julian Corbett in the last. Since Corbett wrote, a great deal of new and exciting information has come to light. Various authors have made most interesting discoveries in the archives, English, French, and Spanish, on all aspects of this fascinating subject. But no one has made a larger contribution than Dr. Williamson himself, with his studies of the Hawkins family, of the Cabots, and early English maritime enterprise : his life of Sir John Hawkins is crammed full of new material and is indispensable to a proper knowledge of the Elizabethan age. Dr. Williamson himself says that

" in recent years new material has been discovered in almost every field of Elizabethan enterprise, and the effect has been to recast and almost revolutionise some parts of the story and very considerably to modify our conception of the whole."

That is very true. Corbett was dominated by the nineteenth-century hero-worship of Drake. He saw the epic story of Tudor sea history in terms of Drake, with everybody else either leading up to or away from his hero. Not so Dr. Williamson : he has a just appreciation of Drake's superb qualities, but also of his failings and his failures. He corrects Corbett's want of perspective and gives us a proportioned and well-balanced account of the whole story. It is in fact much the best book on the greatest age in our sea history, and perhaps the most satisfying of all Dr. Williamson's books. It is written

---

[1] J. A. Williamson, *The Age of Drake.*

K

with that spirit, that freshness and enthusiasm which seem always to go with a love of the sea. We forgive Dr. Williamson when *he* perpetrates that well-worn *cliché* the " ship of state ", for we feel that to him it really is a ship, with all her " gear and tackle and trim ".

On almost every aspect of his subject Dr. Williamson has something new to say or new information to bring forward. A recent work said rather well of Northumberland that " his career is of some significance, since it sums up both the ignoble side of Protestantism and the unresting cupidity of a class ". Dr. Williamson bears out still further how significant that restless, acquisitive spirit was of his class and time in what he tells us of Northumberland's encouragement of maritime enterprise. We learn that he was the patron of Sebastian Cabot and discussed with him an attack upon Spanish Peru ; more important was his direct interest in and encouragement of the voyage of Willoughby and Chancellor to the North East, which go tas far as the coast of Novaya Zemlya and led to the setting-up of trade with Russia. Northumberland was a friend of the great geographer John Dee, the inventor of the phrase " British Empire " ; he made him the tutor of his sons. In short, he stands very typically at the beginnings of English imperialism.

In spite of his title, which was inevitable, Dr. Williamson shows how the work of Hawkins in building the Queen's ships which fought the Armada was no less important than that of Drake, whose genius caught the imagination of the age as it has done of posterity. But we are given new lights upon Drake's career no less than Hawkins', in the course of telling again the story of those famous voyages to Nombre de Dios and round the world : they are better reading than *Westward Ho !* and as good as *Treasure Island*. To the mature taste they are all the better for being solid history rather than never-getting-it-quite-right fiction. Dr. Williamson was one of the first to begin to piece together the extraordinary but largely forgotten career of Sir Richard Grenville ; he now does it full justice and incorporates the newly discovered account of the last fight of the *Revenge*. His expert knowledge of navigation and Tudor geography illuminate the book throughout.

Writing after Professor Neale, Dr. Williamson understands in a way that no previous naval historian has done the limitations that were set by financial considerations to what the Queen could undertake at home and on the seas. After all, it was wonderful what was achieved in those days with very exiguous resources ; and when one compares it with Mr. Chamberlain's England, one's heart sinks, and one fears for the future.[1] Dr. Williamson concludes with legitimate pride in that wonderful age :

" The whole world today might have been unimaginably different, but for the achievements of the age this book has described, and of the great men whose spirits blazed in such a galaxy as was never seen in England before, nor has been since."

It refreshes the spirit, even though it is humiliating, to read about them at a time when all is confusion, uncertainty, hesitation, and a sense of defeat.

[1] Written in 1938.

XVI

THE OLD MUSIC SCHOOL AT OXFORD

FOR this early hour of the summer afternoon, a magic quiet has descended upon the stilled and sleepy room. Like Matthew Arnold, whom I think of, perambulating the class-room, reading poems out of a book while the scholars are bent over their examination task ; like Yeats, an old grey-haired senator walking up and down between the benches where the school children are congregated watching ; so I sit here at the long table in the music school, alone with all the desks and faces.

Outside, the enchantment of the bells of Oxford in summer has fallen upon the streets and green gardens of the city. All we that pass are borne down beneath the sounding waters. Time's tide sweeps by ; no less inevitably, more felt, for the illusion given that this one moment is eternal. The noises of the city are caught up and cherished and given beauty, as if they too should not perish ; the horn of a passing car, bringing back the snowy squares of Munich one February night ; the quick ring of a bicycle ; the rich " gulge-gulge " of sparrows in the eaves, that I shall ever associate with school on hot summer afternoons from childhood. But above all, the bells ; fragile but immutable ; eloquent of what victories, what past devotions ; quintessence of all that remains when we are gone out of the lovely world.

And all around the room there are the pale faces of the dead men who were here before us, looking out from their picture-frames ; all of them looking down upon me with concentrated gaze, as if in accusation that there are others who have come and taken their familiar places.

There is Matthew Lock, a beautiful face, dark and oval, with high arched brows that are even a little haughty. He does not seem jealous that I am here, but looks with surprise that he has vanished out of the world. He looks not dead, but with loving patient eyes with the awareness of sorrow in their hazel lights, looking a little away from us, as if observant of all that passes, yet greeting rather some friend whom we, outside his time and state, cannot see.

Two dark soured faces of the seventeenth century peer direct from the canvases at me : Christopher Simpson and Thomas Blagrave. Who were they, I wonder ? The one a narrow wizened little man, Puritan and sober-sides, a little like Governor Winthrop, with neat tassels at the throat, drawing together the pointed collar. The other jaundiced, supercilious, puffy about the eyes ; a pertinacious, a perhaps unsuccessful University politician.

Here is William Gregory, iron-grey, with grey suspicious eyes and eyebrows puckered. But what is he so suspicious of ? He has his hand upon his heart. One imagines him to have been a high-stomached man, perhaps purse-proud. There in the dark of the corner is Orlando Gibbons in his flowered satin gown. And then the delightful Henry Lawes :

> " Harry whose tuneful and well measur'd Song,
>   First taught our English Musick how to span
>   Words with just note and accent."

He looks jovial enough, though with a querulous upward turn of the eyebrow ; in his hand, a scroll of music for a canon *a tre voci : Regi Regis, Regi Regis, Regum arcana cano*. How devoted they were to the fatal Stuarts, these musicians ; some of them, masters of the King's music, ate the bread of exile ; others, when the call came, entered the field, like William Lawes, whose portrait too is here, looking so much younger than his brother whose elder he was ; for death came early upon him in the field, and left him for ever young. When he was killed, in the time of the Civil War, the King, it is said, had a particular mourning for him when dead, whom he loved when living and commonly called " the Father of Musick ". There he is, so sombre and dusky in the shadow of the sweeping Stuart hat, one can hardly make him out ; only an angle of the lace collar, slashed sleeves, the canvas darkened by age.

In the centre, there is the best portrait of them all : a brilliant Elizabethan picture of John Bull, the Court musician, as bright now as the day it was painted. The portrait says, *anno aetatis suae 27 ; in the year 1589*. There he is, as if time had stayed him just at my time of life ; had laid a finger upon him, and stilled the tide of the ceaseless unchanging waters ; and there he is, a youthful Elizabethan face, long and ridged, auburn hair and candid narrow brow, neat sparse beard and delicate lined lips. But the main feature of the face, the cold grey eyes, full of the awareness of death. He looks so still ; changeless amid all that changes. He must have charmed his contemporaries and been beloved by them. The painter, painting him in the year after the Armada, inscribed around the finished picture :

> " The Bull by force
> In field doth raigne
> But Bull by skill
> Good Will doth gaine."

Dr. Burney is there too ; and Dr. Croft : good stout eighteenth-century faces, more content, something more placid ; certainly less pathetic, less remote, but no less protestant against the ravages of time.

Last of all, among all these musicians, one who was both musician and painter, and prided himself upon his mastery of the twin arts. For he has painted himself as an artist, holding brush and palette ; and on the table by him he has a roll of music, inscribed in a clear and lovely Caroline hand, " Canon a 3 in ye 5th and 6th ". There are the notes, in an old notation, hard to follow ; and the words — but the words express the universal theme : they say in the accent of their time what all these dead men if they had voices would say from the dark canvases :

> " Thus, thus, at last wee must
> Reducèd be
> To naked boanes and dust."

XVII

THE SPANISH COLLEGE AT BOLOGNA

I WENT, in memory of Edward Armstrong — whom I did not know, but for whose historical writing I have a high admiration — to see the Spanish College at Bologna : he wrote a delightful sketch of its history. Yet so many English people who spend a day or two in the town contrive to go away without ever seeing one of its most interesting sights, and what is certainly its rarest, for it must be about the only survival of a medieval college on the Oxford and Cambridge model remaining on the Continent. Perhaps it is due to its being tucked away down a side street on the edge of the town ; or still more, I should imagine, to the fact that the indispensable Baedeker hardly mentions the existence of the College, devotes no more than a sentence to it in fact. Very rarely that Baedeker allows himself to be so caught out ; in a future edition this should be remedied.

The College occupies an island site towards the south-west corner of the town, between the Via del Collegio di Spagna and the Via Urbana with its tram-lines. Along the former runs the charming irregular line of its red-brick buildings, and along the latter a high parapeted wall with overhanging creeper, above which appear the cedars of the garden within. A very attractive place it is, all built of the pleasant baked brick of Bologna, and though the foundation dates from the fourteenth century, the buildings have the appearance of the sixteenth. The point of the triangle at the junction of the two streets is occupied by a patch of grass with a few trees ; the entrance gate is at the side. On entering you come to the porter's lodge with a quadrangle behind, the chapel opposite, and the rooms of the students grouped around : a familiar, homely arrange-ment to a wandering Oxford man on the Continent. Only this being Italy, the sets of rooms give not directly upon the court but upon a loggia that runs round the four sides. Armstrong called it " a small English college translated into Italian ", and described its character, not quite correctly, as

" in a manner the All Souls of Bologna ".

It was founded by the great Cardinal Albornoz, Legate of the Holy See in these parts, " soldier, statesman, and an administrator of the first order ", in the fourteenth century, heyday of collegiate foundations. " At Oxford ", writes Armstrong, " the foundation of Queen's precedes, that of New College shortly followed, the Spanish College. At Cambridge, Pembroke, Gonville, Trinity Hall, Corpus and Clare are all within twenty years of it." From early days favours were showered upon the College by the Spanish monarchs, by the Popes, and by the town of Bologna. Possessing its own lands like an Oxford college today, and similarly governed under statute by its Rector and Fellows, it enjoyed a privileged and independent position in relation to the university.

Throughout its history the great danger to its existence has been the political connection entailed by its national character. Armstrong says that the Spanish domination of Italy, from the sixteenth century onwards, gave it a political complexion " which was not favourable to its best interests ". It shared the ups and downs of Spanish fortunes in Italy, and several times was very near to foundering altogether. In the War of the Spanish Succession, the students were strong in support of Philip V, the choice of the Spanish people ; the College was in consequence closed by the Austrians and only reopened after the conclusion of the war. Under Napoleon it was suppressed again, its properties confiscated, while paintings by Raphael disappeared from the walls and the great fresco representing Charles V's coronation at Bologna was ruined. The establishment of the new Kingdom of Italy brought yet another danger and the College was temporarily sequestrated. An appeal to the Spanish government was, however, successful, and it survived. Indeed the survival-value of the College must be rated extraordinarily high, one of the very few colleges to have come down to us substantially as it was founded in the Middle Ages — Denifle says, " the solitary example on the Continent ".

It has survived to undergo yet a new crisis with the Spanish Civil War. For on its outbreak, in July last year,[1] all the eighteen students departed. The College is shut up, everything

[1] Written in 1937.

well-kept, neat, and in order, waiting for their return. (Who of them will return ? I wondered.) There is always something rather moving about rooms through which so many tides of young life have flown, particularly in the intervals of absence, when they are withdrawn and the old places wait. All was so familiar here : the little sets of sitting-room and bedroom, the small bookcase, the writing-table before the window. A fresh wind blew through the empty corridors like an Oxford college in vacation.

The friendly porter, so accustomed a figure, showed me round the loggia with its polished floor, its pictures and old chests, the tiny little doors of Spanish chestnut inlaid with the Cardinal's hat that lead into the students' rooms. The common rooms were on a more comfortable scale, and more elegantly furnished than junior common rooms with us. There was the *sala da pranzo* with its bust of Cardinal Albornoz over the door, the *sala da te*, which appealed even more to an Englishman's taste, the *sala da conversazione*, a regular drawing-room such as we are not accustomed to in English colleges, with its fine Venetian mirrors and portraits of recent Spanish sovereigns, Queen Maria Christina and others. Then there was the *sala da giocco*, a long gallery with its billiard-table — " a luxury ", Armstrong wrote in the eighteen-eighties, " to which even All Souls has not yet attained " ; nor has it yet, it might be added. I must not forget the chapel with its fifteenth-century altar-piece, its fresco by Gian Bologna, a tablet commemorating Charles V's visit to Bologna, and one recording that of yet another, more recent Spanish king — Alfonso XIII. The famous library, which escaped the French Revolution, I did not see ; for the Spanish consul who occupies part of the College had taken the key with him. His Excellency was away on a cruise for the benefit of his health. So I think should I be, were I Spanish consul at the present time.

I walked a little in the charming, beautifully-kept garden, to the tomb of the founder with its painted recumbent effigy. The paths were bordered with blue irises, the south wall covered with climbing roses from which looked the little windows of the upper rooms. When all this was over in Spain, my companion said, they expected the College would grow, would have to be extended. No doubt it will, if things in Spain turn out a certain way. One sees the future well marked out for the Spanish College at Bologna if a Spain emerges more or less under Italian dominance. But what a reversal of fortune, what an irony of history, one of time's revenges, that would be : after all the centuries of Spanish intervention in Italy, the long period of Spanish rule — Italian intervention in Spain, perhaps even a measure of control. So the senseless revolutions of the wheel, the ups and downs of national fortune, go on — until we find some sufficient means to put a stop to them, to make a new beginning, a new order.

XVIII

TRINITY, CAMBRIDGE

AN Oxford man may say, what a Cambridge man might not like perhaps to claim, that Trinity is the most magnificent of all English collegiate institutions. It always strikes me as a curious thought that Oxford and Cambridge, which must seem so very much alike to those who are outside them, and almost indistinguishable to foreigners, are two entirely different worlds to those who belong to them. Over there the gods, the great influences who have meant so much in the last century, the familiar names — Whewell, Thompson, Henry Sidgwick — are names that we know little enough about. Over here the accustomed deities who mean so much to us are a totally different lot, who must mean little enough to them : Newman, Mark Pattison, Jowett. The spirit of friendly emulation between the two ancient universities, the diversity of contribution each has made (from so similar a background) to English life, form one of the most agreeable, as well as one of the most important, themes in our history. One thinks of the old-fashioned metaphor of the Elizabethans on the subject — the " two eyes " of the English State — and how right they were.

Trinity freshmen are fortunate indeed to have our most distinguished living historian as their Master to explain to them the stones of the College, its courts and the great men who inhabited them. The Master tells us that he thought of calling the book *The Freshman's Guide to Trinity*, since, when he came up fifty years ago, looking round the Great Court and the Cloisters, he wished someone would tell him about them.[1] But such a book, by Trevelyan, would be bound to be more than a guide. It is that — and a very delicious guide too, illuminated by those touches of historical imagination we expect from that hand. It was the Franciscans of the fourteenth century who brought the water to the precincts : " and even now, the Franciscan water is still used for the College Fountain, whose

[1] G. M. Trevelyan, *Trinity College : An Historical Sketch.*

145

splash at midnight has been grateful to the ears of so many generations of dwellers in the Great Court ". Or in the Master's garden, " the bees have made their hive in a blocked-up window that witnessed the Wars of the Roses ". Or again, there is the dying Whewell who had the curtains of his bedroom drawn back " so that his eyes should rest on the Great Court, the place he loved best on earth ".

But more, his little book gives us a good idea of what Trinity has meant in the national life. The College as we know it, though a foundation of Henry VIII's, is really an Elizabethan creation : it was under the great master, Nevile, that the Great Court took its shape, incorporating, linking up, removing the buildings of the two institutions, King's Hall and Michael-house, which occupied that noble space. It was then, too, that Trinity began to draw level with John's in educating the leaders of that age, Coke, Bacon, Essex ; while Whitgift went from being Master to rule the Elizabethan Church. Trevelyan brings out the essentially Latitudinarian tradition of Trinity which developed in the seventeenth century, so that not even the Civil War left much religious bitterness, unlike the case at Oxford. Comprehension was a great strength and proved wonderfully fruitful in the broad sympathies of Pearson (" Pearson on the Creed "), Isaac Barrow, Newton. From that time Trinity took the lead in natural philosophy, studies in which the College has remained pre-eminent ever since. It is, indeed, an astonishing roll of names which may be cited in this sphere : John Ray, the great naturalist, Newton (for whom Barrow resigned his Professorship : how often has a tutor done such a thing for a pupil ?), Clerk Maxwell, Lord Rayleigh, J. J. Thomson, Rutherford.

Besides her unquestioned ascendancy in this sphere, Trinity possesses the greatest figure in English classical scholarship in Bentley, among historians Macaulay and Maitland, among anthropologists James George Frazer, and a quite unfair proportion of poets — George Herbert, Cowley, Marvell, Dryden, Byron, and Tennyson. It is a fabulous record. What other college in the world can produce a staircase like that between the Chapel and the Great Gate, with rooms on the ground floor occupied by Macaulay and Thackeray, upstairs by Newton, Lightfoot, Jebb, Frazer ?

The Master permits himself an occasional reference like that to Laud, " the Oxford busy-body then occupying the see of Canterbury ". Naughty : and yet perhaps quite right for the Cambridge freshman, by way of stimulating a healthy feeling of rivalry for the other university. In return, it is pleasant to think that Trinity owes its greatest glory, the Library, to a Fellow of All Souls, though I never knew that Wren gave them the design gratis. And dare one say that we think there is a certain optimum size for a college, and that things are better balanced over here where there is no college so grand as to outweigh all the rest ?

XIX

THE CAROLINE COUNTRY PARSON :
GEORGE HERBERT

It sometimes occurs to me, as I know it does to others, to see a
historical period in an image, a pictured scene, a landscape of
the mind, as if one looked into some old forgotten mirror and
saw there the shapes, the figures it had beheld in that time
past, the sunlight and clouds passing of three hundred years
ago. When I think of the quiet, peaceful decade before the
Civil War, when Charles was King and Laud building the
lovely garden-front of his college at Oxford, it is always early
summer. I see the blue sky with white feathery clouds and
those figures walking with grave seventeenth-century tread up
and down the terraces of some great house, as it might be
Wilton or Great Tew, where Falkland walked in the shades
with Hobbes and Sidney Godolphin. It is Sunday ; the church
bells are stilled, yet there is music in the village away beyond
the park-pale ; and within, there is the drone of bees busy
among the rosemary and musk and lavender : they have a
nest in the church porch next the great house. The figures
upon the terrace group and regroup themselves while discours-
ing upon poetry and the times. I cannot hear what they are
saying ; now they pause — there is a rustle of satin upon stone
— and look out over the parterres and English fields to where
there is a cloud no bigger than a man's hand upon the horizon.
A rain-storm threatens ; the sky is lowering : the threat of
the Civil War that came to break up that Caroline peace. The
figures are driven in : the terraces deserted.

Such is the world that the very thought of George Herbert
conjures up in the mind. His poetry is, perhaps, the most
perfect, the ideal, expression of it, if not the most complete,
because of its very unworldliness : it reflects the soul of that
world. And now his poetry and prose alike have been brought
together in a definitive edition, a beautiful book, which is a

masterpiece of loving scholarship and understanding.[1]

Herbert is the best known of those religious poets of the seventeenth century who all came from the Welsh Border. Herbert, Vaughan, Traherne : one wonders whether the Welsh admixture in their blood may not have given them their leaning to mysticism, their familiar vision of eternity in the transitory things of this world, their way of hearing

" Church-bells beyond the starres ".

George Herbert was born at Montgomery, that delightful Border town, where his family had been governors of the Castle for generations. As one writes, one remembers the view out over the little town from the height where the Castle stood, the broad street at the foot, the cottage gardens bright with wallflowers, the fine church with the splendid painted tomb of George Herbert's parents, Sir Richard and the Lady Magdalen. Their fifth son was one of those men of genius who owed everything to a remarkable mother, the friend of Donne, who wrote of her :

" No Spring, nor Summer Beauty hath such grace,
    As I have seen in one Autumnal face."

Left a widow, she brought up her family herself, the eldest of whom, Edward, was to become the brilliant soldier-philosopher, Lord Herbert of Cherbury, and early intended her clever youngest son for orders. But though, from the time he began to write, he dedicated himself to sacred poetry, he had other ideas about a career. With such a family background — and we learn that when young at Cambridge, as was perhaps only natural, he " put too great a value on his parts and parentage " — he aspired to a career in the State. He became Public Orator at the university with that end in view. But ill-health dogged him all his life, and instead of becoming a self-important figure in affairs, conspicuous for a moment and then to disappear into oblivion, he became a priest and poet, a figure who will not be forgotten so long as English is spoken. It was long before he could bring himself to take the yoke. In 1625 his patrons, King James and the Dukes of Richmond and Hamilton, died, and Herbert took deacon's orders. Still he delayed, living in

[1] *The Works of George Herbert*, edited by F. E. Hutchinson.

the country in various houses of friends, pursued by illness, consoling himself with music and books, and, within, that struggle going on to subject himself to the Divine Will, from which sprang the poetry which moves us most in him.

Then, in 1630, he took the decision from which there was no turning back. He married, took the living of Bemerton near Salisbury, outside the park gates of Wilton, and the next three years saw him set a standard in his calling which has ever since been remembered in the English Church as the ideal to which the country parson can look for inspiration. Canon Hutchinson, who understands all this with an exquisite sympathy, so sensitive a touch, sums up George Herbert's inner struggle as no one better :

" The letters which Herbert wrote from Bemerton show how far he had travelled since his Cambridge days ; they manifest an achieved character of humility, tenderness, moral sensitiveness and personal consecration, which he was very far from having attained or even envisaged when he was dazzled by the attractions of the great world. Above all, *The Temple*, in which he laid bare the long story of his inner life, with all its faults and its ardours, and *A Priest to the Temple*, which he wrote at Bemerton that he might have a ' Mark to aim at ', reveal the man, both as he had been and as he had become. . . . The inward conflict which had lent such poignancy to the poems written in the period of indecision and inaction was quieted when Herbert went to Bemerton, and there are only occasional echoes of it. Many of the later poems breathe a spirit of content."

Herbert's aim in his prose work, *A Priest to the Temple ; or The Country Parson*, was to portray the character and rule of life of the ideal pastor : " which also I will set as high as I can, since he shoots higher that threatens the moon, than he that aims at a tree ". His ideals, besides being the ripened fruit of his own spiritual struggle, were much influenced by his friend, Nicholas Ferrar, and the circle at Little Gidding. Herbert was minded to set such a standard for the country parson in his office as to lift him out of " the general ignominy which is cast upon the profession " ; the precepts which he enjoined were those which inspired his famous pastorate during the three years when he was Rector of Bemerton. His own example, even more perhaps than his book, has been a lasting influence upon the congenial and charming tradition of the country parson in England.

What is remarkable about Herbert is his combination of great common sense, his feeling for the plain country folk (he, too, whose early ambitions were set upon Courts), with the rigorous standards of a saint. He was an aristocrat to his finger-tips not only in his own spiritual and aesthetic sensibilities (the two were one with him), but in the tone of authority with which he addresses his folk, whether labourers and ploughmen, or gentry, or noblemen. For example, he says :

" If there be any of the gentry or nobility of the parish, who sometimes make it a piece of state not to come at the beginning of service with their poor neighbours, but at mid-prayers, both to their own loss, and of theirs also who gaze upon them when they come in . . . he [the parson] by no means suffers it, but after divers gentle admonitions, if they persevere, he causes them to be presented."

Really, one feels, the Caroline parson would need to be a Herbert to take this high and mighty line with the gentry of his parish, let alone the nobility ! One wonders if this was the course he took with his distinguished and haughty relations beyond the rectory gates and across the park-pale at Wilton.

With the simple country folk no wonder he was a success : his ideal rested upon such a strong foundation of sense and meticulous attention to duty. The country people live hard and by the sweat of their brow ; therefore their parson must avoid all covetousness and give according to his means. He must be strict in keeping his word, plain in speech and apparel. He must know about tillage and pasturage, be well versed in cases of conscience ; he must be moved himself to move others. The saint was a good psychologist.

" When he preacheth, he procures attention by all possible art, both by earnestness of speech, it being natural to men to think that where is much earnestness, there is something worth hearing ; and by a diligent and busy cast of his eye on his auditors, with letting them know who marks, and who not,

L

and with particularising his speech now to the younger sort, then to the older, now to the poor and now to the rich."

Here speaks the practised speaker : the man who had been Public Orator at Cambridge. What would one not give to have heard one of George Herbert's sermons ? He knew his Caroline country folk well, " which are thick and heavy, and hard to raise to a point of zeal and fervency, and need a mountain of fire to kindle them ; but stories and sayings they well remember ". When he was at Cambridge he had compiled a collection of " Outlandish Proverbs " : the accumulated wisdom, the traditional wise-cracks, of our country folk. No doubt he found them useful in the pulpit at Bemerton. It is a congenial trait that he recommends sermons should last no more than an hour : so very un-Puritan !

The parson entertains his parish folk, his farmers, in turn, and helps to order the poor, parting with some of his living to them in hard times and helping them to find employment : one sees something of the age-long work of the country clergy, along with the J.P.s and parish wardens, in this. He does not disdain to enter the poorest cottage, " though it smell never so loathsomely ". He sees that the church is swept, and " at great festivals strawed, and stuck with boughs ". He acts as a lawyer for his flock, reading up the J.P.'s book and deciding issues between them. No less he should know how to effect cures with simples and herbs. One thinks of the old-fashioned plants, neglected now, that are still to be found about old habitations in the country, the simples our forefathers used. Herbert was much in favour of old customs, " if they be good and harmless ; and the rather because country people are much addicted to them, so that to favour them therein is to win their hearts, and to oppose them therein is to deject them ".

In the end we think of Herbert's last days as Izaak Walton wrote of them in his delicate, delicious Life, so well attuned to its subject : of Herbert walking in to Salisbury twice a week to hear service in the cathedral and afterwards play his part at a music-meeting with friends (like many Englishmen of his class and time, he played upon both lute and viol) ; of the simple folk in the fields who " did so love and reverence Mr. Herbert, that they would let their plough rest when Mr. Herbert's saint's-bell rung to prayers, that they might also offer their devotions to God with him, and would then return back to their plough ".

Almost all of Herbert's poetry is concerned with this inner world of experience, as against his contemporary Herrick's frank acceptance of the good things of this world. A charming contrast those two Caroline parsons make, genial Herrick with his quick eye for the flowers (and the maidens) of his Devonshire lanes at Dean Prior, and the " sainted Mr. Herbert ". Yet they had so much in common : their love of music, so true to Caroline England, of flowers and birds and church bells, of the old country customs and the country people ; their devotion to the English Church they served and by which they are remembered. And though Herbert was so centred upon his inner spiritual life, in turning over his pages one comes upon the evidences, so many notes, of his love of the fragmentary beauty of this. Take one of his Easter poems :

> " I got me flowers to straw thy way ;
> I got me boughs off many a tree :
> But thou wast up by break of day,
> And brought'st thy sweets along with thee."

We think of those sweet-scented, rush-strewn churches of that age. Or when he writes :

> " Sweet day, so cool, so calm, so bright,
> The bridal of the earth and sky :
> The dew shall weep thy fall tonight ;
> For thou must die . . ."

one can fancy that long-vanished summer day at Bemerton within view of the trees of the park, within sound of the Wiltshire Avon running softly down to Salisbury. It speaks the very spirit of the English countryside, its lasting contentment and serenity.

XX

THE ENGLISH REVOLUTION

ALMOST all great countries have had their revolution, including England — only ours took place in the seventeenth century, and so people are apt to think of our history as far too sedate and conservative an affair, when it has been as dynamic as any. Foreigners in earlier centuries thought of us as a most restless, turbulent, and changeable people ; and Sir Thomas Malory, in the fifteenth century, says : " Alas ! this is grete defaulte of us englysshe men, for there may no thynge plese us no terme ". The English Revolution of the seventeenth century had an immense influence in this country and beyond : it dominated political thinking for a century after, as the French Revolution did the nineteenth century and the Russian Revolution our own ; it inspired the makers of the American Revolution in their turn.

It is curious, and yet it is right, that the contemporary interpretation of that age which most satisfies the mind of our own is that of a man who fought on neither side in the Civil War and was a member of neither party : James Harrington, author of one big book, *Oceana*, and a score of short political tracts. His is a famous name in English political thought, and yet how little appreciated or understood he has been, for his was a cross-bench, an original, mind. Perhaps he was something of a Laodicean. People prefer to regard, almost exclusively, the more obvious landmarks. In our time he is coming into his own, for his approach to the " breakdown " of his age is in keeping with our way of thinking.

Professor Tawney has now devoted a masterly, a magnificent, lecture to the subject.[1] Engaged for a dozen years or more upon his researches into the seventeenth century, no doubt when the war is over he will present us with a masterpiece : we have no one more distinguished as a historical mind, nor a historian who writes more superbly. In the meantime, while he is away

R. H. Tawney, *Harrington's Interpretation of his Age.*

en mission in the United States, we must be content with fragments from — or perhaps, anticipations of — the great work.
What could be better than this as a summing-up of Harrington's
position ?

" A niche in public life was not easily found by an enemy
of monarchy who was a friend of the King ; a Republican
who denounced the Republic as, not a commonwealth, but
an oligarchy ; an enthusiast for toleration to whom wars of
doctrine, as he had seen them in Germany, were an abomina-
tion, and the rule of the saints a contradiction in terms ; an
aristocrat who, while rating high the public role of an educated
gentry, epitomised the pre-war politics of most of his class as a
settled determination to prevent the Crown from interfering
with their hunting and the lower orders with their shooting."

Harrington was neither an eccentric nor a doctrinaire, but a
serious and scientific student of politics. He had spent six
years on the Continent studying the institutions of foreign
states : " No man can be a politician ", he said, " except he
be first a historian or a traveller ". On his return he became
a member of the larger Privy Council ; later he was much in
attendance upon the King at Holmby House and Carisbrooke :
though Harrington was a convinced Republican, Charles liked
his conversation, his detached mind. There was a mutual
attraction between the two men. Harrington for his part saw
that something so far-going as the Revolution taking place
beneath their eyes could not be imputed to merely personal
shortcomings on the part of the King. His view was that

" The revolution of his day had been determined by changes
in social organisation which passed unnoticed until too late ;
that the old régime had been destroyed neither by the errors of
the ruler on whom the Tower of Siloam fell, nor by the intransi-
gence of Parliament, but by impersonal forces too strong for
both ; and that political stability was not to be expected till
political institutions were brought into accordance with economic realities. Forms must be adapted to social facts, not facts
to forms."

Beneath the surface of the politics of his time a profound
shift in the balance of social forces, going back to the last
decades of Elizabeth's reign, had taken place. The economic

power of the Crown and its allies, the older nobility and the Church, was shrinking : that of the gentry expanding beyond all comparison. The possessors of property were demanding political power, which they were well equipped to exercise. Harrington was the first to realise that " it was not the Civil War which had destroyed the old régime, but the dissolution of the social foundations of the old régime which had caused the Civil War ". His positive doctrine, then, was that political power, and the character of the constitution, should follow the balance of social forces. It is characteristic of human affairs that this most perspicacious of thinkers, whose views were confirmed by the long-term course of events, was completely caught out by them in the short run.

XXI

JOHN HAMPDEN

THREE hundred years ago (24 June 1643) there died a man who has left an undying name in the story of English liberty : John Hampden. Yet I doubt if he is much more than a name to us. We probably remember him as having something to do with Ship Money (though very vague as to what that was), from our school days. And yet it so happens that Hampden's was one of the most attractive characters, one of the finest natures, that have ever come to the fore in English public life.

In our own time there has come about a certain reaction in our way of viewing the struggle between King and Parliament which filled much of the seventeenth century, a reaction led by a school of popular Tory historians and by Mr. Belloc. They have introduced a way of reading our history upside-down, not merely sentimentalising the Stuarts, but making *them* out to be the patriotic caretakers of the nation's interests — even Charles II, who notoriously sold the country's interests, just as Baldwin and Co. let them go by default.

Hampden was by nature, like so many determined men, a moderate. He had no intention of overthrowing the monarchy, but wished to restrain it within the boundaries of the constitution, to see Charles I working *with* Parliament, not against it. And there is no doubt that Charles was proceeding along an unconstitutional course, raising forced loans, imposing taxes without authority, imprisoning people arbitrarily, governing without Parliament.

From his first entry into public life, Hampden joined the opposition to Charles. But it was not until the famous Ship Money Case that he became a national figure. In itself the extension of the charge for building ships from the coastal counties to those inland was not unreasonable. But the point was that it by-passed Parliament. If the King was to be allowed to go on extending the area of taxes in this way, there was no reason why he should not govern indefinitely without

Parliament — and there is no doubt that the people of England, not merely the gentry, had come already to regard Parliament as the defender of their rights and liberties against encroachments.

The Buckinghamshire squire, who came of a family that went back to before the Norman Conquest and was very wealthy in land, rose to the occasion and challenged the King. The case was fought in the courts, and in the end a majority of only seven judges to five declared for the Crown.

It was a great defeat for the King. Hampden leaped at once into the front rank of men of the day. Clarendon says, in that wonderful style of his :

" He grew the argument of all tongues, every man inquiring who and what he was that durst at his own charge support the liberty and property of the kingdom, and rescue his country from being made a prey to the Court."

And when the King was forced to call Parliament,

" the eyes of all men were fixed on him as their *Patriae pater*, and the pilot that must steer their vessel through the tempests and rocks which threatened it. . . . His power and interest at that time was greater to do good or hurt than any man's in the kingdom, or than any man of his rank hath had in any time : for his reputation of honesty was universal, and his affections seemed so publicly guided that no corrupt or private ends could bias them."

Clarendon sketches his character wonderfully for us : as a young man his pleasure " in all the sports and exercises and company which was used by men of the most jolly conversation"; then with marriage and increasing seriousness of mind, his retirement to " a more reserved and melancholic society, yet preserving his own natural cheerfulness and vivacity, and above all, a flowing courtesy to all men ". There was his

"rare affability and temper in debate", his extraordinary persuasiveness, his tactical sense, his moderation and fairness. " He was indeed a very wise man, and of great parts, and possessed with the most absolute spirit of popularity, that is, the most absolute faculties to govern the people, of any man I ever knew."

Such was the character of John Hampden, as drawn by an opponent. If that was what opponents felt about him, you can imagine how he inspired his followers.

The truth was that there was a bond of sympathy between constitutional Royalists and moderate Parliamentarians. If they had had their way there would have been no Civil War. But Charles could not be trusted; he let them both down—fatal, hopeless man that he was. He broke the law by attempting to arrest the five Parliamentary leaders, Hampden among them, and charging them with high treason.

After that, Clarendon says of Hampden, " He was much altered, his nature and carriage seeming much fiercer than it did before ". And then, in a famous phrase, " Without question, when he first drew his sword he threw away the scabbard".

When war broke out he became, though not a professional soldier, a most active commander in the field. He raised a regiment of his own " green-coats ", which soon became one of the best in the army. He was all in favour of forward aggressive action, as against the slow caution of Essex, the professional soldier whom Parliament made its general.

Next year, in June 1643, Essex moved forward as if to attack Oxford, the King's headquarters. The Parliamentarian troops were dispersed about Hampden's home country, with their centre at Thame, where Hampden had been a lad at school, at the grammar school there. Suddenly Prince Rupert shot out from Oxford in one of his swift cavalry raids. Hampden moved forward at once with his usual dash and intrepidity, and with what forces he could collect, to cut off Rupert's retreat. On Chalgrove Field, that great level stretch ten miles out along the road from Oxford to the south-east, Rupert turned upon his pursuers.

There, among the standing corn on a lovely June day — one knows the red poppies in that great field where English blood was shed — the fight took place : Hampden's green-coats against Rupert's horse. Hampden put himself at the head of the attack ; but in the very first charge he was shot, his shoulder broken. He was observed, Clarendon says, " to ride off the field before the action was done, which he never used to do, with his head hanging down and resting his hands upon the neck of his horse ".

There is a touching tradition — and there is usually something in a local tradition — that as he left the field he looked up to the Buckinghamshire hills towards the house where in his youth he had married the first wife of his love, and whither he would have gone to die. But Rupert's cavalry covered the plain between. So he turned his horse and rode slowly back towards Thame. There he died several days later ; local memory points out the " Greyhound " inn as the house. It is said that the King sent over Dr. Giles, the rector of Chinnor, to visit him in his last hours. Such were the courtesies that passed in the Civil War.

Hampden's death caused consternation in the Parliamentarian ranks. " The loss of Colonel Hampden ", said one of their newspapers, " goeth near the heart of every man that loves the good of his king and country, and makes some conceive little content to be at the army now he is gone." Baxter, the great Puritan divine, wrote in his *Saints' Everlasting Rest* that he thought of Heaven with the more pleasure because he should there meet among the apostles and divines of all ages, Pym and Hampden ; and of the latter he said, " One that friends and enemies acknowledged to be most eminent for prudence, piety and peacefulness, having the most universal praise of any gentleman that I remember of that age ".

But perhaps the greatest tribute of all comes again from his opponent Clarendon :

" He was a supreme governor over all his passions and affections, and had thereby a great power over other men's. He was of an industry and vigilance not to be tired out or wearied by the most laborious, and of parts not to be imposed upon by the most subtle or sharp ; and of a personal courage equal to his best parts."

It is idle to speculate what would have happened if he had lived. Probably with his unique popularity and Pym's prestige — for they were the architects of Parliament's victory — they would have made a moderate, civilian settlement, more durable than the régime Cromwell imposed by force of arms.

But that Hampden deserved the people's love in his own time, and to be something more than a name in the story of English liberty — with its reverberations overseas among our kinsfolk — there can be no manner of doubt.

XXII

FALKLAND

OF the three famous men, John Hampden, Falkland, Pym, who died in 1643 in the first year of the Civil War, Falkland was not the greatest — that title must belong to Pym — but he was certainly the most charming : one of the most touching and unforgettable figures in the English tradition. No doubt a good deal of that attraction we owe to the portrait Clarendon painted of him in his *History* : the most moving, as it is the most justly celebrated, of that gallery of masterpieces. Of their friendship the old Chancellor wrote years after in exile at Montpellier, "From his age of twenty years he had lived in an entire friendship with the Chancellor, who was about six months older ; and who never spoke of him afterwards, but with a love and a grief which still raised some commotion in him ". That commotion he still communicates to his readers.

The nineteenth-century historians were tougher — or more obtuse. Falkland, whose heart was not wholly with either side in the struggle, who was struck down in battle against Parliament for which he had more veneration than he had for the King, could not be expected to appeal to their crude, coarser sympathies, their magnificent sense of the obvious. Macaulay has a funny passage, full of high spirits and Philistinism, making a guy of Falkland's career : " He was indeed a man of great talents and of great virtues," it begins, " but, we apprehend, infinitely too fastidious for public life " ; and Carlyle dismisses him in a footnote about his clean shirt on the day of his death at the battle of Newbury (20 September 1643). Falkland's position to us — in this difficult age — is very understandable. To the Victorians, to whom everything was simpler, it was not. His tragedy was that of the moderate in time of revolution : he died in a cause with which he was not wholly in agreement, hating the struggle which rent the country and longing (as the great majority of people did) for a sensible

161

course between the two extremes. But he was *caught* by his fate. A man of the greatest gifts and promise, he was thirty-three when he died. True, we should not know much about him if it were not for Clarendon; but his career has a certain symbolic importance.

Lucius Cary, son of the first Viscount Falkland, was of west country stock, like several of the poets who were the friends of his youth and whom he names in the couplet

" Digby, Carew, Killigrew and Maine,
    Godolphin, Waller, that inspired traine."

His mother was an Oxfordshire heiress, through whom he succeeded to the delectable houses and estates of Burford Priory and Great Tew. Upon the magnificent painted tomb of his grandparents in Burford Church you may see the little figure of the young Falkland kneeling, looking to the altar. In the Bodleian there is his portrait : that affecting gesture of the hand laid upon his heart, the dark, luminous, melancholy eyes, the look of refinement one notices in Caroline portraits against the hardness of Tudor, the brazenness of Restoration, types. Succeeding early to his estates, rich, youthful, with a passion for learning and a gift for friendship, Falkland made his pleasant house at Great Tew in the Cotswolds the resort of the best minds in the university, of the poets and wits from London. His first devotion was to poetry ; and chief among the poets of his circle was Ben Jonson, who wrote a fine ode to celebrate the passionate friendship that subsisted between Falkland and Sir Henry Morison, whose sister he married when the brother died. Thither, too, came the cynical Suckling, who celebrated the gatherings in his *Session of the Poets*, Tom Carew, amorous but somewhat costive of verses, diminutive but gallant Sidney Godolphin, the much-travelled Sandys. As the years went on, Falkland ceased to write verse and turned his attention to divinity and philosophical questions. Suckling lamented :

" He was of late so gone with divinity,
    That he had almost forgotten his poetry,
    Though to say the truth, and Apollo did know it,
    He might have been both his priest and his poet."

The poets were succeeded more and more by the divines from the university. There was Gilbert Sheldon, Fellow, and soon to be Warden, of All Souls, who was — like the young Cosmo Lang — born to be Archbishop of Canterbury. There were the amusing Dr. Earle, author of the delightful *Micro-cosmographie*; the witty Dr. Morley, whose promotion was held up for a time by a too happy reply to a grave, country gentle-man, who, puzzled by the new-fangled Arminian tenets, asked Morley what the Arminians held ; and he replied, " All the best bishoprics and deaneries in England ". Above all, there were John Hales, " one of the least men in the Kingdom ; and one of the greatest scholars in Europe " ; and the subtle, questing intellect of Chillingworth, Falkland's mentor, who gave the philosophical tone to this circle.

It was that of a passionate belief in toleration. Chilling-worth believed that the fundamental truths of religion were few and simple, that they might be ascertained from the Bible; and he wrote an important book which was a plea for Christian unity on the basis of the widest possible toleration. Falkland followed his lead with a *Discourse on Infallibility*, and two tracts. He had determined to learn Greek; and, because he was fond of the society of London, he made a vow not to see it again until he had learned the language. He not only kept the vow, but ended by reading all the early Fathers. One sees the picture : the young patron whose poetry was without inspira-tion, his philosophy without originality, yet whose gifts of mind and sympathy kept the circle together.

Upon this charming society there fell the thunderbolt of the Civil War. What added poignancy to their grief was that it was so unexpected. Clarendon remarks the calm contentment and prosperity of those years before the storm ; and to the trouble of mind they suffered they added the singular faculty of expressing it in perfect, touching words. " All things progresse toward the fatal declination of our time ", wrote an ordinary Kentish gentleman who watched Pym riding into London attended by hundreds of his supporters.

Falkland was elected to Parliament, and henceforth his life was a part of national history. He was thirty when he became at one step a leading figure in the Long Parliament, which contained a multitude of famous men : a contrast to the Parliaments of elderly men since 1918 who have such a record of disservice to their country. (Historians will do the latter, as they have done the former, justice.) Falkland and Hyde were united with Pym and Hampden in the attack on the King's personal government and on Strafford, who was at once its instrument and victim. Falkland voted for his attainder, though he wished to spare his life ; he led the attack on Ship Money ; he went all the way with Pym in the onslaught upon the Prerogative Courts, the institutions of authoritarian government. He had no love for Laud and was willing to see a reform of the Church and the Bishops out of the House of Lords : he regarded that as a matter of expediency rather than of principle. He was a latitudinarian and a tolerationist.

But he stopped short when he saw that Pym was pressing forward to a constitutional revolution. The united House was divided in two by Pym's revolutionary manifesto, the Grand Remonstrance, which demanded that Ministers should be responsible to Parliament. Falkland opposed this invasion of the King's constitutional rights. After the great debate far into the night — Sir Philip Warwick describes the extraordinary scene — Falkland was left at the head of a large minority, the backbone of a party for the King, the origin of the Tory Party. It was to Falkland that the comparatively unknown Oliver Cromwell said that if the Grand Remonstrance had not passed he would have sold all he had and gone to America. " So near was the poor kingdom at that time to its deliverance ", comments Clarendon.

Since he had broken with the Parliamentarian leaders and led the opposition to their course, the onus fell upon Falkland of advising the King. A man of honour, a man marked for responsibility from the moment of his entering into public life, he could not refuse the King his service, though he became Secretary of State with the greatest reluctance. Clarendon has a penetrating and affecting analysis of his dilemma, the call of duty against every inclination :

" He had not the court in great reverence and had a presaging spirit that the King would fall into great misfortune : and often said to his friend that he chose to serve the King because honesty obliged him to it; but that he foresaw his own ruin by doing it."

Undoubtedly the motive that weighed strongest with him was the hope of using his influence to bring about peace. "When there was any overture or hope of peace", Clarendon says, "he would be more erect and vigorous, and exceedingly solicitous to press anything which he thought might promote it; and sitting amongst his friends, often, after a deep silence and frequent sighs, would, with a shrill and sad accent, ingeminate the word *Peace, Peace*, and would passionately profess that the very agony of the war, and the view of the calamities and desolation the Kingdom did and must endure, took his sleep from him, and would shortly break his heart." All through the winter of 1642-3 he worked hard at negotiations with Parliament; if it had rested with him the Treaty of Oxford would have achieved peace. But there were intransigents on both sides, and in the end his efforts were wrecked by the influence of the Court camarilla and Charles' fatal devotion to Henrietta Maria, who had all the Frenchwoman's itch for meddling in politics. She wanted peace to come as a gift from her hands.

Falkland was despairing, and when war was renewed threw himself into the most dangerous and exposed positions: as he had done at Edgehill, so in the trenches before Gloucester, and at last at Newbury, where " in this battle the Chancellor of the Exchequer lost the joy and comfort of his life ".

Historians have been very obtuse about Falkland's mind and motives, and how he came by his death. Clarendon is quite clear, and surely it is very simple. Falkland had courage and was " naturally inquisitive after danger " ; but it was precisely because he was known to long passionately for peace that he thrust himself in battle into the place of greatest hazard.

In the end one thinks of him in those thyme-scented, walled gardens at Great Tew, walking with his friends among the violets and the limes before the War came upon them to scatter them for ever. And yet they will always have their place in the English tradition, thanks to Clarendon's imperishable portrait of them. Such things friendship, illumined by genius, can do.

XXIII

JOHN PYM, CONSERVATIVE REVOLUTIONARY

JOHN PYM was the architect of the English Revolution, which was, above all, a Parliamentary revolution. Though the name of John Hampden is better known to people today, Pym was a greater man : he was the real leader. And very characteristic, too, for an English revolutionary, he was essentially a moderate, even a conservative. He was no extremist, nor a mere talker, mouthing *clichés* which mean nothing, but a practical man of business who did not want a revolution but was impelled by circumstances and his own abilities to take the lead.

Pym was a west-countryman, of good Somerset stock, and owning estates in that county ; one of the gentry whose rise to power was the dynamic force behind the whole struggle. But his father having died, he was brought up from his earliest years in Cornwall, where his mother married Sir Anthony Rouse, friend and executor of Sir Francis Drake. We are to think, then, of the young Pym growing up in that strong Protestant household at Halton among the cherry orchards of Tamar-side. Not many miles away, at St. Germans, there was growing up another young man, John Eliot, who became the first leader of Parliamentary opposition to the Stuarts.

Equally important for a youth whose whole boyhood was spent on the banks of the Tamar running down to Plymouth, in those years of the great voyages of Drake and his fellows, Pym was deeply interested in the colonisation of America. No nonsense about being ashamed of building an empire with these great Puritan leaders ! The interesting thing is that the whole group of Puritan leaders who defeated the monarchy were imperialists. During the eleven years in which Charles I misgoverned the nation without a Parliament, Pym was the leading spirit, and the treasurer, of the Providence Company, formed to colonise one of the West Indian islands off the coast of Honduras.

But with the summoning of Parliament in 1640, a much larger scope opened for Pym : he became the unacknowledged leader of the House of Commons. Charles I's inept mistakes had involved him in a war with Scotland and aroused the antagonism of the whole country. Clarendon himself tells us what magic the name of Parliament had at this time and how the whole country looked to Parliament for a remedy. Pym, by his immense experience, his judgment, his knowledge of business and procedure, his sense of tactics, became the leader of a united Parliament. It soon became evident that he was one of the two men in the country who understood all that was at stake, and had the strategic vision to guide events. The other was Strafford.

There is no doubt that Pym wanted to come to terms with the King and to avoid civil war. He was not an extreme Puritan ; he was prepared to compromise over Church matters and retain the bishops (bishops, though often figures of fun, have never been popular with Englishmen). But Pym saw, as Strafford did on the other side, that the real issue was whether government was to be responsible to Parliament or to the King.

This was a new and revolutionary step to take. Many people wished to burke the issue or to patch up an accommodation. Pym had the statesman's faculty for grasping the essential issue. And he saw further that with Strafford at his back the King would never come to terms. It was necessary to destroy Strafford : the destruction of that great, tragic man was the work of Pym. In all the manœuvres necessary to bring him down, the impeachment, the bill of attainder, the intimidation of the King, the master hand was Pym's. He never made a mistake ; his intelligence service was so efficient that he knew every move of the Court. " Stone dead hath no fellow ", he said of Strafford. And it was so.

But still the King could not be brought to terms. Pym brought forward that masterpiece of propaganda, the Grand Remonstrance, reciting all Charles' misdeeds and demanding that Ministers should be responsible to Parliament. Charles

M

determined to arrest the five Parliamentary leaders in person :
he made his descent on Parliament to find they had taken
refuge in the City. Pym realised that there could be no security
with Charles, and that civil war was inevitable. He now came
out openly as the leader of the war party, and undertook all
preparations, diplomatic, financial, military.

The first year of the war, 1642–3, was full of reverses for
Parliament, before its superior resources could be organised
and brought into play. Pym suffered a grievous loss in the
death of his friend, John Hampden. The reverses of 1643
forced Pym to play his trump card and bring Scotland in
on the side of Parliament. Though stricken with cancer he
carried through the negotiations to success : the alliance made
the victory of Parliament as certain as it could be made,
though Pym did not live to see its triumph. Within a month
of his death he was made Master of the Ordnance — equivalent
to being Minister of Munitions — on top of being his own
Prime Minister and Foreign Secretary. No wonder that in
these last years of his life he became known as " King Pym ".

He died, worn out with the burden of his work, which he
never relaxed in spite of mortal illness. If he had lived, no
doubt there would have been a civilian settlement of the issues
of the war instead of the military dictatorship of Cromwell.
Pym would have had the enormous prestige of having led
Parliament through to success, and he would have seen to that.
For all his Lenin-like ruthlessness as a leader in time of crisis,
he was a civilian aiming at Parliamentary government. For
centuries now it has been our form of government : we were
the first in that field, and it is our model which the world has
followed.

But we owe it to that very English figure, John Pym.

XXIV

CLARENDON'S *LIFE*

How great, how varied and agreeable, are the riches of English historical literature. Perhaps not quite so copious as the French; but there is no other modern literature that compares with ours in this respect. And yet I doubt if many of us realise what delightful and diverse reading there is to be had : so many works infinitely more worth reading than the trash of which there seems to be more than ever in war-time, or at any rate fewer works of quality to keep it in place. Yet there are classics of our literature of which few enough have heard, let alone read. How many have read Clarendon's *History of the Rebellion*, or his *Autobiography*, or Lord Herbert of Cherbury's, or Hervey's *Memoirs*, or the *Verney Letters*? All of them first-class, enjoyable reading, fresh as when they were written — when Books of the Month, of the Year, are dead from the moment of their appearance, the bright yellow covers on the railway bookstalls destined inevitably for the salvage van.

Horace Walpole knew a good thing when he saw one and pounced upon Clarendon's *Life* when it appeared. He wrote to Montagu, on 19 July 1759, " Have you read my Lord Clarendon ? I am enchanted with it ; 'tis very incorrect, but I think more entertaining than his *History*. It makes me quite out of humour with *other mémoires*." (He meant his own.) It is true that Clarendon's *Life* is in some ways a finer work even than the *History*, and at the same time it is far less well known. There are several reasons for this ; the chief, perhaps, being that Clarendon did not intend the *Life* for publication, but for the private instruction of his children, and so he plundered the completed *Life* ruthlessly to enrich the *History*. The whole story of the composition of the *History*, of the reliability of different parts of it, and of its relation to the *Life*, is a complex one, which has been worked out by Sir Charles Firth in the *English Historical Review* (1904). Most of the famous character sketches in the *History* really come out of the autobiography. What Clarendon did was to leave the latter a torso, by robbing it of much of what he had written about the Civil War and Commonwealth period; though the latter part, from the Restoration onwards, is very full. The result is that we are left with only half of what would have been perhaps the finest of English autobiographies, if we had it complete.

Then, too, it has never been properly edited. The only edition we have, published at Oxford in 1857, is a very inadequate text, with no notes at all, no indication of the large passages which have been transferred to the *History* or of others that have not been printed in either. A new edition is what is wanted: a good job of work for some young scholar returning from the war to tackle.

All the same the *Life*, even as we have it, is a wonderful book. Clarendon wrote it when his powers were at their height, freed from the daily preoccupations of politics by his second and final exile from the country. The taste for character drawing, which they did so well in the seventeenth century, had grown upon him since his original composition of the *History* twenty years before; now he could let himself go, and the most fully-developed portraits all belong to this period. Since he was not writing for publication, he could afford to be far more frank than in the *History*, where one of his main objects was to defend Charles I. Clarendon's deep-seated loyalty prevented him from being too outspoken — besides he had the essential justice of mind and devotion to truth of the real historian ; but the *Life* is much more revealing of the hidden causes of events as he saw them. The sense of the play of personalities is absorbing ; the somewhat ponderous politician turns out to be a subtler psychologist than the nimble wits that got him turned out of power. There is an exquisite feeling for the atmosphere of that delicate, fragrant time before the Civil War when such personalities as Falkland, Sidney Godolphin, Selden, Chillingworth, George Herbert, Nicholas Ferrar had come to flower. Most of them had been friends of Clarendon's — close friends to whom his mind and heart were attuned. No wonder he was a *laudator temporis acti*, who spent much of his activity in politics on trying to make those good days come again, and when that failed him spent his last years in the dream of what that time

had been, out of which he recalled those figures of the past with
all their rich, warm colouring and made them live again for us
and for posterity. Above all, his *Life* is what an autobiography
should be, a complete portrait of his own personality, with all
his qualities and limitations, his fidelity, integrity, honesty, his
ability and courage, his warmth of heart — and the truly
monumental self-satisfaction which cannot but astonish the
modern reader.

I dare to disagree with that great scholar, Firth, when he
says that Clarendon was " one of the first examples in later
English history of the man who begins in low estate and rises
by his own abilities to the highest political office ". He came
from a good country family, well connected — his uncle and
patron was Lord Chief Justice. The King himself wrote him
a letter of recommendation as a lad to Magdalen College, of
which the President, for some odd reason, took no notice; and
so Magdalen lost the chance of having a second historian hardly
inferior to Gibbon. (In spite of his great loyalty to the University, Clarendon, too, was distinctly critical of the studies and
diversions pursued there.) He made a good match which
brought him an estate, and as he says himself, lived as a barrister
in good style, much above that of other lawyers. He kept the
best company and enjoyed the patronage of the great. He
" well knew how to cultivate those advantages ", beginning
with the confidence Laud had in him. (There is a most life-like
and characteristic description of the Archbishop walking in his
garden at Lambeth on the occasion when the young lawyer, so
like him, told him candidly how unpopular he was and how
much it was due to the sharpness and inconsiderateness of his
manner. Laud blushed for himself, and, taking it like a man,
had a particular regard for and trust in his young acquaintance
ever after.)

True, Clarendon was not an aristocrat, but a gentleman at
a time when the gentry were extending their power and influence in the State beyond all expectation or precedent. It was
that upward surge of power, a shift of social forces, which lay
behind the Civil War, and of which Clarendon had no notion.
Just like an actor in these events, he saw it all in personal
terms, the mistakes of the King on one side, the aggressions of

Parliament on the other. It makes him all the easier and more congenial reading.

In spite of long his years of exile, twenty-one altogether, Clarendon remained always the country-bred Englishman with his roots deep in the life of his country. From the very beginning of the *Life* one notices this theme, as one does in the *History* : the different characters of English counties, their differences in custom, cultivation, even in weights and measures. It is so much taken for granted that it is not developed as a theme ; but it is always there in the background. Clarendon's father, a Wiltshire country gentleman, served in the last Parliaments of Elizabeth, but after the Queen's death was never in London again, though he lived for thirty years after ; his wife, to whom he was married above forty years, was never in London in her life :

" the wisdom and frugality of that time being such that few gentlemen made journeys to London, or any other expensive journeys, but upon important business, and their wives never ; by which providence they enjoyed and improved their estates in the country, and kept good hospitality in their houses, brought up their children well, and were beloved by their neighbours ".

Clarendon was always an old-fashioned man in his prejudices, not the worse for being a bit out of date, a belated Elizabethan.

There is no more convincing country note than his story of how he was just reading to his father the passage in Camden's *Annals* about that John Felton who affixed the Papal Bull of Excommunication upon the Bishop of London's door " when a person of the neighbourhood knocked at the door, and being called in, told his father that a post was then passed through the village to Charleton, the house of the Earl of Berkshire ", with the news of the assassination of Buckingham by another John Felton. Clarendon deplored the influence of women in politics at Court, dating from Buckingham's removal and the emergence of Henrietta Maria ; and no wonder when you consider the disastrous effect of that French bitch — a veritable Madame de Portes in a higher position — upon the country's affairs, or of Charles II's seraglio, which Clarendon had even more personal reason to resent. One suddenly realises as never before that the

Elizabethan age, to which he looked back as an ideal, was a thoroughly masculine society ; only one woman had her hand in politics then (and *what* a hand ! there was no room for any others).

Clarendon's psychological insight is nowhere better displayed than in his account of the personal relations of Falkland and Culpepper with the King and Queen. Falkland was compliant enough with the weakness and humours of smaller men, where there was no question of flattery :

" Yet towards the King, who many times obstinately adhered to many conclusions which did not naturally result from good premises, and did love to argue many things to which he would not so positively adhere, he did not practise that condescension, but contradicted him with more bluntness, and by sharp sentences ; and in some particulars (as of the church) to which the King was in conscience most devoted : and of this his majesty often complained ; and cared less to confer with him in private, and was less persuaded by him than his affairs, and the other's great parts and wisdom, would have required."

But what a condemnation this is of Charles really ; he preferred to listen to Culpepper, who told him what he liked to hear, and whose judgment was less good even than the King's.

Culpepper, on the other hand, had

" With all this uncourtliness (for sure no man less appeared a courtier) and ungracefulness in his mien and motion, a wonderful insinuation and address into the acceptation and confidence of the king and queen, and flattery being a weed not so natural to the air and soil of the country where he had wholly lived, he was believed to speak with all plainness and sincerity ; when no man more complied with those infirmities they both had, and by that compliance prevailed often over them. He had a very tragical way in expressing himself, to raise the fears and apprehensions of those who were naturally apprehensive of dangers ; and by this means he prevailed marvellously with the queen in those matters to which she was most averse ; by representing things as dismally to her as he could well do ; and on the other hand to the king (who was naturally very sanguine) he was full of compliance ; cherished all his hopes and imaginations, and raised and improved those hopes very frequently by expedients very unagreeable to the end proposed."

One sees the situation so well : the complex play of personalities holding up, and in the end frustrating, the ends they all wanted — as so often, and so intolerably, in human affairs.

And then a reflection occurs to one about Clarendon's rotund, elaborate style : those long involved sentences, with all the parentheses, are precisely fitted to express the complexity of the psychological situation. Better indeed than a modern style, which would split up the qualifications into separate sentences, where Clarendon is able to carry them along with the statements they qualify. Nor is his style for all its richness without edge ; people can be ticked off very precisely in a subordinate clause. There is the Earl of St. Albans, who visits Clarendon in a crisis " with all those compliments, professions and protestations, which were natural, and which he did really believe everybody else thought to be very sincere ; for he had that kindness for himself, that he thought everybody did believe him ". Then when Clarendon had got through the crisis, Henrietta Maria was gracious enough to him, " and from that time there did never appear any want of kindness in the queen towards him, whilst he stood in no need of it, nor until it might have done him good ". There was the treacherous Coventry, " who had never paid a civility to any worthy man, but as it was a disobligation to another whom he cared less for " ; or the slippery Shaftesbury, " who was good at looking into other men's offices ".

But one must not give the impression that Clarendon was in any way peevish, though the *Life* was written as a defence of his career and actions ; nothing is more remarkable than his magnanimity, in spite of being traduced and hounded out of public life. He does indeed betray a particular sensitiveness about the mimicry of him which brought him into ridicule at the easily amused, cynical, heartless Court of Charles II ; and one remembers the scene of that scapegrace Harry Killigrew, with the bellows for the great seal and the poker for the mace, strutting behind the pompous old Chancellor. What a target he must have presented to those wits and rakes, not to mention the royal mistresses, with his smugness and self-satisfaction, his honesty and integrity. And yet he was right : such qualities would never have been allowed to bring him down at the Court of Elizabeth, and after such services to the monarchy. It is not for nothing that the Stuarts became a byword for ingratitude.

Evelyn describes the portraits of his friends that the Chancellor had hung in the days of his glory upon the walls of Clarendon House. For consolation in exile, setting out upon his travels from the Scilly Islands where he had begun to write his great *History*, in Jersey walking upon the sands in the evening with the Governor, the day's work over, or in the hot streets of Madrid, at Montpellier in his last and final exile, Clarendon loved to turn back in his mind to the garden at Great Tew — and remember the friends of his youth, lingering over their names and virtues. To his love for them we owe the unfading freshness, the beauty of his two great books : into them both there comes the scent of the musk, the roses, and thyme of that Cotswold garden in the high summer of the early seventeenth century.

XXV

PICTURES IN A DEANERY

WHAT could be a more delicious setting for an exhibition of old pictures than a house in an English cathedral close — particularly when it is the close at Salisbury, and the house is the Deanery there, perhaps the most beautiful of all the houses set down in that wide space, with views from all its windows across green lawns and water-meadows, across rose-covered walls to the west front of the cathedral, the back with its cut hedges and grass walks leading down to the quiet-flowing Avon ? It is all very satisfying to the eye. The idea that has so much taken on of late, of bringing together in one place a selection of pictures from surrounding country houses, can never have been more justified than here. Nothing of the deadness, the intimidating professionalism of so many galleries : Dr. Tancred Borenius, who has had the arranging of these pictures, has been able to imagine himself as an eighteenth-century dean with a taste for pictures and this superb house to put them in.

There are so many good things here which may not be brought together again for a long time ; best of all are the paintings of the late fifteenth and sixteenth centuries, in the downstairs room, many of them owned by Mr. John Morrison of Fonthill. They have, too, a common character, which makes them the more interesting : that of the Renaissance in Northern Europe, France, the Low Countries, England. In that order, for really the English contribution is very small : a beautiful miniature of Sir Philip Sidney, by Isaac Oliver, and a charming small painting of him in camp at Zutphen, which I do not remember ever to have seen reproduced. If a more English character were to be given to this room, no doubt it could easily have been done by bringing the Holbein portraits of Erasmus from Longford Castle, and of Sir John More from Wilton.

Practically every picture in this small room is of first-rate beauty and interest. There are two of François Clouet's, both well known ; one of Mary Queen of Scots, " *Le Deuil Blanc* ",

in the white cap and high-necked veil prescribed as mourning
for widows of the French royal house — a picture for which
there is a study in the *Bibliothèque Nationale* ; and a charming
portrait of Charles IX, with that pale-olive Medici complexion
and almond-coloured eyes, a small round hat with plume set
on one side of the head, a pearl in his ear. There is a memorable
portrait, by Corneille de Lyon, of Theodore de Beza, the
Reformer, all in black against a green background, with full
grey beard and fine blue eyes set wide apart. A less interesting
portrait of the French school, one of Louise de Lorraine, has
nevertheless an amusing historical interest for us ; for the
daughter of the Duke of Lorraine was one of the ladies whose
hand Henry VIII sought after the death of Jane Seymour,
before he, so disagreeably for himself, became committed to
Anne of Cleves. Surely this portrait must be one of those
specially painted for the King — like the famous Holbein
portrait of the Duchess of Milan — in the hectic rush round
Europe for a wife in the years 1538–9, one that came to repose
afterwards, the lady herself put aside or not being willing, in
some private collection in the country ?

The Sidney portrait — it is not certain whether it is an
Oliver or no — is worth a note. It is a full-length portrait
of him in armour chased in gold from head to toe — indeed
the effect is rather of a medieval picture with much use of
gold leaf. Sidney is standing at a table covered with green
velvet cloth reaching to the ground, at the entrance to his
tent ; in the background a servant is holding his horse richly
caparisoned. It is a curious picture ; and though the face
is a familiar Elizabethan face, with tall fine forehead, brown
hair and moustache, is it certain that it is Philip Sidney ?
Might it not be his brother Robert, who was Governor of
Flushing ?

But the masterpieces in this room are those of the Flemish
school. There is the beautiful Morrison Triptych — the centre
panel a Madonna and Child with angels and saints adoring,
the inside panels occupied by a St. John the Baptist and some
saint holding a chalice, an exquisite figure with a lavender-
coloured cloak over a grass-green vesture : the latter obviously
painted under Italian influence. The backgrounds are filled

with beautifully painted Low Country landscapes, a fifteenth-century brick house with truncated gable by a river with swans ; the centre panel has a large castle with river and wooden foot-bridge : all very well realised and naturalistic, the slow tide of that late fifteenth-century life now vanished for ever, yet leaving this image of what once it was, of those human beings seeking some permanence in things, even as we. They found it in devotion, as we perhaps cannot, in a structure of belief in another world which they brought in to right the disaster of this.

There are other expressions of that faith here : an *Adoration of the Shepherds* by Van der Goes, touching in its simplicity and very satisfying in its grouping of the figures. The hands are remarkably good, distinctly characterised, as are the faces, rustic, awkward, angular, and the little landscape in each corner, the angel appearing to the shepherds, the blue strange light upon the hillside : the essence of Christmas and all that has meant to generations of the faithful :

> " Herdmen beheld thes angelles bright
> To them apperèd with gret light,
> And seid ' Goddes sone is born this night.'
> *In excelsis gloria.*"

Yet somehow this Van der Goes is a little disappointing : it has nothing of the strange power, the ecstasy of passion of that fragment of a *Lamentation* of his in the library of Christ Church at Oxford. Nor are the two Mabuses, each of them a *Madonna with the Child*, more exciting ; they are heavy and Flemish and placid. Altogether more attractive is the *Madonna and Child* of the school of the Lower Rhine, lent by Mrs. Christie-Miller. This has so much more life and rhythm, the figures as round and substantial (if anything more so), but more lively, gay, and happy. The picture exfoliates children, cherubs after the German fashion, expression of their idealisation of the family. The Virgin, a simple German girl, radiant and innocent, is seated on a low cushion, child on her knee, a rich crimson cloth of State held up behind her.

Going from this room up the Dean's staircase (very chaste and Georgian), you pass one or two pleasant unobtrusive pictures of the English eighteenth century, a painting of old

Lambeth from the river, and two pictures of Samuel Scott, one of Covent Garden, the other of Lincoln's Inn Fields : both portraying so regular, so noble an architecture, that if Lincoln's Inn Fields looked like that, one feels, and this picture is faithful reporting, what a disaster it is that has overwhelmed London in the last century !

And so into the Dean's great gallery, a superb room on the first floor looking east and west, to the cathedral and the water-meadows (what a fortunate man the Dean was !). Here are gathered the main bulk of the pictures, an eighteenth-century collection, in keeping with the character of that hypothetical collector, the Dean. There are two charming Canalettos, familiar scenes along the Grand Canal, one of Santa Maria della Salute, the other of the Dogana : with a little cleaning, they would show up, with that lovely light upon them, bright and festive as the day they were painted.

By far the largest number of pictures, as was perhaps to be expected, are, however, English portraits of the eighteenth century : Gainsboroughs, Reynolds, Hoppners, Lawrences, of members of the surrounding families, Herberts, Radnors, Burdetts, Methuens, for the most part perfunctory enough, obvious products of a fashionable practice, which bored their authors as they are dull in their effect upon the observer. But here and there is a picture of interest, occasionally one that is striking and worth lingering over and memorising. There is an attractive portrait by Sir Joshua of Gibbon as a young man — and portraits of Gibbon are few and far between. This one is more carefully painted than most in the room : the sitter, though he can hardly then have been known for what he was to become, evidently interested the artist. The young man has a pleasant green coat with gold facings, freshly painted ; he has the face of the young prig he was, of a fair complexion, with small mouth and pursed lips. One sees in this the Gibbon of the later portrait, the great historian, very conscious, fat, and pursy. There is an interesting early portrait of Nelson, by Rigaud, no doubt painted on his return from the West Indies Station, in 1780 : a pleasant picture in which the most is made of the dominant blue of the naval coat, and the rhythmical line it makes, cut in close to the slender figure. A better picture is

Sir Thomas Lawrence's portrait of W. H. Miller, founder of the Britwell Library : a fascinating young man (or is it only the Lawrence glamour ?) of a rather Jewish cast of beauty, dark and gleaming, in a somewhat Byronic pose, hair carefully disarranged as the fashion was, wearing a rich red velvet coat edged with fur, in a green chair : a little like an Ingres in effect.

But the most exciting portrait in the room is one of Alexander Davidson of Drumhall, Cromarty, Governor of Madras 1785–91, by Tilly Kettle. This indeed is something of a revelation, for who was Tilly Kettle to paint like that ? No doubt the experts may find it not at all surprising ; but to the ordinary person with a liking for pictures, it comes as an unexpected gift. Is it that most of his pictures are in private collections, or remain in India where he lived for some seven years painting, and made by it a considerable fortune which he subsequently lost ? If so, and he is not sufficiently represented in our national collections, let an endeavour be set on foot at once to repair the deficiency. For this portrait — it belongs to Mrs. Devenish — is as good as a very good Sir Joshua. The subject has evidently inspired the painter to his best effort : it is that of a handsome man in young middle age, very dark with black hair and swarthy complexion, the dark red appearing through the brown, an irresistible combination. He has very fine dark eyes and marked brows, with a cupid's bow to his lips. It is a lovely head in shape and poise, round and leaning slightly to one side. He is wearing a sandy-coloured coat of some sack-like material, with dark-green waistcoat and lapels, and gold facings. Altogether a beautiful portrait, with the same suavity, substance, and poise, a kind of golden luminousness pervading it. It should be in the National Portrait Gallery.

No less excellent — though less striking, for these were to be expected — are the two Zoffanys. One is of a family group with a boy flying a kite, very pleasant and lively, full of movement and charm. In the other the interest is concentrated rather upon character. It is a conversation piece portraying the Hon. Charles Hope Vere with his sisters, Lady Christian Graham and Lady Charlotte Erskine : a most satisfying

composition, fresh yet sober in colour, the figures lively but
staid, each distinctly visualised and characterised, yet entirely
subordinated to the general scheme : the quintessence of the
eighteenth century.　Lady Graham and her brother are seated
on a dark blue-green sofa (each gold nail-head distinctly
painted), the man in a bright brick-red coat, one hand in his
waistcoat, the other holding a book dated 1782 : he has a very
aristocratic horsy face, with a large nose and marked profile.
The two ladies are in black satin, with large white lace aprons
and mob caps : the one on the left, Lady Erskine, has a pert
gay expression, looking direct at the painter, with a flowered
damask work-bag on her wrist, her spectacles and a book upon
the little round table by her chair.　Lady Graham in the
middle looks older, more imperious, a less cheerful nature.
There they are : two old tabbies and a tom : a charming
scene, beautifully grouped, their expressions, their very selves
naturally caught and precisely rendered.

In the last room, the parlour, the Dean's own taste as an
eighteenth-century connoisseur has been allowed full play by
Dr. Borenius.　This is exactly what he would have collected
and brought home to the Deanery, if he had ever existed.　The
room is full of little Wouverman and Van der Neer landscapes,
Pieter Neefs' and Saenredam's interiors of Dutch churches :
very nice, very pleasant, rather dull.　One concludes that here
in this room the charming fiction of the Dean has been given
too much scope — these are only too exactly the pictures he
would have chosen, not the masterpieces of the earlier period
in the room downstairs.　But one goes down the Dean's stairs
and out into the Close with a clear vision of the exquisite use
to which our deaneries may be put, when, alas, the sad day
comes when there are no longer deans to occupy them.

XXVI
JONATHAN SWIFT

(i)

IT is perhaps not surprising that of all the books that have come out in late years about Swift, there is hardly one that is completely worthy of the subject. But there can be little doubt that Mr. Quintana comes nearest with his ; he has limited himself to an academic study of the mind and art of Swift as portrayed in his writings, and his book is the better for that.[1] In fact, he shows a very remarkable degree of sympathy with and understanding of that most extraordinary mind — perhaps the most extraordinary in the whole range of English literature. He gives us a very careful and sensible survey of all Swift's writings, connects it up with the vast body of research that has accumulated upon the subject, and gives us enough of Swift's life to make it intelligible.

All the same he has not quite fulfilled his aim of " presenting him against the background of his age ". Mr. Quintana treats Swift in and for himself very sensitively and successfully ; but it is precisely the background to Swift's thought, the various elements that entered into it from other thinkers, where they came from and how they affected him, that might be made more of. Mr. Quintana has this to excuse him, that there is no history of English thought in the seventeenth century, and that it would take a historian to write one. One notices this lacuna most in regard to the problem of Swift's belief — or unbelief ; for there was a strong strain of deism, or of definite unbelief, among English thinkers of that age, which must have powerfully affected Swift's mind. Mr. Quintana notices the influence of Hobbes' materialism upon Swift's view of the imagination and his aesthetics generally ; but it may be opined that that influence went further, to affect the whole foundation of Swift's intellectual position, to instil scepticism into a mind not naturally sceptical, to cause him to doubt the

[1] Ricardo Quintana, *The Mind and Art of Jonathan Swift.*

validity of any but a crudely and narrowly realistic view of the world and of experience. Nor should one forget the very considerable body of deistic or atheistic writing contemporaneous with Swift, which is part of his natural background : such writers as Shaftesbury, Toland, Mandeville. No wonder Mr. Quintana says, rightly and well, that " when the great Dean of St. Patrick's died in 1745 he had already ceased to be understood by the eighteenth century ". All the more reason to consider him fully in relation to his proper environment.

Such a study would illuminate all sorts of things, not only the question of Swift's religious convictions — though that is, of course, central. On this point as on some others, Mr. Quintana shows a youthful and ingenuous desire to defend Swift, to excuse him — though neither defence nor excuse should be necessary in this, the twentieth century ; it is enough to understand him. " It is not that Swift wavered in belief, nor that in conduct he failed to be guided by it ", says Mr. Quintana. " In all these matters he was rigorously consistent, rigorously in accord with his theoretical premises." But the point is whether these premises were in accordance with orthodox Christianity. I cannot but think that the Archbishops, Queen Anne, the instinct of all religious believers since (typified by Dr. Johnson, who could not bear him), and the general attitude of the religious-minded nineteenth century, were right about Swift. They scented that there was no religion about him. As for getting a bishopric, he was lucky indeed to become a dean. Only an age when oligarchical patronage was in the ascendant would have been so broad-minded ; any other age would have expected a dean to believe. But of this there is hardly any evidence in all his writings. Such conception of religion as he had was of an external and political character ; there is no sign of personal belief. Even in the *Prayers for Stella*, the nearest he achieved to belief, there is more evidence of doubt than of faith or hope ; whereas he frequently gives expression to the Manichee doctrine that life is in itself an evil to be endured. That at any rate is the view which he consistently stated and held to in his writings. But one wonders whether one ought to take him so seriously as he took himself on this point ; for if life is so unbearable, why not then suicide?

N

In fact, he clearly enjoyed some part of his own life — the years 1709-14, for example, the exercise of power, his many friendships, writing.

Mr. Quintana is at pains, too, to rebut the charge that Swift was a misanthrope. But why should he be, unless an American audience has to be assured of the larger hope ? Why shouldn't Swift be a misanthrope ? He admits it, indeed states it proudly. Hatred of human beings is as legitimate a subject of art as love of them, and its possibilities more rarely explored. Or again, Mr. Quintana displays a tendency to a prudery quite unworthy of the twentieth century which claims to understand Swift, in the case of the scatological poems with their " disgusting " imagery. They are often aesthetic triumphs, and are as much part of Swift's mind as the " fine, satiric touch " — indeed more intimately part of his mind, and therefore all the more revealing to the student of what kind of mind that was. The discerning should see that the horror and self-torture of these poems are due to an excessive, an unnatural sensitiveness. " I was to see Lady ——," he wrote to Stella, " who is just up after lying-in ; and the ugliest sight I have seen, pale, dead, old and yellow, for want of her paint. *She has turned my stomach.* But she will soon be painted, and a beauty again." In this one has the type of all those poems of physical disgust he wrote : they are due to a morbid degree of sensitiveness, acting upon a disillusioned temperament, to make him torture himself and others. But why complain, or excuse ? Things are what they are.

There certainly was an extraordinary tension between defeatism in his view of human nature and an active temperament in himself, between reason and the emotions, in Swift's mind. He had no illusions about human nature, yet he did expect men to be better than they are. He insisted always, too much indeed, upon the moral responsibility of the person. He believed tremendously in Reason, but found little of it in men's lives. It may be that in his outlook there was too great a dichotomy between Reason and the emotions ; he seems to have thought of them as necessarily in conflict and that increased the strain in his inner life. The tension was fruitful, no doubt, of great art, but it made for greater unhappiness. No one has put the point whether a defective intellectual position did not add much to that unhappiness. Swift believed, for example, in accordance with the materialism of Hobbes, that " self-love, as it is the motive to all our actions, so it is the sole cause of our grief ". It is a very inhibiting doctrine to hold, very repressive of the emotional life, especially when a man is as self-conscious as Swift : it had a terrifying hold upon his mind. *He* at any rate was not under the illusions that most people are as to their motives. He grieved that this was man's condition ; but would he not have attained greater peace, if, realising how little disinterestedness there was in the world or in himself, he had made it more his aim ?

As it was, his intellectual position was at every point that which his interests demanded and with which his person was identified. A churchman, he saw only the interests of his own sect ; a Tory, of his own party ; an Irish Protestant, he stood up for the Irish Church against both Catholics and Dissenters. If he had happened to be a Dissenter, or had remained a Whig, he would have been as vehement on the other side. That is very human. Mr. Quintana appreciates the point and adds the comment, " however ignoble his actuating impulses may have been, the ends which he achieved cannot be judged solely in terms of motive ". That is sound enough ; but what is more remarkable is Swift's complete consciousness of the situation and his acceptance of it. It is on a par with his denial of any place to romance in life, or to imagination in poetry : an abnegation which was due to his fear of disillusionment. He saw very clearly the pains and penalties of the latter, but did not allow for a certain amount of romance being necessary to make life tolerable. Whatever we may think of the greatness of Swift's life, with his convictions and temperament, it hardly was a tolerable one.

Mr. Quintana makes a new point in insisting upon the richness and fertility of Swift's last period. " Nothing is further from the truth than the idea commonly entertained regarding Swift's latter years of activity. He was still the great artist, producing verse and prose of undiminished brilliance and intensity, and he remained an imperious public figure." So often this period is treated merely as an after-math. Yet it is in this period that he produced *Gulliver's Travels* and much of the best of his poetry. All the more reason for not agreeing with Mr. Quintana that *Gulliver* is inferior to *The Tale of a Tub*. There is a universality and a range in *Gulliver* which the earlier work does not touch ; it has, too, a depth of experience and conviction, where *The Tale of a Tub* is to me a trifle cold and academic. *Gulliver* is the work that the world has chosen ; and I do not think that that kind of consensus is likely to be wrong.

(ii)

The poetry of Swift is, it would appear, an esoteric taste. There is hardly anyone in our literary history, so far as I can call to mind, who had a liking for Swift's poetry — that is, since his own time. In ours, Yeats is a notable exception and perhaps the only poet whose verse is directly influenced by Swift ; in fact one may say, what has hardly been noticed, that the reading of Swift has been the chief influence in making the later verse of Yeats what it is, in content, tone, and perhaps even in form. But apart from Yeats, nobody. This lack of appreciation may in large part be due to the dominance of the romantic tradition in our literature, or at any rate in the reading of literature in our schools — the line that runs from Spenser, Shakespeare, the Caroline poets, to the great Romantics, Wordsworth, Coleridge, Shelley, and the later. But for some time it has been observable that such poets as Skelton, Donne, Dryden, Byron have been coming back into their own. One may hope that this great edition[1] — as it is not too much to call it — may have the effect of enabling Swift to do so too.

There is so much in his poetry which should appeal to this age : the uncompromising intellectualism of his attitude to experience, its essential hardness, realism, absence of illusions, its force, clarity and candour, its complete self-consciousness. There is no reason why his poetry should be an esoteric taste, except that the romantic tradition formed an idea of what poetry should be, an extremely rarefied and confined one, excluding much of our experience, and imposing that view upon the rich and natural variety of the subject matter of poetry. *Nihil humanum a me alienum puto.* The attitude of refined

[1] *The Poems of Jonathan Swift*, edited by Harold Williams.

romanticism is one from which the present generation of poets, from Mr. Eliot downwards, is happily delivering us. Of those still younger, Mr. Auden has always insisted on the necessity of bringing poetry into direct contact with life at every point, nourishing and re-vivifying it with every kind of experience, nothing too common, or mean, or — it may be added — abnormal to serve. It is a right and proper attitude ; anything else means the progressive refinement and pining away of poetry as under the pre-war Georgians. Hence it is that the work of the younger poets has meant a great liberation of impulse.

This makes it all the more appropriate that this superb work of scholarship, the definitive edition of Swift's poems, should appear now ; for I am sure that Swift has all kinds of things to say to our younger poets, not only as regards subject matter, intellectual temper, psychological approach, but even as regards form.

Hitherto, it is not too much to say that Swift has been *universally* underestimated as a poet. To some extent he is himself to blame ; for it has been at least partly due to that pride which made him so careless, where Pope was so careful, about the publishing of his poems. It was Swift's foible to care more for the reputation of a gentleman than of a poet : " I do not call him a poet that writes for his diversion ", he said, " any more than that gentleman, a fiddler, who amuses himself with a violin ". Certainly Swift left his poems, from the publishing point of view, in indescribable confusion, a veritable jungle, until Mr. Williams came along to clean it up, in a way nobody had done previously. (" No part of his writing has been so neglected and mishandled by editors ", Mr. Williams says firmly.) Partly again the neglect of Swift's poetry may be put down to the rapid change of fashion that came about after his death, in the latter half of the eighteenth century ; and in part, too, to his consistent, half-humorous depreciation of his own verse :

> " In Pope, I cannot read a line,
> But with a sigh I wish it mine."

But it does not say much for later generations of critics that they have been so ready to take a master of irony *au pied de la lettre*. Nor has the reception of this edition been much more discerning : so far as I have observed not one of the critics has appreciated Swift's poetry at its true worth. Their comments on it have for the most part only displayed the inadequacy of their critical apprehension. In this they have been oddly encouraged by the editor who, in a way unusual to editors, is either over-modest in his claim for his subject, or perhaps has not the courage to state it at its full value. Mr. Williams says that to the unhappiness of Swift's life there was added " the misfortune of falling short of his friends, Pope, Prior and Gay, in the poetic content of his work. . . . In verse Pope was his superior. Gay and Prior had a more lyrical gift. Swift's genius lay in the succession of Samuel Butler." I cannot but think that this judgment comes from accepting at their face-value the statements of the text-books in the schools. Swift was a less accomplished poet than Pope, and he had altogether less charm — though he was a more remarkable, a stronger genius, and so it appears in his verse no less than in his prose. But fall short of Prior ? of Gay ? Nonsense, Mr. Williams.

The truth is that he is one of the great English poets, and this edition makes it abundantly clear if ever. You have to consider first the range and variety of content in the poems. Mr. Quintana has made the point that Swift expressed himself more fully and more continuously in his verse than in his prose. Even Mr. Williams allows that " he was constantly turning verses as a common part of his everyday life, so much so that no part of his writing is as complete an autobiography ". But then he says, incomprehensibly, " Swift was not a poet by profession ". Mr. Williams is a great deal too modest. At the end of his Introduction, he concludes, " We are closer to Swift in his verse, and in his letters, than in his prose-writings " ; and he quotes Dr. Elrington Ball's words, " Without knowledge of his verse a true picture of Swift cannot be drawn. In his verse he sets forth his life as in a panorama, he shows more clearly than in his prose his peculiar turn of thought, and he reveals his character in all its phases." What is this but to say that Swift was just as much a poet, and as essentially, as he was a prose-writer ? He took earlier to the writing of verse, and in an early poem, the *Ode to Sir William Temple*, describes how everything that he writes turns to verse :

> " In vain all wholesome herbs I sow,
>   Where nought but weeds will grow.
> Whate'er I plant (like corn on barren earth)
>   By an equivocal birth
>   Seeds and runs up to poetry."

That in itself has a certain value as evidence of his early bent, not to be disregarded. And though there comes a break after these early poems, six years in which he is not known to have written any verse, it has not been observed before how early the characteristic traits of Swift appear; it is usual to mark a complete contrast between this first group of pindaric odes and the later poems. Yet in these first poems there is the declared intention to lash mankind for its folly :

> " My hate, whose lash just heaven has long decreed
> Shall on a day make sin and folly bleed."

There is " that scorn of fools, by fools mistook for pride ", the authentic note of contempt for the mob, the fatal incapacity for contentment which such thoughts, in the circumstances of human life, induce :

> " Madness like this no fancy ever seized,
> Still to be cheated, never to be pleased."

There is the inhibiting doctrine that all our knowledge comes only from memory, enshrined in a remarkable passage to which Mr. Yeats drew Mr. Williams' attention :

> " But what does our proud ignorance learning call,
>   We oddly Plato's paradox make good,
> Our knowledge is but mere remembrance all,
>   Remembrance is our treasure and our food ;
> Nature's fair table-book our tender souls
> We scrawl all o'er with odd and empty rules,
>   Stale memorandums of the schools ;
>   For learning's mighty treasures look
>   In that deep grave, a book."

All this in those first few poems, the neglected odes : the poems on which it is said Dryden commented, " Cousin Swift, you will never be a poet." It is impossible not to believe that Dryden said something of the sort ; for Swift underwent some kind of crisis, was silent for six years and then emerged with a totally different style, fully-formed, from which he never afterwards departed. But the themes were continuous and received their full development.

There is a case for saying that the more complete Swift is the Swift of the poems. There is nothing which he said in prose which he did not say as well in verse ; only the reputation of the author of *Gulliver* and of *The Tale of a Tub* has overshadowed the fact. There is all the savagery of the last book of *Gulliver* in *The Legion Club* ; and there are a good many things among the poems which are hardly paralleled in the prose. The good-humoured, below-stairs fun of *Mrs. Harris's Petition* is not quite recaptured in the *Directions to Servants* ; there is a note of bitterness in the latter which the poem is entirely without. It is noteworthy too that it was in verse only that Swift expressed the odd, precarious ambiguity of his relations with Vanessa ; nothing like it in his prose. And how well that complex, poised state of mind, neither wholly one thing nor the other, is described :

> " But what success Vanessa met,
> Is to the world a secret yet :
> Whether the nymph, to please her swain,
> Talks in a high romantic strain ;
> Or whether he at last descends
> To like with less seraphic ends ;
> Or, to compound the business, whether
> They temper love and books together ;
> Must never to mankind be told,
> Nor shall the conscious muse unfold."

As to form, Swift's verse was a perfect instrument for the expression of what he intended ; and it too has far greater variety than is usually realised. Even Dr. Johnson, whose criticism of Swift's poems was indolent and perfunctory, allowed this : " They [the poetical works] are, for the most part, what their author intended. . . . All his verses exemplify his own definition of a good style, they consist of ' proper words in proper places '."

It is true that the ends Swift set himself were too limited by his fear of romanticism, of giving himself away, of giving hostages to fortune in the realm of the emotions. One understands so well the attitude to the universe that made him repress his hopes and desires — his determination to have as far as possible his life under his own control, a rational control ; the belief, well justified in his own experience, in the insentience of the universe to the sufferings of men ; his own refusal to lay himself open to such torture. The paradox is that human life is such that it is just those persons who go out of their way to reject experience for fear of the suffering it may entail, who suffer most. And it is the particular irony of Swift's life that the man who imposed so rational a control upon his emotions, should have ended by losing his reason. Mr. Williams is right in saying that if he had been prepared to let himself go, he would have been a greater poet, that " he had something to give to English poetry that he never wholly gave ". On the other hand, it is that very sense of restraint, as was noted of Newman, that gives the impression of such power in reserve. And it is present, perfectly and precisely expressed, in all the metres and verse-forms he chose to write in.

The real criticism against Swift's poetry is not, then, on the score of lack of variety either of subject, or — though here there is more of a case — of metre, but rather a lack of variety in *tone*. Even here may not the same be said of many other poets whom the world has agreed to receive, Spenser, Shelley, Keats — though with them the tone is a different one ? It may be agreed that Swift, for a poet, wrote too much from the head, and not enough from the heart ; and it is not a good thing for a poet to write wholly from the head, never to allow himself freedom from the limits consciously imposed by the intellect. Yet that is what Swift did, and the result we have to take for what it is. It is silly to demand that it should be something other than it is, as so many have done, and say " This is not poetry ". They start from a carefully selective view of the poetic — one moreover which is not sanctioned by the practice of the poets — and then would impose that standard upon poetry like Swift's. As if English poetry were not a house with many mansions ! At any rate, the present generation of poets should have no difficulty in seeing in Swift not only a poet, but one of the major English poets.

Naturally, with a dominantly intellectual approach and with his experience of the world what it was, Swift's creative impulse turned mainly to satire. He might have said with his so much admired model, Juvenal : " *Difficile est non satiram scribere* ". And he was well aware of the criticism that might be pointed against him :

> " Perhaps I may allow, the Dean
> Had too much satire in his vein ;
> And seemed determined not to starve it,
> Because no age could more deserve it."

It is clear that this was the frame of mind which with him released the aesthetic impulse, that this was the psychological groove along which his inspiration ran most easily. There is a strong case for Swift's classicism, that controlled and deliberately directed emotion, as opposed to the romantic inspiration. For one thing his chief emotion was intellectual passion, a very rare thing in an Englishman ; which is perhaps why the English have never properly understood him or his poetry.

There will be the less excuse after this magnificent edition. The editing of the poems of Swift was the most difficult task of its character that could have been undertaken in the whole range of English literature ; its accomplishment is a triumph. Mr. Williams has been at work for years in the wilderness of Swift texts. No English poet offers greater problems or has a more complex and baffling bibliography. Mr. Williams has emerged with a canon of two hundred and fifty genuine poems, as against one hundred and fifty attributions and supposititious pieces. Nearly every one of these poems has its separate bibliography, and what Mr. Williams concludes in this field, it is safe to say, no one can challenge. The Clarendon Press has made what was already a work of scholarship of the first importance, also a thing of beauty.

XXVII

SARAH CHURCHILL IN OLD AGE

THIS is a delightful book,[1] one of those books which give one
so much pleasure, especially in these days, because they recall
an earlier, more agreeable age, adding something new and
fragrant to our knowledge of it, bringing out delicious letters
from the presses of old houses which have meant much in the
history of our country. In this case Woburn, whence Miss
Scott Thomson, with the encouragement of the Dukes of
Bedford, has got so much from which to give us pleasure and
instruction. The editing is all that it should be : Miss Scott
Thomson places the letters perfectly in their setting, tells us all
that we want to know to make the story clear, works them
skilfully into a characteristic conversation piece of the eighteenth
century.

The letters are those of the great Sarah, Duchess of Marlborough, written in her old age to her favourite granddaughter,
Diana, Duchess of Bedford, whom she had brought up and
loved with all the intensity of that electric, vibrant personality.
We all know what an astonishing personality Sarah's was : her
beauty, her passionate devotion to her famous husband, her
forthrightness, candour and sincerity, her possessiveness and
tenacity, the jealous spirit that went with it, her quarrelsome-
ness and next to impossibility for anybody to live with. She
was like a flame that scorched, rather than warmed, everything
that came near her. And yet one would forgive her everything
for her magnificent answer to the Duke of Somerset : "*If I were
young and handsome as I was, instead of old and faded as I am, and
you could lay the empire of the world at my feet, you should never share
the heart and hand that once belonged to John, Duke of Marlborough.*"

Sarah, whatever her faults, had great style : she was a
wonderful woman ; and these letters reveal her at her most
sympathetic. An old woman, crippled with gout so that she
has to be carried about in a chair and often cannot wield the

[1] *Letters of a Grandmother, 1732–1735*, edited by G. Scott Thomson.

pen, she is as indomitable as ever and has such zest for life —
and that is always irresistible. She is all for investigating new
experiences, seeing new sights ; those sharp eyes took in everything, her even sharper tongue commenting readily, and with
a devastating candour, on everybody. The very intensity of
her personality made her an admirable writer : she sees things
with such a direct, clear vision ; as she says about the finishing
of her house at Wimbledon, " My taste having always been to
have things plain and clean from a piece of wainscott to a lady's
face ". The indefatigable old lady in one day jolts along in her
coach from Holywell, near St. Albans, to Woburn, sees all over
the house, wearing out the invalid young Duke in the process
— though here very considerately, " I find he cannot endure
to be thought ill, and therefore did not take any notice that I
saw it, but contrived to sit down often as we talked over the
pictures " — dines there, pushes on to Northampton, and the
same night dictates a letter to her beloved Diana, describing
it all.

So she trundles along all the way to Scarborough — which
was just coming into fashion as a spa — to drink the waters
there for the benefit of her health. She does not seem to
have noticed that she might have spared herself the pains,
since she could have bought the waters bottled and drunk them
at home. Nor did she like the place when she got there :

" My Lord Chesterfield is here and he told me my house
was the envy of the place, but I think it a very bad one, very
dirty and so noisy that I am going to lay straw in the street
before my house to hinder the intolerable noise of the horses
and coaches that go by my window. I have seen nobody yet
that I know, but my Lady Gertrude Hotham and my Lord
Chesterfield, who are both extremely well bred, and if anything
could make this place tolerable, it would be their agreeable
conversation."

She was pleasantly surprised by a visit from the young Lord
Cowper, who brought her a favour,

" which is so extraordinary in this modern way of breeding that
I was surprised at it, and asked one that is acquainted with him
how he came to think of an old woman who was of no manner
of use, to which I was answered that he loved me because I had

been his father's friend. This is likewise a different way of thinking from the present age. He is an extremely honest young man and seems to have good sense. Those that know him say that he has a very good understanding and no vice. I think my Lord Grantham's daughter is a very lucky woman to be married to such a man, for it is certain she has no great title to sense from either side of her family, and had but £10,000."

Courtesy seems to have been hereditary in the Cowper family : for, years before, when Sarah had had to give up her apartments in St. James's Palace, on her quarrel with Queen Anne, the first Lord Cowper had been the only one of the Whig leaders, for whose sake she had sacrificed her favour with the Queen, to pay her a farewell visit. " The only Whig that behaved himself like a gentleman to me ", she wrote.

However agreeable this interlude, it was the same old Sarah underneath, with her scoriating comments on whoever or whatever earned her disapproval : " There is no company here that one would not choose to be deaf and dumb than to be with them ". Her grandson, Lord Sunderland, comes in for a severe wigging :

" if I were a young woman and was in circumstances to choose my lot, I had rather marry a man of sense with good morals than the Emperor of the world, that was a brute and a fool. My Lord Sunderland can't be called strictly the last, for as he speaks very little he imposes upon some. . . . Since he had money in his power, he has never disposed of any, that I have heard of, with any judgment ; nor has he governed himself in any one action by the rules of reason. He seems to be very fond of his person, though not a very pleasing one, and to bestow a good deal of time upon dress, and which is not a great commendation, even in our weak sex."

In fine she winds up, " By some of these accounts I send you, I think it is very plain that there is some tincture more or less of madness in almost everybody that one knows ".

Architects especially come in for her condemnation — she had had such an experience of them with the long warfare she had carried on with Vanbrugh over Blenheim Palace. Sarah, who in a way was very common-sense and hated pretentiousness, had never meant to have such an elephant of a building ;

and yet there she was, in spite of all her efforts, landed in the end with something like an English Escurial on her hands ! Architects ? — " I know of none that are not mad or ridiculous, and I really believe that anybody that has sense, with the best workmen of all sorts, could make a better house than any has been built these many years ". That was all very well in an aristocratic age, with standards formed by an *élite* which imposed its taste upon the whole society. But now that the flood-gates have long been open, the tradition broken, and there is complete chaos of taste, it is of melancholy, if also salutary interest to watch in these letters how their taste was formed, how it asserted itself, how watchful it was of every detail of proportion, how sensitive to beauty.

Sarah greatly admired Southampton House, the town house of the Russells in Bloomsbury — alas, like so many of London's finest houses, completely vanished.

" In this room at Southampton House, there is a set of blue and gold leather hangings which I bespoke and which is as fresh now as when it was put up. And I like it so extremely that I have bespoke the same to hang one of my rooms at Wimbledon. Southampton House is the handsomest, the most agreeable and the best turned that ever I saw either in town or country. There is everything in it that can be wished. He that built it (my Lord Southampton) has a great character, and I think that house represented one part of it very well."

It is a most interesting comment and shows how conscious people were about the lovely houses they put up in those days. It is only in such circumstances that a general standard of excellence and beauty is possible. But the letters are indeed full of the detail which reveals the loving care they lavished upon every aspect of their houses : Sarah's enthusiasm for the rich effect of the fashionable new combination of red damask hangings with white painted panelling, the great pier-glasses hung between windows to heighten the effect ; her preference for simple mouldings as against the elaborate carvings of the previous century, her passion for light in a house.

Sarah prided herself on being a woman of sense. " Sense " and " reason ", the " rules of reason ", were for ever on her lips or the tip of her pen : they were the tribute that the old Eve in her paid to the good form of the age. In fact she was the same impulsive, passionate, possessive woman she had always been ; beneath the formidable exterior of the dowager Duchess there beat the same ever-youthful heart that had exerted such a jealous hold upon John Churchill ånd had battled with such fierce passion for sole possession of the Queen's affections. It was power that was Sarah's foible, and she was so addicted to exacting submission that many of her intimates were forced into the position of being enemies to save their very independence of soul. With Sarah it was always a case of " He that is not with me is against me " ; she had that kind of egoism which forced everyone to choose for her or against her. Most of those who were close to her, it must be admitted, seem to have chosen the latter.

In her old years Sarah met her match in her granddaughter, Lady Bateman, a veritable chip of the old block. We find the Duchess trying to force her favourite granddaughter to choose between her and Lady Bateman : " But for Lady Bateman I must declare that I never can have any satisfaction in the conversation of anybody that has any commerce with her, I mean as to my own relations, for as to common acquaintances, I don't concern myself with what they do ". Diana must have been a clever, tactful girl to have slipped out of that dilemma. And then we find Sarah ending up, " I think I am not in my nature at all partial, and I am the more persuaded my notions are right in this ", etc. etc. Of course ; she was one of those people who are always right. But power was at the bottom of it all, and it was her egoistic, dynastic sense that was outraged. " But this, with a great many other things I know, makes me see plainly, that she is a great favourite at Court, and that must be from the hopes the ministers have of dividing a family, who, if they were wise would be strong enough to make any ministry afraid of disobliging them."

The tragedy of Sarah, as with all such persons of her temperament, was that she brought a good deal of ill-treatment down upon herself as the result of the intensity of her affections, her likes and dislikes. She was hardly treated by her daughters, the Duchesses of Marlborough and Montagu — disgracefully by the latter. For years relations had been broken off between them ; and when the elder daughter, Henrietta, died, Sarah wrote :

" You have judged very right in thinking that what has happened I should feel much more than I should have imagined formerly I could ever do. By which I am convinced that there is such a thing as natural affection, though I have heard many people laugh at that notion. . . . However it is a satisfaction to me that I did all that was in my power. But what do I dream of satisfaction when there are not two things upon earth at so impossible a distance as satisfaction and me ? "

She ends up with a picture of herself, as vivid as ever, reading Job for consolation : " But I can say with Job that my eyes are dim with sorrow, and my nerves are as shadows, and indeed I think my circumstances is more like his, than anybody's that I have heard of or read of ". This from the richest, and about the most famous woman in Europe, with £100,000 a year, widow of the great Duke who had adored her ! But egoism certainly makes for sharpness of outline.

And it is precisely that that makes her such a good letter-writer, for which we have reason to be grateful. *We* — two hundred years away, and not among the exposed circle of her relations, not even " common acquaintances " — do not have to put up with the tantrums, the upbraidings ; we have only to sit tight and be grateful for someone who is so unself-conscious, so natural and immediate in her reactions, that she might even now be in the room with us. There are a good many writers of repute who have not that gift. Sarah was a born writer. We see her as she saw herself, " labouring like a pack-horse every day " to save her grandson, the young Duke, from the cheats ; " it is probable the Duke of Marlborough may think £20 nothing ; but it is a great deal in £46 ". Now she is reading Sir William Temple, having put by the Book of Job. Or she is suggesting that Diana should get somebody " to pick out what is most ridiculous in the reign of King James the first, and read to you. There is a great deal so tedious, that I pass it over, but his love letters to the Duke of Buckingham are incomparable ". Sensible, unsqueamish age ! She cannot abide powdered hair in a picture, though Sir Godfrey Kneller painted her hair like that :

" I never knew anything of it till many years after his death I saw it at his house in the country. . . . But it was a very odd fancy in him to make my hair look like the Queen's [Caroline's] when she came first into England, clotted all over with powder, when I fancy the best thing I had was the colour of my hair."

Sometimes Sarah gives us a whole scene, almost in the manner of the famous, the conscious artists among letter-writers. There is a charming account of what happened to Queen Caroline in Kensington Park :

" Two or three days ago, Her sacred Majesty was in danger of being ravished. She was walking from Kensington to London early in the morning and having a vast desire to appear more able in everything than other people, she walked so fast as to get before my Lord Chamberlain and the two princesses upon one of the causeways, quite out of sight. . . . My Lord Grantham meeting a country clown asked him if he had met any person and how far they were off? To which he answered he had met a jolly crummy woman with whom he had been fighting some time to kiss her. I am surprised at the man's fancy. And my Lord Grantham was so frightened that he screamed out and said it was the Queen. Upon which the country fellow was out of his wits, fell upon his knees, cried and earnestly begged of my Lord Grantham to speak for him for he was sure he should be hanged for what he had done. But did not explain further what it was. And her Majesty does not own more than that he struggled with her, but that she got the better of him."

Caroline, who was a good sort, made no fuss about it, seems indeed to have been amused and taken it in good part. Sarah, for whom Caroline was much too able a woman for her to like, wished somebody would make a ballad of it ; "for when I was at Scarborough, I learned to sing and I fancy I could perform such a one very well without any graces ".

Or there is a charming conversation piece, like one of those so characteristic pictures of the time — a Hogarth, for there is a spice of caricature about it — of Sarah, the Duchess of Manchester and Lady Bristol at play at Tunbridge Wells. Sarah did not approve of the last, " for she is a mighty ridiculous woman, entirely wicked in all things. But though her actions are bad, I can't think her what one calls a fool. She is worthless, but there is a mixture of cunning and sometimes a good deal of wit and sharpness in her answers." In spite of this unpromising beginning, a treaty of peace ensued and Lady Bristol persuaded Sarah to give a party at her house to play, and " one of the chief preliminaries of this peace was that she should stake ". When Lady Bristol sat down to play she pretended to have lost her purse.

" There was no remedy for that : so we played as well as we could. She sent several messages about for this purse and acted the part pretty well. And yet she said, there was eight or ten guineas in it and a double moidore. . . . When the play was over, I told her that I had often looked into my pockets for things and have not found them at first, having four little pockets in one great one. And I desired her to search again all her pockets, which are much the same as mine. She said she was sure, and had not it. Then I desired the Duchess of Manchester and I might search the pockets. And so we went to romps. But she struggled with us and got the better, for I would not carry the jest too far."

One sees in this glimpse, under the formality of the age, the horse-play. At the same time as they had far greater elegance in life and taste, a robust and lovely creativeness in art, they were also coarser and more natural, both more formal and more spontaneous. Who would not prefer such a combination to the insipidity, the erosion of taste characteristic of a democratic age, standards geared down to the lowest common measure of understanding and appreciation, a brave new social order intellectually chaotic and aesthetically null ? It is more agreeable to think of Sarah, going to romps with Lady Bristol and the Duchess of Manchester, at seventy-three : how can one resist that ?

All the best side of Sarah comes out in her love for her adored Diana. Early on in these letters she writes : " Your desiring me to take care of myself for your sake is very kind, and I return it by assuring you that I desire to live only for you ". Her formal " dear Lady Russell ", or " dear Duchess of Bedford ", gives way to " dear Di " and in the end " dear Cordelia ". Sarah loved her for her sweet and considerate ways ; she even fancied that she took after her grandmother in this respect. " Notwithstanding, I have had the same way of acting as yours has been to me, with all those that I ever loved ; but you are charming in all your thoughts and actions."

Over the later letters there is the shadow of a fear : Diana's health was not good. There was Sarah in these years engaged in building yet another house, her fifth, at Wimbledon, which was designed for Diana. Sarah was as insatiably interested as ever in pictures and furnishing, planning and projecting, what she was going to have at Wimbledon and what she was *not* going to have, her zest for life undiminished. But Diana's tenuous hold on life was failing ; a horrid fear gripped her grandmother's heart. At last the day came when Sarah had to get out the great tent which the Duke had used on his campaigns — " to think that it was your dear Grandfather's tent, when he did such wonderful things to secure the nation from being enslaved by the French King " — and have it set up on the lawns at Woburn so that her beloved girl might breathe.

In all the letters we never hear Diana's voice directly, but we can gather how kind and tactful she was with her termagant of a grandmother, how lovable and sweet she must have been. Alas, Diana never inherited the house upon which the old Duchess lavished such thought and care. By the time it was ready, the girl who held such a place in her heart was dead.

XXVIII

HORACE WALPOLE AND GEORGE MONTAGU

VIRGINIA WOOLF has made it impossible for anyone coming after her to review Horace Walpole's letters, with her perfect essay on the impossibility of doing justice to the new Yale edition of them. So much work has gone into it, such mountainous collections of correspondence, photostats of everything extant in Horace Walpole's hand, a great deal of the library he had around him at Strawberry Hill, the books he printed at his press in the garden there, the Gothic lantern that shed its dim medieval light upon the staircase — so complete is the work that it is with a sense of amusement that one thinks one comes across the slightest slip such as the attribution of Mount Edgcumbe to Devon instead of to Cornwall. No doubt a trifle like the Tamar estuary is invisible from the fastnesses of Farmington, Conn., where Mr. Lewis' stupefying collection of Walpoliana reposes. An error, or the omission of a note to tell us which Duke is being referred to (as in vol. ii, p. 261), comes as a shock, though a pleasant shock, like an unexpected, tricky catch of a ball in the cricket field.

The Yale edition has now got as far as the Correspondence with Montagu,[1] the best of all Horace Walpole's series of letters, taken all round. It contains some of his most famous letters, like those describing the executions of the Jacobite lords after the '45, the funeral of George II and the coronation banquet of George III, the description of Walpole's visit after many years to his father's great house at Houghton with all its memories, the celebrated party at Vauxhall, that on the summer of 1759 with its victories and golden weather ("Our bells are worn threadbare with ringing for victories "). But apart even from all these, which have become almost set-pieces with frequent quotation, Walpole is at his best, his gayest and most spontaneous, in writing to Montagu. They

---

[1] *Horace Walpole's Correspondence with George Montagu*, edited by W. S. Lewis and R. S. Brown. 2 vols.

were friends from their school-days at Eton ; they both belonged to the innermost circle of the great Whig families ; they knew everybody. While Walpole lived the busiest and most active social life in London, or constantly entertained at Strawberry Hill, Montagu lazed his time away in the country and was content to hear what happened in the world from the most brilliant and vivacious letters anybody ever got. He was so indolent, and often unresponsive, that he did not deserve to have them. But the indolent and impassive frequently have an unaccountable attraction for the active-minded and sprightly ; and so it was with Walpole and George Montagu.

To all the gaieties and charms of a Walpole correspondence there is added the psychological interest in this case of the curious relation between these two. From the very beginning it is Walpole who makes the pace, the more interesting man making up to the less. " Write soon," he says, " for I love your letters." How often he had to repeat the request in the years that were to come, until even his vivacity flagged against such massive unresponsiveness and he was driven to complain. " I hate you for being so indifferent about me ", Walpole writes ; " I live in the world, and yet love nothing, care a straw for nothing, but two or three old friends that I have loved these thirty years." And again, just before Montagu allowed their friendship to lapse into silence : " But I grow old ; and the less time we have to live together, the more I feel a separa-tion from a person I love so well ".

Montagu was a lazy bachelor, a sort of FitzGerald, who dreamed his life away in the country, drinking his port, nursing the gout, dozing by the fire in his successive country houses. Not that he had FitzGerald's gifts ; but all the same he was not without talent. He was a very good letter-writer, when he chose to exert himself — as we can now see from this first publication of his letters in full ; he was well read, interested like Walpole in antiquarian things, amusing ; he must have had charm. The real passion of his life, as with a good many bachelors who do nothing about it, was for his family, the great Montagu clan, the Cues as they are called all through their correspondence ; anything about the doings of any of them was grateful news to him sunk in rustic sloth at Greatworth or Adderbury ; any family portrait he could pick up, or Walpole for him, was grist to his mill and went into his collection. He, too, was something of a collector, in this a follower of Walpole's ; and they both shared a romantic sensibility to nature. He was as proud in his quieter way, of his own Greatworth as Horace was of Strawberry Hill. " My Greatworth begins to put on its pretty looks ", he writes in April 1763, " and I amuse myself with washing its face and powdering its hair, and I hope for a country lass you will not find her quite inelegant." One misses the lyrical note of Walpole's love for Strawberry, " where [May 1761] my two passions, lilacs and nightingales, are in full bloom. I spent Sunday as if it was Apollo's birthday, Gray and Mason were with me, and we listened to the nightingales till one o'clock in the morning." Or the sharpness of a poet in his observation : " observing [May 1763] all the way I came the proof of the duration of this east wind, for on the west side the blossoms were so covered with dust one could not distinguish them ; on the eastern hand the hedges were white in all the pride of May ".

With such a friend, the nervous, highly-strung, electric Walpole could be perfectly at ease. He wrote Montagu all the gossip of the town, all the events and happenings, the great occasions of public life as well as the tittle-tattle of private life. But we must never forget that the small-talk, the amusements, amenities, extravagances were those of a society that was intensely political at heart, of an aristocracy that ruled England and made an Empire. It is that that gives a solid foundation of rock to all the bubble and effervescence on the surface, that makes all the difference between Horace Walpole's " town " and Proust's Faubourg. Walpole himself was an active politician who worked and intrigued hard for his side — Macaulay forgot this, among other things, when he treated him as a mere *farceur*, and the Victorians followed suit. Almost the deepest thing in Horace was his pride in his father, the great man who ruled England as Prime Minister longer than anyone else and who ended his career under a cloud. His son found it hard to forgive anyone who had contributed, however many years ago, to his father's fall. And so we have the unforgettable portraits of Newcastle for ever behaving absurdly on the public stage, making a fool of himself at George II's funeral :

" He fell into a fit of crying the moment he came into the chapel and flung himself back in a stall, the Archbishop hovering over him with a smelling bottle — but in two minutes his curiosity got the better of his hypocrisy and he ran about the chapel with his glass to spy who was or was not there, spying with one hand and mopping his eyes with t'other. Then returned the fear of catching cold, and the Duke of Cumberland, who was sinking with heat, felt himself weighed down, and turning round, found it was the Duke of Newcastle standing upon his train to avoid the chill of the marble."

The Duke was an Aunt Sally for everybody, but even his Duchess comes in for a *coup de patte* from Walpole : " On Tuesday the operation of shaving was happily performed on the upper lip of her Grace the Duchess of Newcastle by a celebrated artist from Paris sent over on purpose by the Earl of Albemarle."

The two old bachelors talked antiquities, books, projects for planting, building, printing, improving ; and, as bachelors will, they talked bawdy. " Dick Edgcumbe is shut up with the itch ; the ungenerous would ascribe it to Mrs. Day, but he denies it, owning, however, that he is very well contented to have it, as nobody will venture on her ". Lord Calthorpe has gone mad and walks down Whitehall with red ribbons in his hair to insist on seeing the King. Lady Townshend falls madly in love with the Jacobite Lord Kilmarnock at his trial. We are kept well posted in news of the health of Mr. Chute of the Vine : he is always in or out of bed with the gout, and nothing else happens to him at all, except an occasional chaste visit to Strawberry Hill. " Here I am with the poor Chutehed, who has put on a shoe but today for the first time." " The poor Chute rose from the gout, and Lady Carberry who can raise nothing " are now at Frogmore. Mr. Chute has another very severe fit of the gout ; and now again he is out of his bed — one feels it is but for a very short while.

How much we have to be grateful for to this friendship which has left us such a portrait, with all its colours, its lights and shades, of that age and world ! One still derives some sense of it from the gaping windows and broken fanlights of those streets in and around Arlington Street. " From my earliest memory, Arlington Street has been the ministerial street." But how much more one gets it from these letters ! Two days before her death Lady Hervey wrote to her son : " I feel my dissolution coming on — but I have no pain — what can an old woman desire more ? " The brave, stoical, *sensible* eighteenth century, besides its elegance, its colour and gallantry !

As one reads these letters, something happens to one. The eyes wander away from the printed page ; one loses oneself in a dream, as in listening to music ; one sees the world through the eyes of Horace Walpole ; it is his world that one sees. It is the summer of 1753 once more; George II is king, and the garden at Strawberry Hill is at the height of all its sweets ; it is the hottest day of the summer and in the evening the Duc de Mirepoix, the French ambassador at the Court of St. James', walks slowly in the *beau milieu* of Brentford Town, without any company but a brown lapdog with long ears, two pointers, two pages, three footmen, and a vis-à-vis following him. Or it is May in 1763, and Miss Pelham is entertaining a party *al fresco* at Esher : a magnificent dinner, cloaked in the modesty of earthenware ; French horns and hautboys on the lawn. They walk to the belvedere on the summit of the hill, where a threatened storm only serves to heighten the beauty of the land- scape, a rainbow on a dark cloud falling precisely behind the tower of a neighbouring church, between another tower and the building at Claremont. Or it is March 1766, and it is snowing in Paris where Horace is on a visit to Madame du Deffand, and clouds of dust are whisking about the streets and quays, edged with an east wind that gets under one's very shirt : " I should not be quite sorry if a little of it tapped my lilacs on their green noses, and bade them wait for their master ". A few weeks later and he is at Livry in the *forêt de Bondi*, at the little pavilion where Madame de Sévigné used to write to her daughter : " on one side of the garden leading to the great road is a little bridge of wood on which the dear woman used to wait for the carrier that brought her daughter's letters ".

What is it that makes the snow, or the maytime, of two hundred years ago so affecting ? If we could say, we should lay our finger on the nature of poetry or music. We feel about Horace Walpole as he felt about Madame de Sévigné : it is this sense of the past, apprehended through that prism which reflects its beauty, that gives his letters, like hers, their dream-like quality. For Horace Walpole, like Proust, an aesthete to his finger-tips, was a poet : a poet who found the perfect form for his vision and experience.

XXIX

THE LETTERS OF JUNIUS

WHO wrote the *Letters of Junius*? I wish I could tell you for certain. For the authorship of those famous Letters has long been, and still is, one of the greatest mysteries of our literature. Still, it is to the fact that they have provided an outstanding literary puzzle that they very largely owe their fame and fascination. Few people can resist a puzzle, and that this has been found a very good one, very knotty to unravel, may be witnessed by the fact that some fifty different people have been put forward at various times as " Junius " and a whole small library written to settle his identity.

We now know that we shall never be able to *prove* who " Junius " was : the secret in his own day was astonishingly well kept and it seems to have died with him. At the same time, as the result of the careful work of a good many scholars, there is the cumulative probability, I think amounting to virtual certainty, that the author was Philip Francis.

What were the *Letters of Junius*? Why did they make such a sensation in their time and retain their interest long after the original circumstances which brought them forth had vanished? Who was Philip Francis? It is at least possible to answer these questions.

The Letters were a series of contributions to a London newspaper at a very critical period in our history — the early years of the reign of George III. The first appeared in the *Public Advertiser* on 21 January 1769, the last on 21 January 1772, so that this unknown author held the attention of the public, stirring up feeling against the Government, lashing Ministers with all the resources of a brilliant invective, agitating, arousing opinion, exciting the most intense personal animosities, during a period of three years.

The period was in many ways like the disgraceful Baldwin-Chamberlain epoch which we have been living through in the past ten years, and which has landed us in the situation in which we are now.[1] It was a period of decadence after the great triumphs of the Seven Years' War, which under the genius of Pitt had elevated this country to the greatest height of power it has ever known.

After the war was over the governing circle turned away from the great man under whose star it had been won and gave itself up to the delights of faction fights, which were exploited by that obstinate fool George III (who was cunning enough for his own ends). The pity of it was that the one man of genius, William Pitt, played into the hands of these smaller men by the mistakes he made and at times was incapacitated by illness, so that he was effectively kept out of power. Meanwhile, the American Colonies were provoked and teased into rebellion ; our enemies on the Continent, France and Spain, were enabled to steal marches on us, to get ahead of us ; the Navy, which Pitt had left stronger than the combined fleets of France and Spain, was neglected and we were out-numbered at sea ; the Army got demoralised, and Pitt's able generals displaced to make way for yes-men.

Above all there was a fatuous spirit of self-complacency exuded by the Government (so like the National Government of 1931–9), a spirit of levity which led them to appoint second-rate and third-rate men to crucial posts and to keep out men of energy and ability. The Prime Minister, Lord North, who was a sort of Baldwin of the time, popular with both King and people, himself said on one occasion of the army officers he had appointed : " I do not know what effect they will have upon the enemy ; I only know that they make me tremble." The upshot of that disgraceful decade in our history was that we lost the American Colonies, and had to redeem the situation by a twenty-year struggle with Revolutionary and Napoleonic France. *Absit omen !*

" Junius " was a convinced, a devoted follower of the great man, Pitt (Lord Chatham), who at the end of 1768 had recovered from his two years of mysterious illness and re-appeared like an avenging spirit upon the scene of his former labours and triumphs to find all in confusion. George III's contemptible Government — like the National Government —

[1] Written June 1941.

spent all its energy in clinging to office at any price and had none left over to look after the interests and security of the country. They had alienated the people and divided the country by their determined exclusion of the Radical Wilkes from Parliament, who, three times elected by the voters of Middlesex, was as many times excluded from the House and in the end somebody else declared elected in his stead. The House of Commons was bought — as in a way it has been by the Conservative Head Office since 1931 ; the King himself was the chief borough-monger and agent of corruption. He was obstinately determined upon alienating America, while neglecting the real interests of our security and failing to stand up to Spain over the Falkland Islands — which played something like the part that Czechoslovakia did in Mr. Chamberlain's appeasement plans — if " plans " is the word for anything so abject.

Chatham emerged from retirement determined to reverse all this. He formed a united front with the Whigs to drive this effete Government out of power and return to power himself while there was yet time to save the country. In the campaign which he launched, his most effective weapon in the Press was the unknown and terrible " Junius ". The freedom of the Press was all the more important since Parliament was bought. " Junius " made it his business then to fight each and every of these campaigns, since it was the Government's aim to muffle Press criticism as well.

" Junius " was in the possession of weapons which made him a very formidable adversary. In the first place he *knew* everything : he had that great advantage over so many political writers on the fringe of politics that he was inside and did know what was going on — very often things of so private and personal a nature that his letters bordered on political blackmail. That, added to his anonymity, redoubled his power : nobody knew where these blows came from or where or on whom they might fall next. In addition he wrote a singularly fine and effective style. Only one political writer of the time came up to him, and that was Burke, which made some people suppose that Burke was " Junius ". But in reality their two styles were very different ; where Burke's periods are like a resplendent bouquet of rich and variegated flowers, " Junius's " sentences are like the flash of a swift and elegant dagger.

When somebody pleaded that the Prime Minister — as it might be Lord Baldwin — was a virtuous man and had done some good, " Junius " replied in a flash : " You do good, my Lord, by stealth — and the rest is upon record ". Here is his description of the ministry, fiddling while the Empire was foundering :

" While the fate of Great Britain is at stake, these worthy Councillors dispute without decency, advise without sincerity, resolve without decision, and leave the measure to be executed by the man who voted against it. This, I conceive, is the last disorder of the State."

Anybody who came to the defence of the Ministry received more than he bargained for. Sir William Draper, a retired and well-sinecured officer, took up his pen on their behalf. " Junius " asked :

" After selling the companions of your victory in one instance, and after selling your profession in the other, by what authority do you presume to call yourself a soldier ? . . . Are your flatteries of the commander-in-chief directed to another regiment, which you may again dispose of on the same honour-able terms ? We know your prudence, Sir William, and I should be sorry to stop your preferment."

He attacked Ministers and their appointees mercilessly, and in nearly every case he proved to be right. He was justified up to the hilt in his attack on General Burgoyne, whom the Ministers promoted by favouritism :

" Let me ask your Grace for what military merits you have been pleased to reward him ? He had a regiment of dragoons, which one would imagine was at least an equivalent for any services *he* ever performed."

That man was the general who by his incompetence later surrendered the British Army at Saratoga. The Government had withdrawn Carleton, the ablest British general in America. " Junius " was right. We had to pay a pretty price for the years of incompetence and smug self-complacency — " the

years that the locusts have eaten ", as Mr. Churchill has
called them.

" Junius " did not fear to attack the highest in the land and
indict George III, who was at the back of it all — much like
the Conservative Head Office in our time. He did not hesitate
to imply that if they persisted in their course, a revolution
would be the only remedy :

" The prince who imitates their conduct [the Stuarts']
should be warned by their example ; and while he plumes himself upon the security of his title to the crown, should remember
that, as it was acquired by one revolution, it may be lost by
another."

But "Junius" and his great leader, Chatham, were defeated
by the unprincipled gang gathered round George III, who
clung obstinately to power — like Baldwin and Chamberlain
— and went on his way to the downfall of the country and the
loss of America.

All the signs point to the author of these Letters being
Philip Francis. He was a young civil servant who had been in
the Secretary of State's office, had been for a short time secretary
to Chatham, and was at the time of the " Junius " Letters in
the War Office. He had a great deal of inside information
about what was going on, and it seems that he got more
information from sources even higher up in politics — from
Lord Temple, Chatham's brother-in-law, and Calcraft, who
was a go-between Chatham and Francis. It does not appear
that the great man himself knew the identity of " Junius ",
though " Junius " sometimes sent him his advice and Chatham
adopted the very phraseology suggested by Francis.

Francis was a young man of very great ability, immense
industry, and remarkable accomplishments, with a distinct
literary gift. As a civil servant he was debarred from saying
in public all that he felt and wanted to say — though there was
no such stringent rule in those days as in ours. He was one of
the circle of young men who believed that Chatham " could
save the country and that nobody else could ". In that he was
quite right ; and since he believed it with an ardent conviction,
who can blame him for taking the steps he did — if it was he
who did — to warn the country of its danger ? Would that we

had had in the past ten years another "Junius" — some official entrenched in Whitehall who could have told the country from the inside all that was going on and all that was amiss ! But no doubt, as in "Junius's" day, a stupid and complacent people would have refused to listen until the danger was at the door.

XXX

WILLIAM AND DOROTHY WORDSWORTH

(i)

No poet has written more revealingly of the inner processes of a poet's mind than Wordsworth. Certainly not those poets who have taken to prose analysis, for something essential is missed in the process, as Wordsworth himself held :

" danger cannot but attend
Upon a Function rather proud to be
The enemy of falsehood, than the friend
Of truth, to sit in judgment than to feel."

Prose analysis helped to kill the poetic genius of Coleridge. A concrete descriptiveness is necessary, is perhaps the only way, to give a picture of the poetic imagination at work. It can only describe itself in terms of itself, as only music can say what it has to say for itself, and cannot be rendered in words. And this is what *The Prelude* does. It is not far-fetched to compare it with Proust as a rendition in self-awareness of aesthetic experience and artistic creation.

It is, indeed, a most wonderful poem, and of an extra-ordinary modernity. Though not a greater poem than *Paradise Lost*, which Wordsworth always had at the back of his mind in composing it, it is in a way even more interesting. *Paradise Lost* is, in part, a majestic fabric of consolation in art for defeat in the external world of politics. But *The Prelude* has the excitement for a contemporary mind of describing the hopes raised by a great revolutionary movement of emancipation, that of 1789, the betrayal of these hopes, disillusionment, the utter blankness of despair, sickness of mind and heart — and the way out Wordsworth found in a return to his own inner integrity, the solace of a right relation to nature, the with-drawal from the public life into seclusion, the life of poetry.

Professor Havens does not deal much with this side of Wordsworth, though he does say in an aside that it was the reaction from the French Revolution that made him a great poet.[1] His is an analysis rather of the character of Wordsworth's poetic mind in itself. As such, though the Professor moves heavily, not to say lumpily, and is vastly repetitive, it is sure and convincing, even if he had not made it irrefutable by the sheer bulk of the evidence he has cited. He devotes successive chapters to the various characteristics of the poet's mind, his matter-of-factness, anti-rationalism, his attitude to nature and the mystical experience. Of these the best — and it is a tribute to the book's solid sense and learning — are the most difficult : Wordsworth's inner religion and imagination.

We should all probably agree with Professor Havens that Wordsworth was, in a sense, profoundly religious. But what were Wordsworth's religious beliefs ? Was he a pantheist or not ? On these difficult and really rather obscure questions the Professor has a very just and convincing summing-up. Wordsworth was certainly not orthodox, neither in the first half of his life, as is well known, nor really, according to Professor Havens, in the latter half when he was externally more conforming.

In short, Wordsworth's real belief seems to have been in the transcendent power of the imagination, as not only the chief means of communication, but the creative instrument in the relation between man and nature ; his religion that of the poet who believes that the apprehension of the world *qua* beauty is the supreme value in life and gives sustaining power to man. On this side he was even more insistent upon its ethical than its aesthetic value. But its source and sphere are the mind of man, which, in the light of this belief, as Wordsworth says in the very last lines of *The Prelude*,

> " becomes
> A thousand times more beautiful than the earth
> On which he dwells, above this frame of things
> (Which 'mid all revolution in the hopes
> And fears of men, doth still remain unchanged)
> In beauty exalted, as it is itself
> Of quality and fabric more divine."

Professor Havens has devoted fifteen years of research to this

[1] R. D. Havens, *The Mind of a Poet*.

P

immense tome of nearly 700 pages, which we must regard, for its learning, accuracy, and sense, as a standard study of Wordsworth's mind, particularly as revealed in *The Prelude*. But it would have been better to divide the work into two short practicable volumes : the first consisting of a shortened introduction to Wordsworth, the second of the admirable, if only briefer, commentary on *The Prelude* in detail. The intending purchaser could then have taken his choice.

(ii)

On a June morning in the year 1800 a coroneted landau passed by a little cottage in the Lake District. The ladies turned an eye of interest upon the garden and the two figures sitting on the sodded wall, and well they might, for the figures were those of William and Dorothy Wordsworth at the beginning of those wonderful years together at Dove Cottage, Grasmere, which made such a difference in the history of English poetry.

There never can have been, I suppose, in the story of literature another case of a poet who owed so much to his sister — hardly of any who owed so much to anybody else — as Wordsworth did to Dorothy. There was an extraordinary unity of sympathy and sensibility between them — to such a degree that they almost saw the world through the same eyes, noted the same lights and shadows and meanings in its changing aspects. Dorothy, herself " more than half a poet ", was in these years a half of William's mind ; it might be said that she lived in and for his mind. It is not too much to say that she was deeply in love with her brother. Not surprising then that the " Grasmere Journal " which she kept from 1800 to 1803, those years when Wordsworth's creative inspiration was at its height, when much of *The Prelude* and many of the loveliest lyrics were written, is an astonishing record from close up of the ways and workings of a poet's mind, a document of the first importance in our literature.

Hitherto it has been known only in selection : Professor Knight printed the high lights, chiefly passages showing her minute and loving observancy of nature. Those were enough to reveal a prose writer of extreme sensibility and distinction : a poet who wrote in prose (sometimes Dorothy only just falls behind her brother's best poetry, as in her exquisite description of the daffodils by the lakeside ; often her prose rendering of the same scene is better than William's verse). But now for the first time we can view their life in the round, with the planting and hoeing, mending and baking, along with reading Chaucer and Spenser and Shakespeare, the writing of poetry. It makes it all so much more vivid and moving, the poverty, the simplicity, the dedication. Never was there a household more dedicated to poetry than theirs was : they lived poetry, as nobody except perhaps Shelley and Keats did, and Tennyson later. And all the while there is the sense of happiness and the enjoyment of life that rises like a fragrance from these journals. Then, too, there were the intimate friendships, " dear Coleridge " coming and going, the letters going to and fro to Annette in France : there was no mystery made about it, and the Journal includes, what is quite new, an account of the journey William and Dorothy made to Calais to see Annette and her child for the last time before William married Mary Hutchinson.

But apart from the light these Journals throw upon the greatest of English poets, after Shakespeare and Milton, they stand on their own feet as the work of one whom Professor de Selincourt describes as " probably the most remarkable and the most distinguished of English prose writers who never wrote a line for a publisher ". Dorothy's chief prose work, in a sense, was her delightful " Recollections of a Tour made in Scotland " (1803), which circulated among her friends in manuscript. It is deservedly famous now. But Professor de Selincourt prints much fuller versions than have hitherto been known of the " Journal of a Tour on the Continent " (1820) and her " Second Tour in Scotland " (1822), besides other excursions.

This definitive edition of the Journals is a distinguished contribution to English literary scholarship ; and it makes one proud of English publishers that at such a time so beautiful a book can be produced.[1]

[1] *The Journals of Dorothy Wordsworth*, edited by E. de Selincourt. 2 vols.

XXXI

THE YOUNG FROUDE

COMING up through Devon the other day, the slopes of Dartmoor in view from the train, succeeded by the lovely spacious landscape from Ivybridge to Brent, then the reddened waves curling in to the foot of the red cliffs by Teignmouth, I derived a peculiar, pointed pleasure from reading that book of a Devonshireman, Froude's *The Nemesis of Faith*.

Of all the great Victorians Froude, it seems to me, is the writer least estimated at his proper worth and most worth while reviving. There is so much in him that should appeal to our age ; in many ways he had more affinities with the twentieth century than with the nineteenth : the strain of scepticism in him for one thing, the historian's relativism that made him see all religions as myths and men's philosophies as rationalisations of their interests and desires; his independence of mind, detached from either party in politics, which saw the cardinal importance of good leadership to a people rather than the emptier *clichés* of demagogic appeal, so dangerous if believed in.

And what a magnificent writer ; what a stylist ! So infinitely better than Carlyle, to whom he deferred, like the rest of the Victorians, as a great man and a major prophet. And I am not so sure that in addition to writing better, he had not more to offer in what he said, at any rate more sense, than Carlyle had. Give me Froude every time : a better historian, a better writer, a more sceptical, a more subtle, intelligence.

Perhaps one should not wonder why such a man was so controversial a figure to the Victorians — so downright they were, so unsubtle, so censorious and convinced, so sensitive to any departure from orthodoxy, so crude. And yet it is a little difficult to understand quite why Froude was so much harassed and attacked. Every book of his provoked an outburst of criticism and controversy from the first to the last. His person-ality itself was regarded, I think very unjustly, as in some curious way questionable. It was a strange, and characteristic, fate that shrouded his greatest friendship and the chief intellectual influence in his later life, that of Carlyle, in a more resounding storm of controversy than any other.

Yet he was read. He held people's attention. He had admirers, if few defenders and no followers. He was a lonely figure, at the same time as he was much sought after and a distinguished person in society. But one cannot doubt that all this criticism and controversy had a deep effect upon him, though he kept himself in restraint and hardly referred in his writings to the detraction which followed him all his days. Lytton Strachey has tried to put the vendetta with which Freeman pursued Froude in a comic light ; it was anything but comic really, and shows up Strachey in a rather deplorable role, always ready to sacrifice truth to a joke, even a poor one. On Froude the ceaseless attacks had the effect of driving him in upon himself, making him aloof, and giving him a rather cynical and sardonic air in public — though with his intimates he was an open and brilliant talker on all subjects. It had the further, and regrettable, effect of forbidding any official biography, and most of his letters and papers were destroyed.

The result is that he is much less well known than many lesser men among the Victorians. Think if we had only had something comparable to Sir G. O. Trevelyan's classic *Life and Letters of Macaulay*. The materials for it were there all right : the background of that brilliant family of brothers, the masterful figure of Archdeacon Froude, the lovely countryside of the Dart where they were all brought up, the Oxford of the Oxford Movement with Froude's close contact with its leaders, the friendships with Matthew Arnold, Clough, Carlyle, the life in Wales and on the Devon coast with its open-air interests, angling, sea-fishing, sailing, the voyages he made all over the world, like his west country forebears, the Forgotten Worthies whom he caused to be remembered in a famous essay. Alas, I am afraid there will never be a *Life and Letters of Froude* worthy to stand by Trevelyan's Macaulay now. It is sad to think that there might have been.

But that is just like Froude's luck. I cannot help thinking that he was an unlucky man to have had so much trouble.

The Nemesis of Faith is chiefly known for having been publicly burnt by the Sub-rector of his college at Oxford when Froude was a young Fellow. It is deserving of attention on more serious grounds and for its own sake. Its subject is the ferment of thought about the foundations of faith stirred up by the Oxford Movement, the dilemma of belief which was such a critical issue to sensitive minds in the mid-nineteenth century and especially to those brought up in a clerical environment like Froude, whose livelihood and career were involved in it.

We need not pay much attention to the story : it is the auto-biography in it that counts. And though Froude was forced to disclaim that it was autobiographical, in the way in which authors sometimes are, in a preface to the second edition (1849), in fact there was no mistaking the parallel between his hero's case and his own. Markham Sutherland has the same struggle with his father, the same difficulties about the clerical career — which, like Froude, who stopped at deacon's orders, he drops — the same intellectual doubts about the inspiration of the Bible, the divinity of Christ, the historic and exclusive claims of Christianity, the same horror at the wicked nonsense of the doctrine of eternal punishment. Religions were all myths ; truth was not to be found in either of the rival armies that claim so loudly to be her champions. At the same time as he dis-believed in any of the particular revelations which made such exclusive — and mutually conflicting — claims to allegiance, " a profound belief in God and in God's providence lay at the very core of his soul ". The stage is set for the historian of the Reformation in England, when God had shown himself to be distinctly on the Protestant side.

Incredible as it may seem, Froude was sometimes charged, on the basis of what he wrote about himself under the guise of Edward Fowler in his first story, " The Spirit's Trials ", with moral cowardice. Any stick would do to beat a dog who had left the comfortable kennels of orthodoxy ; " it's the banana that leaves the bunch that get's skinned ", as the egregious Buchman said in his palmier days. It seems to me very brave, and not merely youthful or ingenuous, on Froude's part to have published the book. It lost him his Fellowship ; it lost him (fortunately for him) a job in Tasmania ; for a time he had to depend upon the generous-hearted hospitality of Kingsley. The old archdeacon, who had bought up and destroyed as many copies as he could of Froude's previous book, *The Shadows of the Clouds*, published anonymously (1847), cut off supplies at this second offence.

Both books are chiefly interesting from the autobiographical point of view. The story " The Spirit's Trials " in the first book contains a terrible indictment of the bullying rampant at Westminster when Froude was a boy there. There can be no doubt that he suffered deeply and that it left a mark on him. He certainly had to be taken away, and he fancied that it made him a moral coward. Later, he tells us, he had to face the weaknesses that such treatment germinated in him, and he was able to conquer them — but not till years after. These two books of the eighteen-forties tell us, under a thin disguise, the story of his intellectual and moral struggle. Those years in which he wrote them were the formative years, when he worked out, after the immense disturbance that Newman made in his mental life and the agitation had subsided, the position from which he confronted and carried out his own life's work.

There is a great deal more to interest the reader in both books, especially in *The Nemesis of Faith*. I doubt if anywhere one gets a closer or more intimate sense of the source of Newman's hold over the young men of his generation at Oxford. Froude could never forget his fascination, and, far as he moved away from him in intellectual position, he always thought of him as one of the two men of genius of the age : Newman, Carlyle. Forty years later when himself a famous man, he wrote a study, " The Oxford Counter-Reformation ", in which he speaks of Newman, now a Cardinal, immensely old and celebrated, with the same inner feeling for him as when an undergraduate he heard that voice from the pulpit at St. Mary's. He had brought Newman in as the *deus ex machina* at the end of the *Nemesis* — an extraordinary instance of the fascination, almost a kind of wish-fulfilment, for the man from whom he had departed :

" How often in old college years he had hung upon those lips ; that voice so keen, so preternaturally sweet, whose very whisper used to thrill through crowded churches, when every breath was held to hear ; that calm, grey eye ; those features, so stern, and yet so gentle."

He finds exactly the right phrase to describe the personality that arose from such sensitiveness under such self-discipline ; he speaks of the " silvery loveliness of character " that resulted from it.

Then, too, we can trace in the moving descriptive passages of these little volumes the evocative cadences, the foreshadowings of famous pages he was to write at the height of his powers :

" The old black wood lies round the house as it lay then, but I have no fear now of its dark hollows, of the black glades under its trees. There are no fairies and no ghosts there any more ; only the church bells and the church music have anything of the old tones, and they are silent, too, except at rare, mournful, gusty intervals."

Where did he get the secret of such silvery cadences ? Where, indeed, but from Newman himself ? The apologist of the Protestant Reformation was the Cardinal's greatest pupil.

XXXII

CARLYLE'S *PAST AND PRESENT*

IT is difficult for us of our time and generation to appreciate
Carlyle. So many things come between us and him. In the
first place that appalling style, with its repetitiveness, its over-
emphasis, its perpetual note of adjuration, its shrillness and
exaggeration, with no soft tones at all, the trumpets always
braying and that rather discordantly : it makes him almost
impossible to read. Then there is the insensitiveness, the
dislike of art for itself, of music and painting, the philistinism
of the Scotch peasant. And, no less serious, there is his German
monomania, the confusion about what he thought of the relation
between Might and Right, his intellectual muddle. There is
no doubt that the Victorians overrated him ; and that current
text-books on the literature of that age are quite wrong in
placing him at the head of it. (Newman, for whose intellect
Carlyle expressed great contempt — so much the worse for
him — should take a much greater place than he does : in
some ways his mind foreshadows the subtlest and most crucial
intellectual issues of our time.)

Yet for all his defects Carlyle was unmistakably a man of
genius. He was that very unattractive kind of genius, a prophet.
All prophets are misfits ; and that throws a flood of light on
the source and conditioning of their " message ". (Perhaps
one should not complain of their repetitiveness, or what would
become of the books of Jeremiah, Isaiah, Amos, Hosea, etc. —
or for that matter, of Marx and Lenin ? Repetitiveness is
one of their strongest weapons, the way they get their message
across.) But the very fact of their being misfits means that they
see more vividly certain shortcomings and defects in society
and people around them. It also means that they often miss
the unobtrusive good which is being done quietly by ordinary
folk to whom they give no credit. What the understanding of
their prophetic character in terms of modern psychology does
is to make us chary of accepting their *judgment* about the things

they so vividly, so vehemently (and often so usefully) condemn. Judgment is precisely what they have not got ; what much-despised statesmen like Peel and Gladstone and regular thinkers like Mill had, Carlyle not. On the whole, considering his vehemence, and how much he lived by his intuitions, it is remarkable how much he was in the right.

Anyone who wishes to tackle Carlyle anew — for it is a question of tackling : one cannot promise pleasure — might do best to take *Past and Present* as an introduction. It is a book very symptomatic of its time and still has something to say to us today. It is the best and the most balanced of the books Carlyle devoted to the Condition-of-England question, which so exercised men's minds in the eighteen-forties and left such a mark upon contemporary literature.

And well it might ! For the hungry forties were the turning point in the development of the Industrial Revolution, a dark and dangerous tunnel which the country had to traverse before it emerged into the daylight and prosperity of the Victorian era proper. There was mass unemployment on an unprecedented scale, fruit of the maladjustment of the new powers of production to the mechanism of distribution ; the price of corn soared while men went hungry in the country districts no less than in the towns ; the discontent of the working class expressed itself in the agitation of the Chartist Movement, that of the new middle class in the campaigns of the Anti-Corn Law League. It was a very disturbed decade, which culminated, on the Continent, in the revolutions of 1848. All these forces the writers of the time were conscious of in their different ways, Dickens, Disraeli, Tennyson, Arnold, Clough. In his *Life of Carlyle* Froude has a most interesting passage on the intellectual ferment of those years, and what it was that made younger men like himself turn to Carlyle.

Carlyle focussed these discontents and gave them expression in a way which arrested attention. It is not that the thoughts which he had were very original ; the actual thought is not subtle, or remote, or difficult, but simple and even platitudinous. It was his way of putting it that was striking, his vehemence and sincerity. And he had a peasant's horse-sense about ideas : his intuitions were often more right than the intellectual views of the academic thinkers — for example, about *laissez-faire*, the Poor Law, and factory legislation. The sublime certainty and self-righteousness of the Victorian economists has a modern parallel in the equally fatuous fanaticism of some L.S.E. economists against any form of economic planning in our time. (Or rather a few years ago ; for *Où sont les merdes d'antan ?*) Carlyle, for all that he was no economist, was often quite right as against these *a priori* second-raters.

He begins his book with the contrast of an England wealthier than it ever had been before and yet with two million people out of work, in workhouses " pleasantly so-named because work cannot be done in them . . . they sit there, pent up, as in a kind of horrid enchantment ", or in receipt of out-door relief. It is a very impressive beginning that his book has ; he had been shocked by the scenes of want he had witnessed in East Anglia the autumn before on his ride through it in pursuit of material for his *Cromwell* ; he was still more shocked by the condition of things in Glasgow, Manchester, Stockport, and elsewhere revealed by the papers and blue-books, the reports which Edwin Chadwick was beginning to compile and of which Marx was to make such use later. He went on to point to the dilemma of over-production and under-employment which is a recurrent trouble of *laissez-faire* capitalism. He put it very effectively : so many shirts that " hang there by the million unsaleable ; and here, by the million, are diligent bare backs that can get no hold of them ". The operatives who made them are in want, without bread ; and yet " there is not a horse in England, able and willing to work, but *has* due food and lodging ; and goes about sleek-coated, satisfied in heart. And you say, It is impossible." Carlyle replies : " It is impossible for us to believe it to be impossible ", and to those who are responsible, he says : " Do you depart quickly ; clear the ways soon, lest worse befall ".

He addressed himself to the aristocracy, the ruling class ; quite rightly, for they had all the power and only they could amend it. It is interesting that the mission of this son of the people should have been directed to the upper and middle class ; and that Marx and Engels, those scions of the middle class, should have turned to the people. Both had their influence in different ways ; it would be a pity to exclude the effect of either upon the social amelioration which was a grand feature of the nineteenth century. Carlyle appealed to the conscience and political interest of the rulers ; Marx and Engels did their best to organise the workers to push themselves. (They must have been wonderfully disillusioned after a lifetime of entertaining such hopes of them.) Carlyle, with more immediate point, tells the ruling class that since they are in possession of the land, they owe it good governance ; and if they did not do their duty, worse consequences would follow. He always had the vision of the French Revolution at the back of his mind. So had they, and in fact, in the confusion of the forties, led by Peel, the " pilot who weathered the storm ", they did not do so badly. The English governing class gave this country infinitely better leadership in the nineteenth century than the governing classes on the Continent gave their countries.

There were, of course, spells of faltering leadership, as at the end of Whig rule in the late thirties, or the way in which we muddled into and through the Crimean War. Carlyle hated the popular humbug of the age and the politicians whose ideas of leadership were publicity and playing down to the mob. He has an excellent ironical portrait of Sir Jabesh Windbag, type of all these. " Windbag, weak in the faith of a God, which he believes only at Church on Sundays, if even then ; strong only in the faith that Paragraphs and Plausibilities bring votes ; that Force of Public Opinion, as he calls it, is the primal Necessity of Things." The regular type of the politician who tells the people what the people like to hear, until they wake up and find themselves where they did in 1939–40. Have you never, dear reader, come across a Sir Jabesh Windbag in our time ?

Carlyle's anti-democratic bias is well known. But in this book it is held in restraint ; he does not lose all sense of balance as in his later political writings, *Latter Day Pamphlets* and *Shooting Niagara*. In *Past and Present* he is content to insist upon the need for sincere, candid, able leadership.

In these years, while he was writing *Cromwell*, he had the great days of the Commonwealth all the time before his mind. Since he knew that in fact only a few rule, he was above all anxious that the right ones should be chosen. Liberty he attached less importance to than economic security : in that a true man of the people. " Liberty, I am told, is a divine thing. Liberty, when it becomes the ' Liberty to die by starvation ' is not so divine." It is here that Carlyle links up with the socialist trend of thought in his age. He goes further :

" Liberty ?   The true liberty of a man, you would say, consisted in his finding out, or being forced to find out the right path, and to walk therein.   To learn, or to be thought, what work he actually was able for ;   and then by permission, persuasion, and even compulsion, to set about doing of the same."

This leads on to his gospel of work :

" Consider how, even in the meanest sorts of labour, the whole soul of a man is composed into a kind of real harmony, the instant he sets himself to work ! . . . Blessed is he who has found his work ; let him ask no other blessedness.   He has a work ; a life-purpose ; he has found it, and will follow it."

Carlyle had been struck by the medieval Chronicle of Bury St. Edmunds and its portrait of Abbot Samson, who bore rule there nobly and restored the fortunes of the house : a fine figure of a man such as Carlyle loved, the hero as man of religion, one might say.   This middle section of the book, the historical, which most people will find the most readable, sets off the rest of the book very well.   Carlyle, who had such difficulties with his writing and filled the house at Cheyne Row and his correspondence with his groans, had no difficulty with *Past and Present* : he wrote it straight off at white heat in the first seven weeks of 1843.

There is a good deal in the book which we may take to heart in the difficulties of the period of social transition to which we are committed.   It may be that, for all the unattractiveness of the role, what we shall need is, as in Carlyle's time, a prophet who does not fear to say the unpopular thing.

XXXIII

MACAULAY'S *ESSAYS*

NOT the least among the number of remarkable books whose publication distinguished the year 1843 was Macaulay's *Essays*. We owe their appearance at that time to the Americans. Macaulay had previously considered publishing his reviews in book form and turned the idea down. For all his cocksure certainty he was a modest man. He did not think so highly of his essays as the public did. "The public judges, and ought to judge, indulgently of periodical works", he wrote to the editor of the *Edinburgh Review*. "They are not expected to be highly finished. Their natural life is only six weeks." But his hand was forced in the matter. When, not content with collecting and publishing his reviews (without permission or remuneration) in the United States, American publishers sent over copies in their hundreds to this country, Macaulay was forced to act. We have reason to be grateful. So far from being confined to a natural life of only six weeks, the *Essays* have survived a hundred years. Few works have been so severely criticised, or shown to have more serious errors ; and yet there is no doubt that they will go gaily on to their second century. To what do they owe their survival ?

First and last, they owe it to their immense readability. The inscription upon Macaulay's statue in the ante-chapel of Trinity at Cambridge, which says that he was the first to write annals in such a way that the truth was more readable than fiction, has an element of exaggeration in it, when you think of Gibbon and Hume before him, not to mention Tacitus. But all the same it lays hold of the essential fact about Macaulay: he is the most readable of historians. The difficulty with him is not, as with some others (the uncongenial Freeman, for example), to take him up, but to put him down : the eye races through those exciting, easy pages, fearful lest the chapter or the essay come to an end too soon. And the *Essays*, though not up to the standard Macaulay reached in the *History*, reveal this particular quality at its highest.

Whatever we may think of his point of view, and however much we must take exception to what he says, there is no doubt about the pleasure he has given now to generations and will continue to give. Sir G. O. Trevelyan says that the demand for Macaulay varies with the demand for coal. It is a pleasant nineteenth-century thought. But I can imagine no more cheerful and stimulating companion for winter evenings in war-time, in conditions of the black-out. As Macaulay himself says of the pleasures of reading : " Plato is never sullen. Dante does not stay too long."

And the *Essays* are incomparable for young people who are just beginning to take an interest in things of the mind. How many people owe their first intellectual stimulus to the *Essays* ! (The appreciation of the *History*, a maturer work, comes later.) Arthur Balfour, in his *Autobiography*, has expressed the obligation of those hundreds of people, with minds worth speaking of, for whom the *Essays* opened a door to higher things. One can see why this should be : for all that Macaulay was a man of affairs, and even a man of the world, there was something curiously unadult, ungrown-up about him. After Dickens the most famous writer of his day, he remained something of a boy to the end of his life. (Some people — It is obvious that Strachey was one of them — have the impression that we do not know all there is to be known about Macaulay.)

What, then, are the qualities which make the *Essays* such a prodigious success ?

They have a power of holding the attention in a most extraordinary way. And this arises from the fact that their style is essentially conversational — but the conversation is dramatic, declamatory, exciting. In fact the *Essays* are debates. Macaulay in his usual generous way gave Southey the credit for first hitting upon this form of historical essay ; he merely said that he had improved upon it. But what life and vivacity Macaulay gave to it ! You can hear the voice, the torrent of that astonishing conversation, which made some people protest (cf. Greville's *Memoirs*), though, like Greville, they usually ended by submitting, fascinated, conquered by him. Again and again one has the sensation of listening to a wonderful discussion among that brilliant circle of young men at Cambridge, or to the famous talk at Holland House. There is all the dramatic excitement of opposing ideas being argued out. There are the intellectual high spirits on every page — always an irresistible quality. There is plenty of good knockabout fun. One cannot but enjoy his attack on Montgomery's *Poems* — would there were someone with a pen like his to deal with the Montgomerys of our day ! — or his onslaught upon the intolerable prolixity of Professor Nares :

" The work of Dr. Nares has filled us with astonishment similar to that which Captain Lemuel Gulliver felt when first he landed in Brobdingnag, and saw corn as high as the oaks in the New Forest, thimbles as large as buckets, and wrens of the bulk of turkeys. The whole book, and every component part of it, is on a gigantic scale. The title is as long as an ordinary preface : the prefatory matter would furnish out an ordinary book ; and the book contains as much reading as an ordinary library. We cannot sum up the merits of the stupendous mass of paper which lies before us better than by saying it consists of about two thousand closely printed quarto pages, that it occupies fifteen hundred inches cubic measure, and that it weighs sixty pounds avoirdupois. Such a book might, before the Deluge, have been considered as light reading by Hilpa and Shallum. But unhappily the life of man is now three-score years and ten ; and we cannot but think it somewhat unfair of Dr. Nares to demand from us so large a portion of so short an existence."

And so on.

I used to think that this might be somewhat unfair on poor Dr. Nares ; but having tried to read his book, I now sympathise with Macaulay.

Besides high spirits, ceaseless vivacity, great sense of phrase, a vivid historical imagination, clear-cut and accurate, something more is needed to explain his success as a writer. On the technical side the clue is to be found in his admirable, his infallible power of construction. Whatever it may be, whether argument, or scene, or narrative, he carries the reader irresistibly along with him. Other factors help to explain his almost unexampled success with the public in his own time. He was a deeply conventional man, a Philistine of genius ; his work appealed to, was the very expression of, the conventionalism, the Philistinism of the Victorian age. He was a moralist of a rather crude kind ; he spoke straight to the heart of a society which, almost inexplicably to us, saw everything in crudely moral terms. To him, as to them, everything was either black or it was white. And so we get the fatiguing antitheses in which he saw, altogether too simply, the characters of Warren Hastings, Clive, Marlborough, Bacon, Dr. Johnson, Horace Walpole. Whatever we may think of it as history, there is no doubt that it makes for good reading.

Macaulay's defects were the defects of his qualities. He was very square-cut, definite, downright. Altogether too much so. He had much of the positiveness of the eighteenth century about him. His taste was formed on Addison, that proto-Victorian, and the writers of the age of Queen Anne. This meant a great limitation of sympathies — though, even then, those were broader than many of his latter-day critics realise. It was Macaulay, somewhat surprisingly, who said : " We know no spectacle so ridiculous as the British public in one of its periodical fits of morality ". (If it had not been for that magisterial " we ", it might have been Matthew Arnold speaking.) His essay on the Restoration dramatists shows him a good deal less sympathetic to Puritanism than might have been feared from the son of Zachary Macaulay, brought up in the strictest circle of the Clapham sect, the darling child of Hannah More.

The pity is that Macaulay had such power, such unique vividness, that when he was wrong, as he often was, he has impressed his own version upon the English mind more firmly than the truth. His treatment of Warren Hastings and Marlborough are outstanding cases in point. One might almost say that his misrepresentation of Hastings was responsible for the Indian attitude towards the history of our rule in India. What people other than the English would have been so careless of their own case, so unjust to themselves, as to prescribe the reading of Macaulay's essay on Warren Hastings in their schools and universities ? The English have a singular faculty for depreciating their great men. (Is it perhaps a form of superiority-complex ?) Most people must still be under the impression that Marlborough, though a great soldier, was a bad hat. That is the view that Macaulay has fixed upon us. It is quite untrue that he was a bad man : he was a cold, wonderfully controlled man ; but in addition to his genius, he was not without a heart. The Prime Minister's life of his ancestor has disproved Macaulay once and for all.

Nevertheless, the exaggeratedly high standards which Macaulay stood for were an important element in forming the Victorian outlook. Though the Victorians kidded themselves a lot, they were genuinely high-minded ; which we are not — and we lose something by it.

It is interesting to note Macaulay's own modest estimate of his *Essays* :

" In spite of the applause and the profit, neither of which I despise, I am sorry that it had become necessary to republish these papers. There are few of them which I read with satisfaction. Those few, however, are generally the latest, and this is a consolatory circumstance. The most hostile critic must admit, I think, that I have improved greatly as a writer. The third volume seems to me worth two of the second, and the second worth ten of the first."

That gives a very useful little clue to the correct estimation of the *Essays*. What is needed is a dependable guide to them for the use of the unwary.

XXXIV

KILVERT'S DIARY

(i)

KILVERT is a real literary discovery.[1] Last year there came to light some twenty-two note-books containing the diary of this young Victorian clergyman, and of these we are given selections from the first eight in this volume. I find it fascinating reading; for, even apart from a liking for diaries in general, this one has quite exceptional qualities. It gives an extraordinarily sensitive and observant picture of country life in the seventies, mostly of Radnorshire and central Wales, where Kilvert was a curate, but also of the west country, for his home was in Wiltshire, and during this year, 1870–1, he visited a good deal in Cornwall, Devon, and Somerset. But, more important, he wrote like an angel; his gift was for prose rather than verse — though his verses are quite charming too. The result is an addition to literature. In an odd way, the discovery of this unknown curate reminds one of the resurrection of Gerard Hopkins, though Kilvert was a gentler, less striking genius than that.

Kilvert came from a good old west country family; and, though he spent most of the years covered by his diary as a curate in a remote part of Wales, he did not think of it as exile, but lived a very full and enjoyable social life. He was a welcome guest at all the country houses round, especially at Clyro Court, in his own parish, with the family at which he was on friendly, affectionate terms. He clearly had great social gifts, though he had a real gift for solitude too, and can say : " I have a peculiar dislike to meeting people, and a peculiar liking for a deserted road ". He was an out-of-doors man who liked riding, fishing, and, above all, walking — that favourite pursuit of the intellectually-minded. Not that he was an intellectual ; he does not appear to have been a great reader ; his reactions to public events — the Franco-German War, the Mordaunt case — were conventional enough. He was something more and

[1] *Kilvert's Diary*, edited by William Plomer, 1938.

better than that ; he was an artist, with a passionate love of life.

He noticed everything ; and his position as parson opened all doors to him. It is safe to say that very few people could have kept such a diary. It was not only the life of the country gentry that he knew, but of all the country people — farmers and their labourers, the villagers, the poor. He notes their superstitions and beliefs, their good looks — he was extraordinarily sensitive to physical beauty whether in women or men, though particularly in girls : a susceptibility which he shared with Lewis Carroll, whom he knew. He was no less attracted by natural beauty, by mountains and hills, birds and flowers. But he was an artist in expressing his passion. The Diary is full of such passages as this :

" The peewits were sweeping, rolling and tumbling in the hot blue air about the tall trees with a strange deep mysterious hustling and quavering sound from their great wings."

Or this, which reminds one of Hopkins by its phrasing :

" Last night there was a sharp frost, the crescent moon hung cold and keen, and the stars glittered and flashed gloriously. Orion all in a move of brilliance."

There is a beautiful passage describing what he calls the Easter Eve Idyll — the custom of dressing the graves in the churchyard with flowers on Easter Eve — and concluding with an astonishingly imaginative phrase :

" As I walked down the Churchyard alone the decked graves had a strange effect in the moonlight and looked as if the people had laid down to sleep for the night out of doors, ready dressed to rise early on Easter morning."

It was a very varied, pulsating, natural life in that Welsh countryside which he observed so lovingly. There was always something interesting happening in Clyro ; there are stories enough in the Diary to make a short-story writer's reputation. And Kilvert's account of the funeral of his great-aunt, Miss Maria Kilvert, the house in the College Green at Worcester, the haughty, unfriendly servants who knew that the wilful old lady was leaving her money away from the family, the service, the Canons, the reading of the will, show that the diarist had the makings of a remarkable novelist in him — perhaps a Trollope.

What would he have become had he lived ? With his social gifts, perhaps a canon, or an archdeacon ? But that we shall never know ; he died when he was still under forty, leaving behind him this exquisite Diary and a few poems. But we are grateful for what we have, for he is a real addition to the Victorian age. And oh ! what nostalgia that peaceful Victorian life gives one to read about — archery and croquet on the lawn, tea under the trees, picnics on the unspoiled Cornish coast, grapes and claret on a grassy bank, pleasant dinner-parties at Clyro Court, the busy, kindly life centring upon the Church. The characters of the Diary have a greater reality than all but the best novels ; they have the substance of life, and live in the imagination.

(ii)

The publication of the second volume of *Kilvert's Diary* maintains and strengthens the impression that here we have a really original work of great delicacy and beauty, a book that is an addition to our literature. The work to which it most closely approximates in character is Dorothy Wordsworth's *Journals*. That is a classic, and I have no doubt that this will be. *Kilvert's Diary* does not come behind hers in its quality of observing physical beauty of every kind, whether of landscape, sky, flowers, men, or women, and in the power of rendering it directly, sometimes with an acute nostalgic effect ; in this respect he was not unlike a quieter, Victorian D. H. Lawrence. He even surpasses Dorothy Wordsworth, exquisite writer that she was, in the humanity of his diary : he had an extraordinary quality of sympathy for people, as great as that which he had for flowers and animals ; it is clear that they loved him, and the result is in the breathing lifelikeness of his book, the stories of their lives simple people tell him, the intimate apprehension of character, the delicious portraits of the people of his Welsh and Wiltshire countrysides, his susceptibility to the charm of women, especially of young women and girls, which, held in as it had to be by the restraints of his position as a Victorian

clergyman, went near at times to overwhelming him. It is clear
in this volume that he was spoiling for marriage. That he was
not already married was not his fault: it was due to the difficulty of his social position; after seven and a half years of his
curacy at Clyro, to the lovely Brecon and Radnorshire background of which the Diary owes so much, he was still without a
living. He does not seem to have had any push ; he was a man
of extreme sensibility and charm, an artist, and, there can be
no doubt, a man with a touch of genius.

The one advantage which Dorothy Wordsworth has over
him is that she lived among men of genius. Kilvert, though he
was of good family and passed his life with the best of country
society, knew nobody in the literary world ; this volume of his
Diary ends with a visit to William Barnes, the Dorsetshire poet,
also a clergyman — and that was his highest flight in this
sphere. In a sense he lived ultimately to himself, and wrote
for himself; hence the integrity, the transparent sincerity, the
perfection — it is not too high a word — of his Diary. Is there
not a romance in the discovery of this unknown figure, a young
Victorian clergyman whom nobody knew, yet who wrote as
well as Dorothy Wordsworth ? It makes one think what in-
exhaustible reserves of talent, of gifts of mind and character,
of genius, there have been among our countrymen. The discovery of Kilvert in only the past two years is on a par with the
discovery of the poet Gerard Hopkins in our time, forty years
after his death ; but even Hopkins knew Coventry Patmore,
R. W. Dixon, Robert Bridges. Kilvert knew nobody, except
plain people.

I should place his Diary among the best half-dozen or
dozen ever written in England. It is the quintessence of
England, and the English attitude to life, to the country, to
people, even though most of it, and the best part of it too, was
written against that beautiful background of central Wales, the
Breconshire Beacons, the lovely mountains and valleys in view.
Kilvert died, still in the thirties, only a few years after the end
of this volume, it is pathetic to think — he had such a thirst for
life and loveliness in every form. But the Diary in the end is
his *raison d'être*, and for that he had every qualification : a
subtle ear and eye, a nostalgic memory — like Proust, he

remembered everything — an interest in folklore, he took down the stories and beliefs of the old people, he noted their sayings and looks and songs.

No need to illustrate now how well he wrote, the direct physical impact of things :

" The oatladen waggon came creaking and swaying and sweeping the hedge along the edge of a brow high above the house and then down a steep rough path into the rickyard ".

Or again :

" A group of people were sitting in the churchyard among the graves, and one woman was dressing a green grave with scarlet and white flowers near one of the vast black yews."

Or :

" The western sky was in a splendour and every branch and twig stood out clear against the glow and the two twin sister silver birches leaned towards each other and kissed each other in the dusk."

(iii)

What is the secret of Kilvert ? Ah ! — if only one knew that, one would have the clue to so much more of life than one has. But there, Kilvert has this mark of genius, among others, that he has the faculty of making us insatiably curious about him. We want to know *all* about him, as we long to know what sort of man Tennyson was at heart, or Newman, or what was it that happened to Gerard Manley Hopkins ? We should like to know so much more about what went on in him, and what happened to all the girls he was so much in love with, and what to him in the end. Alas ! we shall never know : he has the attraction of holding a secret for us. It is partly what makes his fascination, his spell so complete : there is something mysterious and elusive about him. At the same time as we are in such close touch with him, share his own intimate and tremulous sensibility, there remains something withdrawn. He was that very rare creature, a diarist who was not in the least egoistic, nor even introspective. What he shares with us is his own apprehension of life, completely and without any reserves ; but life viewed always in its aesthetic aspect, *qua* beauty, as one who was essentially an artist saw it. There remains something about the inner man that escapes us, to which we have not the key.

Kilvert's is not the usual clergyman's diary at all ; nor even like Parson Woodforde, who was so much concerned about eating. Very little in Kilvert's Diary about eating : only the dinner he gave to his farmers his first year at Bredwardine.[1] (But that sounds a good one : "white soup, roast beef, boiled chickens and ham, curried rabbit, stewed wood-pigeons, beef-steak pie, potatoes and stewed celery, plum pudding, custard, plum tart, mince pies, apricot jam tart".) No, the point about Kilvert is that he was the master of a most exquisite and lovely prose, and the Diary that he kept is not merely a revealing document of the social life of the countryside in his time — it is certainly that — but one of the first half-dozen diaries, and that not the least moving, in our literature. When the first volume came out, I described it as the nearest thing to Dorothy Wordsworth's *Journals*. It is pleasing to find here Kilvert's mother presenting him with Dorothy Wordsworth on his birthday, and her name invoked on his very last page. He pays a visit to Brinsop Court and the sitting-room where " dear Dorothy Wordsworth spent much of her time ".

For those who know and love Kilvert, looking forward to the appearance of another volume this autumn has been a pleasure of its own ; but now, alas ! it is countered by the sadness that this is the last. There is no more. That is, unless some of the missing volumes of these last years should turn up ; but I am afraid there is little hope of that.

When this volume opens, he is still acting as curate to his father at Langley Burrell in Wiltshire, having returned from Clyro in Wales, where so much of the action in the first two volumes passes. At once, from the first page his spell is upon us. Here is Seagry Mill in May, Kilvert lying back on the river bank while his father fishes :

" It was a glorious afternoon, unclouded, and the meadows shone dazzling like a golden sea in the glory of the sheets of buttercups. The deep, dark river, still and glassy, seemed to be asleep and motionless except when a leaf or blossom floated

---

[1] *Kilvert's Diary* : Volume III, edited by William Plomer.

slowly by. The cattle by the mill plashed and trampled among the rushes and river flags and water lilies in the shallow places, and the miller Godwin came down with a bucket to draw water from the pool."

It is a perfect little landscape, like a Constable ; and that is the kind of thing that Kilvert can do on every page. More often, he is rendering life, from close-up observation and with the tenderest, most exquisite sympathy for every sort of human being. It was here that his being a parson was such an advantage : it meant that every door was open to him, not only the squire's and the surrounding gentry and clergy, but the farmers and their labourers, the poor, the wretched and derelict. Still, the world they all inhabited was a secure and a quiet one : their greatest disasters an occasional railway accident, or a shipwreck. What occupied much more of the foreground were such matters as the Squire's dismissal of old George Jefferies from leading the singing in church, the installation of a harmonium which almost led to a breach between manor-house and rectory. " How strange it is that the Squire is such a distant man about music ", says Alice Matthews. It is a world of rural deans, and tea on rectory lawns under the trees, and, after tea, archery or croquet, or picking flowers in the flowery meads of Wiltshire for decorating the church, of pretty Victorian girls looking over the parapet of the bridge while the river flows by. And all the while there is one, a little apart, watching life itself flowing by, trying to catch it on the wing, to ensnare a momentary aspect of its beauty, with what quivering sensibility, with what nostalgia for what is passing, even as it passes, in a paragraph, a sentence, a phrase. Here is Christmas Day, 1874 :

" This morning we plainly heard the six beautiful fatal bells of Bremhill ringing a Christmas peal through the frosty air."

Next day, St. Stephen's Day, he goes to visit a sick child who is in great pain, hoping to read her to sleep :

" The light shone through the night from the sick girl's chamber window, the night was still, an owl hooted out of the South and the mighty hunter Orion with his glittering sword silently overstrode the earth."

On Childermas Day :

" As I came home the sky was black and thick with snow, but through the gloom one great lone star was burning in the East. We have seen His star in the East."

There is, however, more to Kilvert than this lonely recording of natural beauty. It is when he gets back to Wales that his Diary quickens with an intenser life ; he loved the Welsh, their warm, sharper, more percipient, more emotional life — so much so that he fancied he had Welsh blood. The characters become more vivid, more strange ; there is Priscilla Price, who lived with her idiot stepdaughter, could remember the coronation of George IV and tell him all sorts of human oddities such as he loved. He once asked James Meredith :

" ' James, tell me the truth, did you ever see the oxen kneel on old Christmas Eve at the Weston ? ' And he said, ' No, I never saw them kneel at the Weston but when I was at Hinton at Staunton-on-Wye I saw them. I was watching them on old Christmas Eve and at 12 o'clock the oxen that were standing knelt down upon their knees and those that were lying down rose up on their knees and there they stayed kneeling and moaning, the tears running down their faces.' "

It is like Thomas Hardy : curious to think that these two who were so near each other in spirit, and writing at the same time, should have known nothing of each other. But then, it is part of the romance of Kilvert that nobody should have known of him as a writer, and then within the last few years a new figure should have been added to English letters from that vanished world of the seventies.

XXXV

THE PUBLIC RECORDS : A NATIONAL HERITAGE

(i)

WHAT an extraordinary institution the Public Record Office is ! I do not mean from the point of view of the general public. To the ordinary man in the street I suppose it is an institution like any other institution. The passer-by, going up or down Chancery Lane, probably takes not the least notice of that heavy barrack-like building in bogus Tudor (curious how fond the Victorians were of mock Tudor) with its suggestion of Princetown gaol combined with a transept tower of Exeter Cathedral. But the man in the street — I always feel as I pass the familiar policeman and the gate, so to say, clangs behind me — has no conception of the esoteric excitements of the place, the oddness of the experience.

To appreciate it you have to be a regular habitué ; for the P.R.O. — as it is fondly called by its initiates — is a sort of prison, or to vary the image, a kind of drug. I well remember my tutor at Oxford warning me against its fell enchantments. But there, I succumbed to it in the end ; it takes time, it consumes time, it lives on time. It is the sort of place a young man goes into dark-haired, fanatical, full of hopes and desires, and emerges from grey-headed and old, rather gentle and courteous, old-fashioned and left behind by time, the dust having settled steadily upon him and all his ways. What has happened to him in the interval ? — ah ! that is the point ; for he himself can hardly tell you.

To get the full savour of the experience, you need not only to have become an initiate, but to return to it from time to time. The P.R.O. is one of those places, like Venice or Oxford, to be always returning to, rather than to live permanently at. For I suspect, or rather I know, that if you live there long enough, you lose your sense of time and space.

It is a curious confraternity we form, and one of the strongest bonds we have in common is that we all know we are slightly mad. Not so mad perhaps as the old gentleman who spent all his life researching into the Falkland Islands, or the endless procession of females you hear inquiring at the desk for defunct relatives in the Navy (" He died a post-Captain in 1776," you hear them say, or it may be 1811 or any year under the sun) ; or that frightening old woman with the glittering eyes and the dangerous hat-pins, gaunt, *raide*, and six feet tall, who believed in the Evil Eye and worked ever at the same books for twenty years, standing up behind one's chair in a most advantageous position for cracking one's skull with a heavy paper-weight, occasionally forking out her fingers at anyone she suspected to have the Evil Eye. I found that a terrifying experience and in that atmosphere : the silence, nothing but the rustling of paper, the turning over of leaves, of age-old parchments and rolls, the slow raining down of smuts from the domed glass roof, covering oneself and one's work in a like oblivion.

Yet we are not without our excitements. We may look a little dingy, moth-eaten, the dust powdering our temples. But we have before us, under our hands, the actual letters, State papers, secret instructions written by kings, queens, princes, cardinals, ministers of State, spies. Somebody over there is reading the very instructions written by the great Pitt with which he breathed his spirit into the conduct of the war over three continents (would there were a Pitt to inspire and lead us now) [1] ; somebody else has out charters signed by the greatest of our medieval kings, magnificent men of action though a trifle illiterate ; I myself, cold with excitement, am turning over the very letters which Drake wrote from on board the *Revenge* to the Queen when the Spaniards were already in the Channel. It seems that the sand he sprinkled on the paper, having folded it up hastily for the messenger, still glitters ; or is there something in my eyes ?

You see that we have our consolations.

(ii)

Various happenings of late — the centenary of the Public Record Office this summer,[1] the issue of the triennial report

[1] Written in 1938.

of the Historical Manuscripts Commission — serve to call attention to a subject which might otherwise be overlooked in the stress of national life just now : our public records. For they are a great national heritage, and worthy, not only of a little notice now and again, but of rather more public attention than they usually receive. It is said of an Oxford don, a distinguished classical scholar, who was asked what he was doing in the late war, that he replied : " I am the civilisation they are fighting for." It might similarly be claimed for our public archives that they are some part of the civilisation to protect which we are pouring out hundreds of millions on armaments these days. They do contain something of the essence of our traditions as a nation, a sort of documented memory of much that has been forgotten by the English people, a silted-up deposit of what was once living and active, even as we. They have their significance all right, and upon us a special claim.

The most highly civilised European nations — at any rate those whose civilisation has been at all long-established, France, Italy, Spain, the Netherlands — can perhaps rival us in the possession of numerous collections of historical documents. Yet it may be doubted whether any nation has such long and comparatively unbroken series of national records — State records. We have lost a great deal, but we have had no such cataclysms as the French Revolution, the burnings of Continental jacqueries, the rape of Belgium or the sack of Rome, the firing of the Four Courts.

In this our public archives afford a true reflection of the national life, a long record of happy success (except for Ireland, and a bad patch about 1776–82) going back to our emergence from the trials of the seventeenth-century Civil War, and, most would say, substantially from the time when the Tudors planted our feet firmly upon the way to success as a modern state.

What we have lost has been due mainly to mouldering and decay and damp — " Fier, Water, Rates and Mice, Misplacinge ", as a seventeenth-century archivist wrote — rather than to wars and cataclysms. So many of the numerous repositories where the nation kept its records, before the Public Record Office was set up to remedy this state of affairs, were thoroughly unsuitable. In 1830 the King's Mews at Charing Cross were fitted up to receive documents ; but by 1835 they were found to be " in a state of inseparable adhesion to the stone walls ", and some 4000 cubic feet of them were described as " a mass of putrid filth, stench, dirt, and decomposition ". Documents are delicate things, and yet properly cared for live for ever. The nation's archives were scattered all over London, at the Tower, in the Chapter House at Westminster, in the old Houses of Parliament, the State Paper Office, Somerset House, in the Rolls Chapel, and a score of other places, some suitable, others not. For some time a public conscience was growing on the matter — the early nineteenth century did a great deal of useful work in publishing State records : there are great series of them dating to that time, the Rolls of Parliament, the Statutes of the Realm, State Papers. At last the building of the Record Office was undertaken to centralise and house properly these scattered collections ; and bit by bit there rose gradually throughout the later nineteenth century, upon the old Rolls estate, that familiar, that sepulchral, prison-like building in Chancery Lane to which we are all so devoted, with its peculiar atmosphere, the like of which exists nowhere else — the British Museum is light and gay, positively flippant compared with it — those long stone corridors, one's footsteps falling dead as one goes, the excitement as soon as one enters and the doors shut behind one, the fascination of a world of its own.

Some people call it a drug ; and like (I imagine) a drug, it is both delicious and irresistible. Only an addict can understand that fascination ; and it is hardly possible to be a good modern historian without becoming an addict. It is so exciting ; you never know what you may find. You may have days and days of drudgery, and then suddenly stumble upon pure gold. I shall never forget the cold thrill of excitement when I came upon the young Richard Grenville's pardon for manslaughter on the threshold of his minority, and the whole story of it. I was, of course, not looking for it, but for something else : it was quite unexpected. The best discoveries seem always, alas, to be made that way. It is that that explains something of what holds one to work in the P.R.O. ; it appeals to the gambling instinct, the hope of something turning up.

And the good thing about it is that, unlike the roulette table, something always does turn up to reward one. Robert Louis Stevenson stipulated that if ever he joined the Catholic Church, he should be made Bishop of Noyon-sur-l'Oise (I think there was a good Bishop's Palace there). Of the various alternative lives I propose for myself when day-dreaming, one of them is to spend all my days, all my time, all my life, burrowing away in the Record Office.

There are such lovely things to be found there, so much consolation for the miseries and defeats of the contemporary world : things so affecting, so moving, human beings at their best, not, as in the realm of politics, at their worst and stupidest. Even if you are not a researcher, you need only step into the Museum (I am glad to learn that it is growing in popularity) and you may see a letter from Leicester, written when all the strain of the Armada's passing was over, to Elizabeth, and her inscription in her own hand upon it : *His last letter.* Or you may see letters of Nelson, that familiar, backward-sloping hand, after he had lost his right arm, or the less familiar, forward slope of his earlier writing, altogether bolder, less pathetic and exciting. You may see Domesday Book, any number of fine seals and parchments ; there is no end to what you may enjoy.

All the same, the essential thing is that the public may come to the treasures locked away in those store-rooms and purlieus into which one never penetrates. One wishes that it were possible to publish these materials for our history on a larger, more generous scale. The Government grant is far too small and we have to wait far too long. I believe all the material is assembled, for example, for the publication of the Patent Rolls of Elizabeth ; a magnificent series, too, it would make. But we have to wait while the Patent Rolls of Mary emerge slowly one volume to two or three years. It is, one understands, simply a question of finance. The Historical Manuscripts Commission, which before the last war had an income of £1800 a year, when pounds were pounds, has now only £700. The case must be not dissimilar with the Record Office. And yet what dangers there are in waiting, nowadays, when the documents themselves may be destroyed ! Once in print, they are indestructible. Perhaps the Government, of its goodness, when we are spending such astronomical amounts upon armaments, could afford just one little thousand pounds more per year upon publishing these evidences of our past, if only by way of suitably celebrating the centenary of the Record Office ? This granted, their aforesaid orator will — in the time-honoured formula — for ever pray, etc.

XXXVI

THE USE OF HISTORY

(i)

WHAT is the use of history, say the unintelligent, the ultra-utilitarian, and do not pause for an answer. Yet there is an answer, a pretty direct and effective one, which they knew very well in the sixteenth century. Machiavelli and Erasmus, Montaigne and Bacon, all the superior spirits were agreed that history was the sovereign study for the prince, the statesman, the politician. History played, and has always played, a large part in the education of rulers. (One gathers from the picture papers that it has done, quite rightly, in the education of the Princess Elizabeth.) It was the favourite reading of Napoleon, as it is of Mr. Lloyd George. The proper study of history — or rather remembering its lessons in time — would have saved innumerable disastrous errors and blunders in affairs. Everyone needs, if he is to *understand* politics and not just take part in them, a historical background. Indeed we might go further to say with Sir Walter Ralegh, that a knowledge of history is necessary to a fully intelligent life, " the end and scope of all history being ", he says, " to teach us by example of times past such wisdom as may guide our desires and actions ".

If people of recent years, in schools and places where they teach, have been inclined to give history the go-by, it is to some extent the fault of the historian, who has not been confident enough, indeed not arrogant enough. He should make his proper, and so much better authenticated, claims heard against the clamorous demands of chemistry, physics — and for all I know accountancy, shorthand, and typewriting. The *use* of chemistry was so much more obvious to the stupid, though actually it is far less : it produced something, if only a smell.

There will be the less reason for such diffidence after Professor Williams' book.[1] He has had the excellent idea of

[1] C. H. Williams, *The Modern Historian.*

collecting from contemporary historians, or rather those of the last half century, passages showing how they think of their subject and its difficulties, what they mean by history and its place among social studies, and illustrating them by others which reveal the historian at work : the tradesman at his trade. What emerges from the book is that these historians he quotes from have a far more large-minded and comprehensive conception of history than they are usually given credit for. In this respect they are not unworthy successors of Gibbon, Macaulay, Froude. (Of course, Mr. Williams' bias is with these, the humanist historians rather than with the technical, the unliterary, one might almost say, the illiterate, for there are such.) Yet why were the public in the earlier years of this century less inclined to lend ear to the claims of history than they were in the nineteenth century ?

Increasing specialisation among the historians is one answer. Not that that made them necessarily unreadable ; Maitland was one of the most specialist of historians, yet he is " read-able ". This specialisation was part of a tendency at work in every sphere. Poetry, it seemed, was being written for poets, music for musicians, economics for the economists, and history, it might be said, for historians. Mr. G. M. Trevelyan in these years was a notable exception to this, a conscious upholder of an earlier and sounder tradition.

But I am inclined to think that the answer has even more to do with the public than with the historians. Professor Powicke notices that the last war gave an impetus to the interest in history — in itself a most interesting observation like so much that Mr. Williams quotes from him. And it seems certain that the preoccupation of a younger generation with problems of the social and economic order is sustaining and will increase the general interest in history, the necessary background and the proper training for understanding the political problems that threaten to overwhelm us if we do not understand them. It is this that is reflected in the concern of the younger historians with the complex of questions and with the general attitude to them that goes by the name of Marxism : the relation of the various factors, intellectual, cultural, spiritual, to the economic and social structure, the subtle and various ways in which one is linked up with the other and is often expressed through another. It is here that Mr. Williams' book is less adequate, is already even a little out of date. He seems to think that, the chief controversy of the early twentieth century over — that whether history is a science or no — there is much less division of opinion now than then. Actually there is a more significant division between those affected by the influence of Marxism and those who are not. This it is that makes the work of R. H. Tawney and G. N. Clark so significant to the younger school, and they are followed by quite a long tail of still younger men who are prepared to go further.

The whole balance of this book might then be shifted with advantage to the left ; it would bring it more up to date and more into conformity with its title. Mr. Williams intends to illustrate the attitude and work of the twentieth-century historian. From that point of view it was a mistake to make Acton the starting point, unless by way of contrast : nothing more perfectly nineteenth century than his preoccupation — for a historian, too ! — with ethical issues. The Gladstonian Liberal ! It is surprising to find the two Oxford professors, York Powell and Firth, much nearer giving the keynote of the modern attitude. " The New History ", says the one, " deals with the condition of masses of mankind living in a social state. It seeks to discover the laws that govern those conditions and bring about the changes we call Progress and Decay, and Development and Degeneracy." And Firth says, even better : " It seems to me to mean the record of the life of societies of men, of the changes which those societies have gone through, of the ideas which have determined the actions of those societies, and of the material conditions which have helped or hindered their development ". Excellent. Any Marxist might practically subscribe to that. Firth was a great man, though his greatness was not appreciated by the general public. He was essentially a historian's historian, as some poets are the choice of their brother poets. For all that, the real patron saint of the modern English historian is not an Oxford, but a Cambridge man, Maitland ; and Mr. Williams' book should have begun with him. For it is his work that is so characteristic of the modern age, with its emphasis on the specialist, the technical ;

and he was concerned — who more profoundly, or with more originality and genius ? — with the analysis and description of a whole society.

The selection in Mr. Williams' third section might well have been bettered, too ; we could easily have spared Belloc, Guedalla, Walter Raleigh, Fortescue and some others for more Tawney, and something from Edward Armstrong, J. L. Myres, Stenton, Collingwood, the Webbs, not to mention some representative passages from younger writers. But no doubt every reader of an anthology is convinced that he could have improved on the anthologist.

(ii)

Mr. Crump has written a charming and delectable book,[1] on a theme which is only too often productive of dullness in the author and of boredom in the reader. Historical research may well be thought to be not the liveliest of themes for a book ; and yet this book invests the subject with a singular suaveness and humanity. It is true at the same time that its title hardly represents the contents of the book : Mr. Crump is not engaged here in telling us what he thinks History means, nor in describing the minutiae and paraphernalia of historical research ; his subject is really the researcher himself, or more explicitly, the mind of the historical inquirer.

" For it is the mind of the historical inquirer at which this book is aimed, his mental processes and his ways of thought ; not indeed the mind of the accomplished scholar to whom inquiry has become a second nature, but the mind of the beginner, the tentative struggler, or even that of the worker who has never attained to any confidence in his own methods."

And further, " The object of this book is to discover the characteristic qualities which mark a certain habit of mind ".

The effect of the book depends not only upon its manner and style, which is delightful, but upon the vision and comprehensiveness of its conception of history, of which one is conscious at every point in the argument, however minute. To take the case of the orthodox division of history into " political ",

[1] C. G. Crump, *History and Historical Research.*

" constitutional ", " economic ", " social " : it is evident that such a division has a defence in its convenience for utilitarian purposes ; but it is equally evident that a too rigid adherence to the classification is responsible for the sterility of a good deal of present research. It is refreshing to turn to Mr. Crump, and find his opinion on the interrelation of these categories in the study of history :

" They are all interwoven and interrelated. To study successfully any one of them the others must be kept in mind. A change in an administrative process may be due to a political change or to an alteration in the economic condition of a country. An alteration in the economic condition of a country may lie at the back of a change in opinion on questions of religion or politics ; and yet such a change may take place and its results may be concealed by the natural inertia of men's minds, which will cling to established institutions and accepted opinions long after they have become inapplicable to the new conditions of life. In the case of law this ' lag ' in time has already been noted, and the same factor is of equal importance in all the other classes listed above."

There is no mistaking the influence of his general position with regard to history, in his advice to beginners as to the way of research. He is quite explicit for instance about the futility of making impartiality the ideal of an *intelligence déliée*, the ultimate end of the historian's endeavour. The characteristic note of Mr. Crump's advice is that of naturalness, of taking for granted what one starts out with and not bothering with overmuch criticism of the medium in which one intends to work : " The beginner, who aims at impartiality and objectivity, will assuredly hamper himself and fail to achieve them ; it is far better for him to put all such ideals on one side, and let his mind work freely on its own natural lines ". And the way of research into history will formulate its own logic through the necessity of the mind to connect event with event : " The student works in the main by noticing new relations between known events, and using these new relations to suggest the possible existence of unknown events ".

One might have wished that Mr. Crump had emphasised the logical approach to historical research equally with the artistic ; but it is obvious that the latter has his heart's favour. He illustrates the starting point of historical inquiry by a perfect little anecdóte of a walk in Rome in the year 1909 ; when starting from the bottom of the Via Cavour he went along the new street which runs from the Forum up the base of the Viminal hill ; then from the *piazza* before the Church of San Pietro in Vincoli, he turned down the Via della Polveria, the street of the Powder Magazine, which leads to the Coliseum. On the left-hand side of the street there was in 1909 a long wall covered with stucco : nothing of interest except a large arched doorway, and a pair of rickety doors. But over the arch there was an inscription, probably all vanished now ; in that year it read : " *Empire Français. Dépôt de Poudres et de Salpêtres.*" And in those words there lay a hundred years of unavailing effort, of turmoil, and of forgetfulness in the end.

That is one way of approach to history ; and we know where Mr. Crump's favour is, both from this and from the importance which he attaches to the reconstruction of the drama of history in the individual mind, a theme which he developed more fully in an earlier work, *The Logic of History* (published, somewhat curiously perhaps, by the Society for Promoting Christian Knowledge). It is because of this artistic parallel in his mind that Mr. Crump entitles his second chapter " The Discovery of a Subject " : to my mind the idea of awaiting the discovery of a subject for research — " expecting " it is his word — is going a little too near the process of creation in the arts. Whereas there is considerably closer analogy between historical and scientific research. And it is for this reason that Mr. Crump insists much more upon the independence and originality of the researcher than one would have thought desirable. After all, when one has a rational notion of what history is, to begin with, a subject of research is much less likely to arrive from the heavens than to be chosen in accordance with a deliberately planned system of social study. Where this is not so, the piece of research, as in too many cases, bears all the signs of being written round a subject that had occurred haphazard to the mind and been written up for the sake of writing something. In such cases it would probably be better that they should give up the attempt at independence which Mr. Crump emphasises (and rightly, with the right people) and place themselves under the direction of others who at least do know what they mean by history, and would find something for them to do which was both useful and significant. Unfortunately, directors who possess such encouraging certainty are not always professors.

(iii)

I have sometimes wondered, since reviews in this age have rather taken the place of sermons in the last, why our writers have not the courage to republish their reviews as the Victorians did their sermons. It might have a good effect on the so much criticised art of reviewing, since it has been held that the test of a good review is whether it stands reprinting. Here are two historians who do not fear to reproduce their reviews along with more substantial articles, and they certainly survive the test well.

These two books [1] afford interesting comparisons and some contrasts. They are both collections almost entirely of historical and political essays : offshoots from the main work of these two distinguished writers. Mr. Fisher recognises the occasional character of his : they convey " a gentle invitation to humane studies and a rebuke to the menacing barbarism of the age ". To Professor Namier, the margin of history means something more profound : practically all of the main stream of history that is grasped by the conscious intelligence. " History is a river ", he says, " not to be harnessed in action nor to be mastered in thought ; our conscious work is done on its margin." The first book is that of an eminent but disillusioned Liberal, who finds that " the prime source of evil in the world today is the eclipse of Liberalism " ; the second that of a distinguished and valued recruit to this country from Eastern Europe, who regards himself as a Tory, with the realism of the Tory outlook and the added disillusionment which has come from the experience of his people. They both, like all the best historians, have an active interest in politics, to which these books bear witness : they are not products merely of the study with no knowledge in practice of the subjects they are writing

[1] H. A. L. Fisher, *Pages from the Past* ; L. B. Namier, *In the Margin of History*.

about. Mr. Fisher quotes, evidently with approval, one of the eminent qualifications in Macaulay's view for a historian : that he should have " spoken history, acted history, lived history ". Mr. Fisher himself has been a Cabinet Minister ; Professor Namier has been much concerned with Zionist politics and would regard himself as a practising Tory.

They share an interest in Napoleon. A section of Professor Namier's book is given up to essays and reviews in that immense field ; while Mr. Fisher's historical might-have-been, " If Napoleon had escaped to America ", with its very convincing ending, is excellently done and most enjoyable. (But, by the way, is not a steamer on the Hudson in the year 1815 a little premature ?) Mr. Fisher's essays, as might be expected, are the more polished works of art, with their conscious classicism continuing the flavour of the last century into this : I like " John Buchan, a familiar name, throwing off the sepulchral integuments of an English peerage, comes forward once more, despite the heavy charge of his proconsulate ", etc. But Professor Namier has more to say to us.

Mr. Fisher will not regret that : he regards the present with a certain disdain, and turns from the disgraceful spectacle to the age of Augustus, and that other Augustan age of the great, and the belated, Victorians, Gladstone, John Morley, Arthur Balfour, Sir Edward Grey, their House of Commons. (But again by the way, was the age of Augustus " the most wonderful century of human history " ? I should have thought there was as much, or more, to be said for fifth-century Athens, or the full tide of the Renaissance.) Like so many other writers nowadays, Mr. Fisher writes out of nostalgia for the nineteenth century. But that can be overdone : there are great achievements in our time, too, it is time for people to be reminded. Mr. Namier writes bitterly that the experiences of the past few years have brought home to him the meaning of the line :

" l'horreur de penser et l'honte d'être homme."

But without being an optimist — and how can a historian be an optimist ? — I am not sure, with all respect, that these eminent authors are not mistaken. After all, this is an exciting age to be living in : anything is possible, and things may yet go right with us. It is agreed that since 1931, that disastrous turning point in recent history, things have gone very wrong. Mr. Namier has a section devoted to Lawrence (T. E.), about whom he has written better than anybody ; but an age which can in this country alone produce two such Lawrences, T. E. and D. H., will not go for nothing.

Neither of these historians disdains to draw lessons for the present and future from the study of the past. After all, if a historian cannot advise us from the mistakes of the past, who can ? Professor Namier, with his strong vein of common sense, his realism, has some salutary, if depressing, things to say about the recent past. He said of the too much maligned Treaty of Versailles in 1933 :

" The bearing of the peace settlement on recent developments in Germany should not be overrated. The rise of a pathological nationalism ten or fifteen years after a national defeat seems a recurrent phenomenon, practically independent of the terms imposed on, or accorded to, the defeated country."

There is a great deal of sense and observation in this. The English have a wonderful faculty for sitting gratuitously in a white sheet. The primary causes of what has happened in Germany are internal ; the external factors, regrettable as they have been, are secondary. It is interesting to observe in these essays, dating back to before 1933 as they do, how right, how utterly right Professor Namier has been all along about Hitler. But then, he knew. These contemporary essays, which occupy more than half the book, are the best and the most informative : Professor Namier has not forgotten his Eastern and Central Europe, to our great advantage, for all that he has become our leading authority on the reign of George III.

Of Mr. Fisher's studies, the most substantial, as he tells us, is that on " The Whig Historians " ; though the most instructive is " The Real Oxford Movement ", on the brief and brilliant flowering of scientific studies in Oxford in the middle of the seventeenth century. And I have never known Mr. Bertrand Russell so well dealt with as in " A Philosopher's Paradise ", with an irony equal to his own and a great deal more sense.

(iv)

Miss Elizabeth Bowen has a place of her own that is yet difficult to define in contemporary English letters. Possessor of an admirable talent that is seen to perfection in her short stories, a novelist of distinction and of a high seriousness, a sensitive critic, there is something at once stylish and amateurish, in a good sense, about her work. With this book the novelist turns historian : one is very curious to see what she will make of it.

True, it is family history that she is writing. But what better kind of history can there be ? I find it fascinating. Besides, the family is often more important and more rewarding to study than the individual as the unit in society ; yet family history has nothing like the *réclame* that historical biography has always had.

This book is very much a case in point.[1] One sees both the strength of family history as such — and perhaps the reason why it has less appeal with the public than biography. The value of the book lies precisely in that it is the record of a typical family of Anglo-Irish gentry from the Cromwellian settlement onwards, not in that there are any particular individuals who make history or stand out in any way. The record of the Bowens is singularly unexciting, particularly, one would have thought, for an Anglo-Irish family : no murders, no hair-breadth escapes, no highway robberies, no romantic elopements, no serving man like Mrs. French's in Yeats' poem

> " that could divine
> That most respected lady's every wish,
> Ran and with the garden shears
> Clipped an insolent farmer's ears,
> And brought them in a little covered dish."

The Bowens seem to have been on much better terms with their tenantry : perhaps that is how Bowen's Court escaped burning when so many other houses went up.

The appeal of the book is more subtle than any such excitements : it lies in the atmosphere of the house, most

---

[1] Elizabeth Bowen, *Bowen's Court.*

skilfully rendered, the deep current of love for it and that bare, beautiful countryside with mountains all round and many rivers, the nostalgic, pulsating sense of the family life and its tradition, the fairness and understanding of the historical background. In the portrait she gives of her family Miss Bowen depicts the historic life of a whole class, that of the lesser Anglo-Irish gentry, with extraordinary justice and no attempt to conceal. "My family got their position and drew their power from a situation that shows an inherent wrong ", she says. " In the grip of that situation, England and Ireland each turned to the other a closed, harsh, distorted face — a face that in each case their lovers would hardly know." She sums up the Anglo-Irish who followed Grattan's lead and wished for an Ireland in free and independent association with England under the Crown better than I have ever seen it put :

" Ireland had worked on them, through their senses, their nerves, their bones. They had come to share with the people round them sentiments, memories, interests, affinities. The grafting-on had been, at least where *they* were concerned, complete. If Ireland did not accept them, they did not know it and it is in that unawareness of final rejection, unawareness of being looked out at from some secretive, opposed life, that the Anglo-Irish naïve dignity and, even, tragedy seems to me to stand. Themselves, they felt Irish, and acted as Irishmen."

As was to be expected, Miss Bowen, with the sure hand of the novelist and a passionate sense of ownership, of having succeeded to all those memories, plants the house and its countryside firmly in one's mind. The countryside is that undulating limestone country of North-east Cork, through which flows the Awbeg, the " gentle Mulla " of Spenser's *Faerie Queene*. Kilcolman Castle, where Spenser lived and discussed his poem with Walter Ralegh, is but a few miles away — the ruins of it — from Bowen's Court. It is a country of ruins, and of every period : Desmond castles burnt by the Elizabethans or Cromwell, eighteenth-century houses burnt down by the Irish, barracks fired by the Republicans in the Irish Civil War. A countryside that has been much fought over and now has a melancholy emptiness, a spareness of its own, and there is poetry in it and in its life. Of this Miss Bowen is conscious at every point and renders its atmosphere subtly, transparently, beautifully. One feels one knows the house as if one had lived in it : the hall, the shut-up Victorian drawing-room, the library, the Long Room that was to have been the ballroom, where so many generations of Bowen children have played on wet days. And that is as it should be : it means that the author has succeeded, imposed the desired image upon us. For Bowen's Court is the subject of the book, and ultimately the house is more important than the people, the family than the individual.

The story begins with the dour Cromwellian Welshman from the Gower peninsula, the doubter, the sceptic, who declared he would give ten thousand pounds to know the truth about God. A congenial, if not exactly a genial, figure. Men said that he lived a haunted, solitary life, and the godly Richard Baxter wrote a pamphlet on the shocking apparition which Colonel Bowen sent over the water to his wife in Wales. The story is that Cromwell granted him as much land as Bowen's hawk would fly over. From that moment the Bowens seem not to have looked back : their story is one of suitable marriages, well-arranged dowries, the building of the house, a devotion to their patrimony. But no figure emerges who so appeals to the imagination as the original Bowen, spirit-haunted, sardonic, a scoffer.

A great deal of work has gone into the making of this book. It must have been difficult to gather so much material about so many obscure persons. A charming bloom of amateurishness, of a slightly *égaré* distinction, rests upon an occasional historical touch, perhaps in keeping with the life it describes. To Miss Bowen, who speaks of Charles I's " kingly looks ", it would evidently come as a surprise to know that he was under-sized, had a stammer and a red nose. She clearly sees him through the mirror of Vandyke. Nor was Killiecrankie a rout for the Highlanders : it was, on the contrary, a victory, rendered barren by the death of Claverhouse. But these mere knots of the historian are as nothing compared with the tenderness that inspires the book, the ripe womanly wisdom one comes upon, such as this observation :

" With characters dynamic, shapely in youth, the reverse too often happens : something vital is sacrificed to the reconciliation with life. . . ."

Or :

" Early rising would get one up only a little after the birds, which is to say, awake for their chorus whose most unearthly note is lost as the day hardens."

Or, of the old life at Mallow and Fermoy, the coming and going between the army officers and the country houses, such as Tolstoy and Turgeniev have described it :

" Though pleasure may not be very much, so much of the human heart goes into it that its memory can command tears."

At such moments the historian is touched with poetry.

XXXVII

OXFORD IN WAR-TIME

A FEW weeks ago, about the end of the summer term, if you, a visitor to Oxford, happened to be wandering about the old dead centre of the University town, which was, no doubt, what the wit had in mind when he called Oxford the " Latin Quarter of Morris-Cowley ", you would notice vivacious, chattering little crowds of undergraduates in gowns and white ties, and undergraduettes in caps and gowns and black ties, waiting at the doors of those old, dead buildings for their examinations to begin. Very important for most of them, for these examinations at the end of the Trinity Term are those which give them their classes in the Final Schools ; upon them largely depend their chances of a career in life.

But only someone who knew Oxford would spot that there was anything unusual in those little crowds being there at that particular time. For ordinarily in peace-time it would be the High Street that would be dominated during the weeks when " Schools " are going on by these groups, these droves of black-gowned young men and women, all dutifully clad in *sub fusc*, occasionally relieved by the white fur of a B.A.'s hood, the crimson hood of a don going by in his glory — the examiner alongside the examinee. You see, the Examination Schools, that large, lugubrious building with its great Jackson-Jacobean windows which overshadows the lower High, has ceased to fulfil its gloomy function for the " duration ". It fulfils a nobler and more pressing purpose. And so the examinations have to be held in all sorts of holes and corners in the old dead buildings, which, in former centuries, were the real heart of the University — the Divinity School, with its Proscholium (the " Pig-market ") in the old Schools quadrangle ; even the Sheldonian Theatre and the Taylorian have had to be roped in for the emergency.

Now isn't that just like Oxford ? The buildings of the twentieth century being requisitioned for national purposes, we go back quite easily and naturally to those of the Middle Ages which have lost their former use. I must say it gave me pleasure to see those quiet, deserted yards around the Bodleian, which were once the hub of University life, filled once more with the laughter and excitement of the young.

This leads me to the first and most obvious difference between peace-time and war-time Oxford which must strike everybody's notice, for it is on the surface for everybody to see. The life of the streets, even in the old centre of the town, has ceased to be dominated by the University. So many thousands of evacuees and refugees have flooded into the area, mainly from London : it is said that the population has gone up by some twenty per cent, perhaps twenty thousand people. Then there are all the men in uniform, who crowd into this convenient centre by all the bus routes from round about. So that the streets of Oxford which were calculated to accommodate a population of some twenty thousand with dignity and space, and had long ceased to serve modern Oxford adequately, now have an extra and almost impossible strain upon them. Pavements are incessantly crowded ; shopping has become torture (not that that much concerns dons and undergraduates) ; theatres are packed with unknown faces — as the war wears on it becomes rarer and rarer to recognise a friend, one greets a distant acquaintance with spontaneous effusiveness and genuine relief. The place is filled, one feels, with people who know not Joseph. The few decrepit old dons who are left, and crocks like myself, are driven to take refuge within their ample college walls, cross the High or the Broad furtively, looking neither to the right hand nor to the left, to scuttle for their daily constitutional into the cover of Christ Church Meadows, or Addison's Walk at Magdalen, the gardens of Trinity or St. John's.

So much for outward appearances.

But they do in fact reflect pretty accurately what has happened to the inner life of the University. On the one side, a great influx of strangers from outside ; on the other, a great outgoing of the younger dons and third-year undergraduates to the war and to Whitehall. Even before the war the influx of academic refugees from abroad was beginning to be noticeable. Oxford, like the other British universities, has given a magnificent example of generosity and of the ties of intellect and scholarship transcending national boundaries, in this respect. But somehow Oxford is a magnet for them, which exerts an indubitable attraction, over and above the quota for which the University has made itself responsible. One notices this very much in the café life of the town, which has become distinctly more Continental. From the languages being spoken all around one, one might be inhabiting a bit of old Vienna or some Central European university town. The New Bodleian has an enormous raised terrace, a little *piazza*, just above the pavement level of the Broad : it only needs my suggestion to be adopted, the little tables with the stripy awnings to go up, the shrubs in painted tubs and the sunshades, for the resemblance to be complete. One sees Bodley's Librarian as the chief *cafetier* ; the profits, of course, to go to paying for the New Bodleian Library.

Quite seriously, if there is one town in this country, one town in Europe, which has taken something of the place of Salzburg in pre-Anschluss days, it is Oxford. It has become very much more of a " cultural centre ", in the modern sense (old-fashioned persons may deplore it), not only because of the presence of many distinguished cosmopolitans, but so far as this country is concerned, partly, no doubt, because of the winging of London. Never have there been such wonderful concerts, such an *embarras de musique*, as Oxford has enjoyed in war-time. Not only orchestras big and small, the London Philharmonic, under Malcolm Sargent, the Boyd Neel, the Sidney Beer Orchestras, have come down regularly in term time, but there have been our own Wednesday night concerts, following the National Gallery model, right through the year and drawing a good deal from artists now living in Oxford. It has been a pleasure to see these concerts packed with young people, many of them in uniform, particularly in R.A.F. uniform ; often performers as well as the audience.

In addition, there have been the art shows. Oxford has benefited from the residence of a distinguished Spanish painter, Gregorio Prieto, who has been engaged in drawing types of undergraduate good looks and some of the celebrities of the Oxford scene. An excellent exhibition of his drawings and paintings was held at Lady Margaret Hall. Even more exciting is the exhibition of those younger English painters, the Euston Road School, who owe so much to the judicious encouragement of Sir Kenneth Clark and to the somewhat Puritan genius of their leader, William Coldstream. Their very representative show — it was one of the most stimulating I have ever seen and offers great hope for the future of English painting — was held in the Ashmolean ; which somehow puts an official imprimatur upon their work.

Some whole institutions have moved to us from London, mainly educational schools and colleges like Westfield College, which is part of London University, and now occupies St. Peter's Hall. Then there is Chatham House, the Royal Institute of International Affairs, installed in Balliol College — you may run into a number of eminent figures on the international scene, not merely experts, but statesmen, almost any day crossing the Broad. Somehow it seems all very appropriate.

But how does all this affect the life of the University, above all of the undergraduate ? That is the most important point.

There is no doubt that the life of both has suffered a great deal. That was to be expected. You cannot take away the top layer of undergraduates, the third-year men, and the most active, junior dons, without dealing a great blow to the University. Those who remain do their best to carry on, though University life has lost much of its spaciousness, the leisureliness which enabled young men to develop their minds in the best of all possible ways in the most formative years of their life.

But I must say how struck I am by the wonderful way undergraduates have responded to the emergency and the difficulties of the situation. Think of what happened in the first year of the war. Many of them who were of military age had their undergraduate careers cut short at a stroke, in the middle of their degree course. It was very hard lines. Then the universities got together with the Government and worked out a reasonable scheme by which those who were in the midst of their degree courses were to finish them. Shortened degree courses, at Oxford known as " Sections ", were introduced,

s

which could be taken in from three to five terms and a war-time degree achieved.

In consequence the men have to get their work into much shorter time ; and on top of that they mostly have a day and a half a week taken out for O.T.C. parades, lectures, exercises in the country. In addition they have their college rotas for fire-watching and so on. I am filled with admiration at the way they have carried on their work in these circumstances ; there is no doubt that undergraduates work much harder than ever before. Last year I was examining in one of these " Sections " — Politics and Economics ; as I looked down the serried ranks of young men before me, mostly men in their second year only who were finishing their University life for good and would " come to Oxford no more ", I could not but be moved. When I came to read their papers I was still more impressed ; for in spite of all the distractions from their work, the invasions of their time, they had all worked seriously and hard — far more generally so than in peace-time. There was hardly anyone to plough — just one or two out of a large number ; and many of them had earned distinctions.

Let us look at a typical week of an Oxford undergraduate in war-time. Here is my friend Bill, a heavy fellow who played in this past year's University Rugger Fifteen.[1] Monday all day he has O.T.C. ; work in the evening for his tutorial. (He has two tutorials a week, for each of which he has to write an essay : one on history, another on political theory.) Tuesday morning and afternoon he has lectures and is writing his essay for that evening. He has that evening off and can go to a concert or a cinema or a party of his friends. Wednesday morning and evening, reading up for his next essay ; the afternoon taken up by a practice match. Thursday morning, lectures ; after-noon, O.T.C. ; evening, reading for his next tutorial. Friday, mostly given up to writing his essay for his tutorial that evening. Saturday, all day, a rugger match away ; if at home, he has the evening free. Sunday, all day, rather the worse for wear, reading hard to catch up with his next essay. On top of that, he has a night or so up a week fire-watching. It so happened that the very night before his examination he was up for five

[1] Written in 1941.

hours during an alert. You will be glad to hear that he got through both his Sections !

Let me conclude with a word of advice to parents. For all the handicaps to University life in war-time, or rather because of them, it is a very good thing to send your sons up to the University a year earlier than usual. During their last year at school, boys are very often marking time. It is much better that they should be up at the University getting on with their work, widening their horizons, equipping themselves for life. If they come up at seventeen instead of at eighteen, they have a chance of getting something like their complete course instead of the rather hectic rush of the shortened war-time degree. Seventeen is not too soon to be coming up to the University. Their ancestors came up at fifteen, and in the Middle Ages at eleven or twelve. You cannot but expect an Oxford man to welcome a step that so clearly has the sanction of the past !

XXXVIII

THREE AMERICANS ON ENGLAND

(i)

NATHANIEL HAWTHORNE, perhaps the most distinguished of American novelists, was in England as Consul at Liverpool for four years, from 1853 to 1857, the time of the Crimean War. It stands to reason that his *English Notebooks*, kept with conscientious care and a trained eye for detail in observation, hold a great deal of interest for us as a faithful portrait of the Victorian age in its heyday by a very critical and curious observer. Yet it is only now that a full and reliable text, edited from the manuscripts in the Pierpont Morgan Library, has been published in America.[1] After Hawthorne's death Mrs. Hawthorne published a bowdlerised version of her own, conceived at every point in the interests of Victorian decorum. The new editor claims, I think justly, that " out of the restored journals . . . a new Hawthorne will emerge : a more virile and a more human Hawthorne ; a more alert and (in a worldly sense) a more intelligent Hawthorne, a Hawthorne less dreamy and less aloof than his biographers have represented him as being ".

Perhaps Mrs. Hawthorne then was responsible for the unfavourable judgment on the journals which Henry James expresses in his admirable little book on the novelist. All the same, I cannot but think that Henry James was very obtuse and wrong about the *Notebooks*. He could not see what Hawthorne's motive was in keeping them. In fact, Hawthorne's creative faculty, though very distinguished, was not a strong one. He had just finished his three chief novels, the American romances. This was his first journey abroad. He was by instinct and long years of solitariness a most minute observer. What more natural than that he should record the Victorian scene — and from a very advantageous look-out post, the Consul's office at Liverpool ? There, there were the extraordinary stories he came in contact with every day, of American

---

[1] Nathaniel Hawthorne, *The English Notebooks*, edited by Randall Stewart.

sailors maltreated to death on their ships, of the odd flotsam and jetsam of American life upon the European tide-line floating through his office, the drunken and disreputable Doctor of Divinity to whom the innocent and eminent novelist (greatly to his surprise) has to read a lecture in morals. What more natural than that he should write down their stories? The pity of it is that he had not more years of life in which to write them up when he got back to America.

For an English reader the *Notebooks* provide a fascinating pictorial record of that vanished world. It is like turning over a book of Victorian plates, an early volume of the *Illustrated London News* (the editor of which, Dr. Mackay, father of Marie Corelli, was an acquaintance of Hawthorne's). But what comes as a surprise is how intensely and sensitively patriotic an American Hawthorne was. Himself the most English of American writers, he was acutely touchy and on the *qui vive* about America ; and there was much in the robust and insensitive Victorian attitude that made him wince. He was torn between two feelings : the resentment which made him cry out at the beginning of his stay, " I shall never love England till she sues to us for help ", and the underlying emotion which made him speak, when his stay was over, of " the deep yearning which a sensitive American — his mind full of English thoughts, his imagination of English poetry, his heart of English character and sentiment — cannot fail to be influenced by, the yearning of the blood within his veins for that from which it has been estranged ". In the *Notebooks* one can watch Hawthorne passing in the course of his stay from the one point of view to the other. The editor, Professor Randall Stewart, writes admirably and sensibly about it all in his introduction.

Above all, there is the interest of Hawthorne's everyday life in England : his fascination for the street life of Liverpool and London ; the civic banquets (" turtle-soup, salmon, woodcock, oyster-patties, and I know not what else " — alas !) ; Ambassador Buchanan dropping a hint about the Presidency (he became President) and calling Victoria " a fiery little devil " ; literary breakfasts with Monckton Milnes, the Brownings, Miss Martineau and her trumpet ; Herman Melville dropping into the Consulate for a chat ; Sebastopol night at Liverpool ; the bells of Westminster ringing for the opening of Parliament. " Really, London seemed to cry out through them, and bid welcome to the Queen."

Published by the Modern Language Association of America, the book may be obtained through the Oxford University Press. With more than 300,000 words of it, it would be a good thing if the World's Classics would give us a handy selection from this new complete text.

(ii)

The particular quality of this book,[1] and its value, are due to the fact that its author is an American. Only an American could have written it, observing us and our ways through the ages so closely and yet from the outside, with affection yet with a spice of irony, noting the things we take for granted, the unconscious assumptions, the codes of conduct in our past. In this book a number of English men and women out of the last four centuries are studied almost as museum pieces : the types which are so continuous against the background of our country-side, yeoman and labourer, tailor and shopkeeper, country gentleman and his lady, the old county families.

Yet they are not merely curiosities out of our past; they are studied and recreated for us with too much of inner sympathy and understanding for that. Professor Notestein is one of the most distinguished of American authorities on English history, to whom we owe the magnificent edition of the Commons' Journals coming out under his guidance. He is Professor of English History at Yale ; but not content with devoting years to research among documents and in our archives, routing out old diaries and letters, he knows our countryside as few of us do ; has walked over it, meeting country people, staying with them, talking with labourers in the pubs, learning by heart the village lore.

Now he has written a book about England, drawing not only upon his store of information about the past, but revealing his care for what has lived on into the present, a knowledge of places and persons which is a very graceful compliment to this country.

[1] Wallace Notestein, *English Folk*.

It must have given him pleasure to be able to say with a little flourish, when writing of Nicholas Ashton, a hunting squire of the seventeenth century, who knew Ribblesdale and his Lancashire well : " Two points that he spoke of, Scout Stones and Brennan Stones, are not set down in the ordnance maps today, but the latter is still known to keepers and shepherds ". And there are similar touches everywhere to remind us that here is someone who knows his England well.

His appreciation of the country is wide and varied, and he paints his characters firmly in the setting of their respective landscapes : Parson Woodforde in his Norfolk, Lucy Lyttelton riding about Worcestershire as a child — and very well she described it in her diary — the Berkeleys in the lower Severn valley, so much of which belonged to them. All the same, one suspects that Professor Notestein has a particular liking for the North Country and its people : he has drawn so many of his figures from there : Thomas Tyldesley, the Jacobite squire, a Catholic, and a good hunting man, whose estates lay in the Lancashire lowlands, between Myerscough and the sea ; Thomas Bewick, the engraver, who was born and bred in the upper valley of the Tyne ; Adam Eyre, whose farm looked down upon the little River Don. Of this last, he says :

" Yorkshire yeomen were possibly of a tougher fibre than those of the Southern Shires. They lived in a country from which it was hard to extract a living ; they were used to long, dark winters and raw, searching winds. . . . Even the epitaphs in the churches of the moorlands are those of a stern people, who knew their rights and remembered their wrongs."

As a Cornishman, I cannot repine at this pleasant partiality for the North Country ; but I could wish that he had come far enough into the West to give us some Devon or Dorset portrait (with landscape) to set beside the others.

I suspect, too, that he loves best the England of the seventeenth century ; and who can blame him ? For it was then that the language was at its freshest and loveliest, and English society on the whole had most of chivalry and mutual respect. A tailor will write in his diary of his wedding night, " the music hearing that we were awake came and saluted us with pleasant lessons and choice tunes, and with them many more to know what rest we took ". Or there is the Lady Brilliana Harley's gardener who, being sent as a messenger to her son Ned at Oxford, " fell so in love with travel that he would fain be sent again ".

The book is in the best sense a conservative book : it stands by the values that have lasted so long in our country life. It is all the better witness for coming from the outside. Though Professor Notestein has a tendency proper to the historian to think of these things, these standards of conduct, the friendliness, hospitality and mutual courtesy of great and small folk alike, rather in the past tense, one does not need to assure him that they still exist, if only in part, in that so familiar, well-loved background of the English countryside.

(iii)

A book on England [1] by a Mr. Baldwin does not, at first sight, inspire confidence, but we are reassured to find that the author is an American. And indeed, that is its whole point. It is an attempt to portray what he calls the " Anglo-Saxon spirit " as it has emerged from this country's history. What he has to say is very interesting and, for some people, very salutary.

He tells us that his book arises from his discovery that the point of view about this country in which he was brought up in the United States was quite inadequate, and that he could get no peace until he had written it. The process of discovery is not yet wholly complete. He begins with a number of misconceptions. " No other people so sternly resists the temptation to become cosmopolitan or more obstinately sticks to its insularity." What about the French ? There is no people more insular, more clear-cut, and intellectually uncompromising. We are a rather compromising people, with no such clear-cutness, or, if you like, insularity of mind. We think England " has the best home-life, the best butlers and — God save the mark — the best cooks ". But do we ? In fact we defer, perhaps over-readily, to the French in the matter of cooking. " The Englishman's patriotism . . . allows him to

[1] Leland Dewitt Baldwin, *God's Englishman*.

admire no one else. The Anglo-Saxon, being what he is, does not need to learn." The truth is that all through our history we have been subject to foreign influences, rather more than most countries, and have been very ready both to admire and to learn. Throughout the Middle Ages we learnt from the French ; at the Renaissance from Greece and Rome, and from Italy ; in the seventeenth and eighteenth centuries from the France of the *grand siècle,* and a great deal from Holland ; in the modern period we have learnt something from German science and American mechanical technique. The time has come when other peoples — to judge from the state of the world around us — might well learn something from us.

And why should one not say so ? I simply do not understand why this country, which has made by far the most creative contribution to the modern world, should be expected to be apologetic about it. Many Englishmen, it is true, are — especially if they are intellectuals : an intellectual feels, apparently, that he must apologise — *c'est son métier.* But there is no reason why we should be defeatist about ourselves ; it does no good at home, and abroad people are often silly enough to take it literally. When Mr. Baldwin begins by saying that the Englishman's " way of life is the very best of all possible ways ", one is tempted to ask : " Well, isn't it ? " Looking round the contemporary world, one doesn't see any that is noticeably better in being. I hasten to add that I write not as an Englishman, but a Cornishman : I am merely anxious that the English should have justice done them.

From this point of view Mr. Baldwin's book is of immense value. He is in fact deeply sympathetic to the spirit of this country, now that he has discovered what it really is. But if such misconceptions are possible to the friendliest and best informed Americans, what must the others think of us ? It is an alarming thought. Talk about the re-education of Germany — it looks as if the most important desideratum for international understanding after the war is the re-education of American opinion about this country. And the first thing is not to be afraid to stand up for ourselves. In fact, it is the only basis of mutual respect.

There is no doubt about the deep respect, and understanding, Mr. Baldwin has achieved as the result of his study of our history. He sees that the essence of our effort as a people — and it speaks for our kith and kin overseas — has been the struggle towards individual freedom, the belief in the personality of man as man. It speaks in our history as much as in the American Bill of Rights. It goes along with a certain tolerance of outlook, and a pragmatism of method. In our policy we have followed English interests, quite naturally, as other people have theirs ; but Mr. Baldwin has the honesty to add that those interests have proved to be those of human liberty. He comments : " If one doubts the importance of this coincidence let him try to imagine the course of world history had autocratic Prussia been set upon the British isle." He answers our anti-imperialists at home and our critics abroad : " Certainly England had no intention of becoming the sole colonial and maritime Power, for time after time she returned conquests to her rivals ". The censure that he has to pass, " The threat of war has never failed to catch the British off their guard ", is not really discreditable to us, for it proves that as a people we have pursued peace.

INDEX

273

THE END

Printed in Great Britain by R. & R. CLARK, LIMITED, *Edinburgh.*